THE
MAGNIFICENT
MASTERS

THE MAGNIFICENT MASTERS

JACK NICKLAUS, JOHNNY MILLER,
TOM WEISKOPF,
and the
1975 CLIFFHANGER AT AUGUSTA

GIL CAPPS

DA CAPO PRESS
A Member of the Perseus Books Group

Printed in the United States of America.

For information, address Da Capo Press, 44 Farnsworth Street, 3rd Floor, Boston, MA 02210.

Set in 11.5 point Adobe Caslon Pro by Marcovaldo Productions, Inc. for the Perseus Books Group

Cataloging-in-Publication data for this book is available from the Library of Congress.
First Da Capo Press edition 2014
ISBN: 978-0-306-82041-0 (Hardcover)
ISBN: 978-0-306-82185-1 (eBook)

Published by Da Capo Press
A Member of the Perseus Books Group
www.dacapopress.com

Da Capo Press books are available at special discounts for bulk purchases in the U.S. by corporations, institutions, and other organizations. For more information, please contact the Special Markets Department at the Perseus Books Group, 2300 Chestnut Street, Suite 200, Philadelphia, PA, 19103, or call (800) 810-4145, ext. 5000, or e-mail special.markets@perseusbooks.com.

10 9 8 7 6 5 4 3 2 1

For Julie, Katie, and Ellie
And Mom and Dad

CONTENTS

| Introduction | 1

1 | The Masters | 16

2 | Monday, April 7 | 32

3 | Tuesday, April 8 | 47

4 | Wednesday, April 9 | 62

5 | Thursday, April 10 | 77

6 | Nicklaus | 102

7 | Friday, April 11 | 127

8 | Miller | 155

9 | Saturday, April 12 | 181

10 | Weiskopf | 205

11 | Sunday, April 13 | 231

| Epilogue | 265

Appendix 287
A Note on Sources and Bibliography 291
Acknowledgments 297
Index 299

INTRODUCTION

The greatest golfer of all time squatted down to study his line. Thousands upon thousands of different putts existed on any of the course's eighteen greens, with various hole locations, infinite angles, and boundless distances. None were more difficult to judge than this one—forty feet, uphill, along a pronounced ridge with a break to the left that was nearly impossible to read.

Arriving on the teeing ground just 170 yards behind him, his two keenest rivals watched intently. They had been chasing him, not only through the dramatic twists and turns of this final round, but their entire lives, each dreaming of the day they would eclipse this man on the game's most exalted stage. The next thirty seconds would alter the careers of all three men, and therefore, the game of golf.

What brought them to this juncture? A simple invitation.

3160 CARISBROOK ROAD, COLUMBUS 21, OHIO

The area most sensitive to touch are the fingers. Doctors believe that some people have extraordinary senses, allowing them to process information through feel that others can't. Elite golfers are such a group. This nineteen-year-old boy from the suburban Upper Arlington neighborhood of Columbus knew nothing about that. He did know that he'd never felt an envelope like the one that arrived at his parents' house in February 1959 addressed to him. It was larger than a normal letter envelope—six-and-a-half inches by four-and-three-fourths inches—and ivory-colored with a first-class four-cent stamp pasted in the top-right corner. Its weight stood out, conveying an importance of its contents. The pair of hands, smaller than average for a boy of his six-foot height and stocky build, opened the envelope with great care, only to find another inside. Handwritten on this one was a name: "Mr. Nicklaus."

What the young man saw upon opening the inner envelope could not have made Emily Post prouder. It was perfect. All of the elements of a formal invitation had been carried out with precision. It was printed on the finest of quality paper stock with a raised border just inside the edges. The words were engraved and centered below the invitee's insignia. The invitation was phrased in the third person. Punctuation was placed for separation of words only on the same line—for heaven's sake, never at the end of a line. The state, month, days, and year were all spelled out—no abbreviations. The who, what, where, when, and how to respond were clear as he read the dark green lettering: "The Board of Governors of the Augusta National Golf Club cordially invites you to participate in the Nineteen Hundred and Fifty-Nine Masters Tournament to be held at Augusta, Georgia the second, third, fourth, and fifth of April." At the bottom was the name of his hero: "Robert Tyre Jones, Jr., President."

Jack William Nicklaus had been asked to play in what was becoming the world's most prestigious golf tournament—the Masters. For any young aspiring golfer, this was their debutante ball.

No one was more excited than his father Charlie. He knew the proper etiquette. R.S.V.P. was tagged on the bottom left of the invitation. A prompt, handwritten reply needed to be sent to the return address on the back of the envelope. The elder Nicklaus quickly began drafting a response—mindful to find just the right phrases to match the significance of the invitation. Once satisfied, he would have his son copy what he had composed and send the letter of acceptance back to Augusta National Golf Club.

At the Nicklaus house, the invitation had not been unexpected, but as any good host knows, all of its guests must be invited the same way. On January 31, Nicklaus had been one of nine Americans named by the United States Golf Association for the upcoming Walker Cup—a biennial match-play competition between amateurs from the United States and amateurs from Great Britain and Ireland. Being a Walker Cupper at the time meant a trip to the Masters—one of thirteen categories in which players could earn an invitation to the tournament. His short-term goal had been the Walker Cup; however, his long-term one was to be the best golfer ever to play the sport.

The Masters and the Walker Cup presented a unique opportunity, but Nicklaus was a freshman at Ohio State University. His trip to Great Britain in May would be a four-week endeavor. The team was staying afterward to compete in the British Amateur Championship as well. Nicklaus consulted with his college golf coach Bob Kepler, and they both agreed Nicklaus should take off the spring semester.

With no classes standing in his way, Nicklaus decided to head to Augusta early. He filled up the car with gas—the average price per gallon being thirty-one cents that year. The interstate highway system had been authorized only three years earlier, so the 600-mile journey south wouldn't be speedy. His childhood friend Robin Obetz—"Bob" to Nicklaus—tagged along. Obetz, on spring break, was one of Nicklaus's best friends growing up and would serve as the best man in his wedding the following summer.

They arrived in Augusta on Friday, March 20—a full thirteen days before the first round—and the naïve collegians quickly learned about club protocol. "I didn't know I couldn't take anyone with me," says Nicklaus. "Nobody even said a word about it." Luckily for the boys, Alec Osborne, a club member and advertising executive, recognized the situation and quietly stepped in to take Obetz on as his guest.

Nicklaus was the youngest player in the field in 1959—a distinction that drew media attention. "I've been looking forward to qualifying for this tournament for three years now," Nicklaus told *Augusta Chronicle-Herald* sports columnist Johnny Hendrix. The day after arriving, Nicklaus played his very first round ever at Augusta National. He bogeyed the 2nd, 4th, and 14th holes before recording his first birdie on the par-five 15th, where he hit the green in two shots and two putted for birdie. He made another birdie on the following hole, knocking in a five-foot putt on the par-three 16th. Nicklaus shot a one-over-par 73.

"I liked it. I enjoyed it," says Nicklaus of his first experience there. "I felt the golf course was very much suited to how I played."

Nicklaus practiced and played and played and practiced for three days. He had planned to stay longer, but he hadn't played competitively all year. So he made a call to officials at the Azalea Open in Wilmington, North Carolina, that week's stop on the professional tour. "They said, 'Sure you're a Walker Cup player, you can get right in the tournament'," says Nicklaus. But what they meant was he could play in the qualifier for the tournament, which a displeased Nicklaus found out about when he arrived. He qualified anyway, and being nineteen, says, "I was kind of ticked off because they backed out of what they said they'd do." Nicklaus shot 74–74 the first two rounds and sat in 18th place, ten shots behind Art Wall. "I said, 'I've had enough tournament golf, to heck with this'," recalls Nicklaus. So he withdrew and headed back to Augusta for more practice. That didn't please Ed Carter and Joe Black—the two leading PGA officials at the time. They would catch up to Nicklaus at Augusta and remind him of his responsibilities to sponsors, fans, and himself. "What I did was wrong," says Nicklaus, who, had he stayed, could have finished 4th in the tournament just by shooting 70–70 in the final two rounds.

Nicklaus drove back west to Augusta and registered early for the tournament, the sixth player to do so. He would soon be joined by his family. His father, mother, sister, and girlfriend of six months, Barbara Bash, drove down in a car without air conditioning, singing songs such as "Blue Skies" and "Tennessee Waltz" to pass the time. While Jack stayed at the Crow's Nest at the club, they checked into the Bon Air Hotel, a majestic structure that stood on top of a hill overlooking downtown. The hotel had no air conditioning as well—presenting only slight discomfort with springtime temperatures around 80 degrees that week.

Any golf fan who wanted to attend had easy access to tickets. Series badges for four days of practice rounds and four days of tournament competition were $12.50, available by mail or from more than a dozen retailers around town, such as King's Way Pharmacy, Bill's Barber Shop, and the Municipal Golf Club. And it was quite the local event. There was even a Masters Parade Wednesday afternoon, with 25,000 people lining Broad Street in downtown Augusta to watch a procession of bands, balloons, Cadillac convertibles, and floats, one of which carried the finalists from the Miss Golf Pageant held two days earlier in Bell Auditorium. The parade was led by the mayor and Robert Tyre Jones, Jr. himself. A dozen golfers rode in the parade, including Byron Nelson, Billy Casper, and the defending champion, Arnold Palmer.

Traditions abounded at the tournament, one of which was that each of the amateurs was paired with a Masters champion in the first round. Nicklaus got Jimmy Demaret, who at age forty-eight was three years older than Jack's father. Demaret was the tournament's first three-time winner, having captured titles in 1940, 1947, and 1950. The Houstonian stood out with his gregarious personality and fashionable style—quite the opposite of young Nicklaus. They teed off at 10:42 a.m., and Nicklaus couldn't have gotten off to a worse start. He bogeyed the very first hole, and after a birdie on the par-five 2nd, three more bogeys beset him. He was three over after five holes with momentum going against him. He made a bogey on the 14th and then another on the reachable par-five 15th. He shot 76, seven shots behind leader Stan Leonard, while Demaret managed a 78.

In the second round, Nicklaus was off at 2:06 p.m. with Roger McManus, an amateur from Cincinnati. Again, Nicklaus failed to take advantage of the par-five holes, making only one birdie on them. On the par-three 12th, after watching McManus fly the green with a 6-iron, he took a 7-iron and hit his tee shot in the water. The double bogey would ultimately cost him. He shot a 74 and missed the cut by just one shot.

"I played pretty well. I hit thirty-one greens, managed eight three-putts, and shot 150," remembers Nicklaus. "Arnold (Palmer) hit nineteen greens and was leading the golf tournament at 141, and I was on my way down the road." The previous week's winner Art Wall, who was only three shots better than Nicklaus after 36 holes this time, went on to win.

The generous fairways and absence of penal rough should have been an advantage for the long-hitting Nicklaus, who received plenty of attentive stares from fellow competitors while hitting balls on the range during the week. He found out there was much more to playing Augusta National well. "I figured out, man, you better learn how to putt these greens if you want to win," he says.

These, and others, were lessons to be learned by Nicklaus sooner rather than later. For now, Nicklaus was in a car again, returning to North Carolina for the North & South Amateur at Pinehurst the following week. But Augusta National was anything but in the rear view mirror.

---

94 KEYSTONE WAY
SAN FRANCISCO, CALIFORNIA 94127

John Laurence Miller's first recollections of the Masters came from the headlines in the *San Francisco Chronicle* and *San Francisco Exam-*

iner in 1956. Only eight years old, Miller had already been playing golf for more than three years, and someone he looked up to, local amateur Ken Venturi, appeared to be on his way to winning the tournament. He led after each of the first three rounds and built a six-shot lead with 18 holes to play; however, an 80 in the final round left him one shot behind Jackie Burke in the end. That was also the first televised Masters. Although disappointed for Venturi, Miller kept watching the Masters and became enamored by the great finishes of Arnold Palmer, who won in 1958, 1960, 1962, and 1964. "It was all pretty cool," he says of watching those tournaments.

By 1966, Miller was pretty cool in his own right. Now nineteen, he was a standout golfer at Brigham Young University, and the U.S. Open was coming to his home course, the Olympic Club. He and his friends all signed up to be caddies for the championship, but Miller went a step further. He was one of 2,475 golfers to mail in an entry form—the fee was $20—to try to qualify as a competitor. He made it through the local qualifying stage at Salt Lake Country Club in Utah, chipping in during a playoff to edge out seventy-five-year-old Chick Evans, the 1916 champion, for the lone spot. A few weeks later in sectional qualifying at San Francisco Golf Club, a layout he knew well, Miller finished third to make it into the field as a contestant, not a caddie.

For the first two rounds of the Open, Miller was paired with two other first timers: a twenty-four-year-old long hitter named Harry Toscano and Lee Trevino, a twenty-six-year-old pro from Dallas. Two weeks before the championship, Miller had borrowed a 5-wood from his best friend Steve Gregoire. Miller was a skinny kid and definitely not a long hitter, but this new club would pop the ball up high and stop it on a dime with a slight fade. So he conceived a game plan. Off the tee, he would hit a 3-wood or cut a little driver, whatever he needed to reach 5-wood distance. "I started milking that 5-wood for all it was worth," he says. Miller rode Gregoire's club to a 70, tied for 5th after the opening round. The USGA's press notes reported a telling observation, "He was nervous at first about his putting, but that was all."

With subsequent rounds of 72-74-74, Miller failed to match his opening day success, but a score of 10-over-par 290 earned him low amateur honors. "I wasn't that excited that I finished 8th to be honest with you," says Miller, who actually thought he should've won on a course he knew as well as anyone. "I was pretty disappointed." As the weeks passed, Miller reassessed his accomplishment and the opportunities it would open. For starters, his finish meant that he was exempt for the next year's U.S. Open. And by finishing in the top-sixteen, he was eligible for an invitation to the 1967 Masters.

"I knew I was going to play in it someday," he says, "but not that quickly." Miller was back at school in Provo, Utah, when his first invitation arrived at his parents' San Francisco home in the winter of 1967. "It was surreal," he says. "I knew I was in the Masters, but it looked so cool to get that. It was to John Miller, not Johnny Miller." His mother filed the invitation away.

"My dad was as excited as anyone," says Miller, "but he didn't fly." His father had some unnerving experiences in planes during the Second World War; therefore, Miller's golf coach at BYU, Carl Tucker, accompanied him to Augusta. Miller had been recruited by all the big golf schools and thought he would land at UCLA, USC, Stanford, or the powerhouse Houston, which had knocked the loudest. But his family were members of the Church of Jesus Christ of Latter-Day Saints, and his mother asked him to visit BYU, even though it was not a traditional golf school. Once there, Miller fell in love with the place and felt a spirit throughout the campus. Tucker, however, was there to win. He became paranoid Miller would change his mind and had him enroll early at the age of seventeen. Miller missed his high school graduation, even though as a freshman he wouldn't be eligible to play on the varsity team.

Prior to his first Masters, Jack Nicklaus had traveled around the nation, playing in multiple U.S. Junior Amateurs, U.S. Amateurs, and even U.S. Opens. Miller had not. This trip would be his first east of the Mississippi River, and the first time he'd been on a commercial plane. Provo to Augusta wasn't the easiest of journeys either in 1967. It was an all-day adventure with multiple stops.

Once at Augusta, Miller was taken aback by the amenities and surroundings. "I'd never been where you got treated like that, old-fashioned Southern hospitality," says Miller, who stayed in the Crow's Nest just as other first-time amateurs did before him. "I'd never been to a course that had been maintained that beautifully."

He played a practice round with Billy Casper, who was a mentor to Miller at the time, and Sam Snead, who imparted wisdom to the inexperienced Miller. Miller quizzed him as to what he thought about the swing. "You're either going to hit your short shots good or your long shots good," said Snead while they were standing on the 7th green during one such round. "Nobody hits 'em both good." Miller thought, "Really?" He'd never heard that before.

Like many, Miller didn't realize the course was constructed on the side of a ridge with a 150-foot drop from its highest point to its lowest. "That's the first thing anybody says when they get to Augusta is, 'Whoa, I didn't know it was this hilly'," he says. For years, Miller had watched the same holes on television—15, 16, 17, 18—and the history they produced. "I was pretty enamored by that back nine and by those charges guys would make. I wanted to see what that was like," he says.

The state of Miller's game was not conducive to great golf. Hardly any grass was visible in Provo during the winter. He hadn't played any golf in months. With no place to practice, Miller had been spending his free time skiing. During the informal Par Three Contest held the day before the tournament, Miller made an ace on the 2nd hole, sucking the ball into the hole with a wedge, and finished a shot out of the playoff.

As an amateur, Miller would be paired with a Masters champion, and like Jack Nicklaus, he got Jimmy Demaret. Now sixty-six,

Demaret's best golfing days were behind him—this was his twenty-fourth and final appearance—but his colorful demeanor wasn't. He provided what Miller describes as "the most embarrassing thing that ever happened to me playing golf." On the 8th hole, Miller hit his drive right toward some trees, only to have the ball ricochet back into the fairway. There was a commotion as he and Demaret made their way over. A woman was lying on the ground. Demaret asked her if she was okay and where it hit her. She pointed to her crotch. Demaret turned to Miller. "Hey John," he said, "You almost made a hole-in-one. You missed by one inch."

"I was so embarrassed in front of all these people," says Miller, who, as a Mormon, didn't drink, smoke, or curse, but wasn't naïve. "Of course they all thought it was very funny. But it was pretty embarrassing to me. I had never heard anyone say that in front of a lady before."

But Miller persevered through the red face. He made birdie on the hole and shot a 72 in his first competitive round, matching Nicklaus's score that day and besting other champions such as Palmer, Demaret, Gary Player, and Ben Hogan. He followed with a 78 to make the cut on the number before ballooning with scores of 81–74 on the weekend to finish tied for 53rd. "It was a miracle I even made the cut," he says. "I wasn't practicing for the Masters at all. No golf at all."

Miller struggled to learn the intricacies of the course, particularly the firmness, speed, and break of the greens, which consisted of Bermuda grass, a type of warm-season grass common in the South that was coarse with a deep root structure. "I had no idea what I was doing. I'd never even seen Bermuda before," he adds. "I had no clue how to putt and chip on it."

"Everything was a bit of a blur for me—almost like it wasn't a tournament to me. It was like an experience," recalls Miller. "My eyes were big. I had no expectations. I was just taking it all in."

But after the tournament, he had one overriding thought: "I'll be back."

2295 PINEBROOK ROAD, COLUMBUS, OHIO 43220

Thomas Daniel Weiskopf was not an ordinary first-time invitee to the Masters, not in the mold of Jack Nicklaus, Johnny Miller, or other youngsters. He wasn't a wide-eyed teenager—he was twenty-five years old and married. He wasn't an amateur—he was in his fourth year as a professional on tour. He wasn't an after-thought—he was a favorite with, in his mind, a good chance to win. In 1968, Tom Weiskopf pulled into Augusta National for his first Masters as the leading money winner on the PGA Tour with thirty-one of his last thirty-three rounds at par or better and a victory already on his resume.

Weiskopf received his initial invitation by finishing in the top-sixteen of the previous year's U.S. Open, just as Miller had the season before. With a 15th place finish at Baltusrol, Weiskopf was well aware that he was headed to Augusta. So it wasn't a surprise when the invitation arrived at his English Tudor house with a large walnut tree in the front yard—a little over two miles from the address where Nicklaus received his first invitation. Weiskopf responded just as his mother and father taught him. A prompt reply in the affirmative was sent to the club.

"It's a place that you're familiar with even though you've never been there before," says Weiskopf. "You watch it on TV, what has happened good and bad to everybody. And you just don't forget those things."

The course was everything he thought it would be when he experienced it for the first time during a practice round on Thursday, March 21. In the next morning's *Augusta Chronicle*, Robert Eubanks wrote prophetically: "Tom Weiskopf, the man with the long frame and an even longer game, Thursday decided to strike up an acquaintance with the Augusta National Golf Course which promises to be a lengthy friendship."

"It was the best hole-after-hole, shot-after-shot, risk-reward championship golf course I'd ever played," says Weiskopf. "It defines parkland golf." He was struck by its beauty—some of the early blooming plants were just beginning to show their colors—and the uniqueness of each hole. His formal education of the game had taken place on the Scarlet Course at Ohio State University—an Alister MacKenzie design just like Augusta National. "There were a lot of characteristics that were duplicated in various ways," says Weiskopf. "A lot of similarities—green contours, false fronts, false sides, big greens, bunker placement, wide fairways, big golf course. It really fit my game, there's no doubt about that."

Weiskopf played one of his practice rounds that week with Nicklaus, a fellow Buckeye nearly three years his senior. Bobby Jones was riding around in a golf cart on the second nine, and Nicklaus introduced them. "It's always impressive to me when you met these icons and they know about you," says Weiskopf. Jones asked him about Columbus, Ohio State, and the putt that gave Weiskopf his first win on the PGA Tour at the inaugural San Diego Open two months earlier. Tied for the lead coming into the 72nd hole at Torrey Pines, Weiskopf rolled in a twenty-five-foot putt for eagle on the par five for his maiden title. But Jones didn't mention March when results hadn't gone his way. At Doral, Weiskopf bogeyed his final two holes in the final round to finish a shot behind Gardner Dickinson. The next week at the Citrus Open in Orlando, he missed an eight-foot birdie putt on the 71st hole to finish a shot behind Dan Sikes. The stats showed seven top-three finishes in his career, but just one win.

Aware that outside the first Masters only Gene Sarazen in 1935 had won in his initial try, Weiskopf teed off in the opening round of the 1968 tournament at 10:03 a.m. paired with Canadian George Knudson. While he took advantage of the par fives with his length, making birdie on three of the four, Weiskopf struggled on the par threes, bogeying all four of them—the 4th, 6th, 12th, and 16th. He shot 74. Just as those before him, inexperience bit Weiskopf. No matter the talent, there was a reason that since the first two tournaments, no first-time participant had won the Masters. "I probably didn't realize the little nuances, the little things that only experience can give you until after my second year," says Weiskopf, who shot under par the rest of the way (71–69–71) to finish in a respectable tie for 16th.

Just like for other first-timers, it was a week of celebration. He and his wife Jeanne rented a house. His mother, father, and brother came down from Ohio along with some friends. But trepidation tinged Weiskopf's Masters week.

At the time, every American male between ages 18–25 was eligible to be drafted into the U.S. Army. If chosen by Selective Service, young men were required to go before local draft boards and submit to physicals. Each month, thousands were being conscripted into active duty to serve in Vietnam as long as they met the physical, mental, and moral standards of the board. When Jack Nicklaus, still a college student, informed his local draft board of his marriage in 1960, they told him they would never see him again. After the birth of his first child in 1961, they were right as men with families were exempt. Johnny Miller's number had come up while at BYU, but during his physical doctors noticed a fresh scar on his left knee. Miller had suffered a torn meniscus while playing intramural football, and the stitches from his surgery had just been taken out. Both were classified 4-F: not available for any military service.

Weiskopf underwent his initial physical in 1963 shortly after leaving Ohio State. The Army classified him as 1-Y. He wasn't given a reason why, but the classification was usually given to men who had minor physical ailments or injuries that were limiting in nature but not disabling. This meant he wasn't available for military service but did qualify for duty in the event of war or a national emergency.

By April 1968, the situation in Vietnam was looking more dire. The Tet Offensive launched by the North Vietnamese two months earlier was taking its toll on U.S. troops in South Vietnam. Just before the Masters, Weiskopf received the same notification that thousands of other 1-Ys would in the coming weeks. His classification had been rescinded. Weiskopf was married and six months shy of turning twenty-six years old when he would be free-and-clear of any service obligations. Instead, he was now going to be either 4-F, like Nicklaus and Miller had been, or 1-A, available immediately for military service. The Army originally scheduled his physical on the Tuesday of Masters week, but deferred it until the following month. Weiskopf would have to wait until then to find out when his next trip to Augusta would be.

BY 1975, INVITATIONS WERE a foregone conclusion for this triumvirate. Going into the 1975 Masters, these men were the top-three players in golf—and the three most talented. They had combined to win six of the thirteen tournaments so far that year. Miller was first on the money list with $128,226, Nicklaus second with $109,242, and Weiskopf third with $91,238.

In 1959, Jack Nicklaus was a year removed from playing high school sports for the Upper Arlington High School Golden Bears. Now, Jack Nicklaus was known as the Golden Bear. His career took off following that 1959 Masters and hadn't stopped. Now thirty-five years old and in his fourteenth year as a professional, his resume listed four Master titles, twelve major championships, fifty-six PGA Tour wins, and $2.3 million in career earnings on the PGA Tour. He could still hit it far but had long since learned how to hole clutch putts and utilize his mental strengths. These qualities had brought him fame, fortune, and universal acknowledgment as the game's best player—until 1975.

Now challenging his position was Johnny Miller. The twenty-seven-year-old had come a long way from the scrawny, undersized teenage beanpole he was eight years earlier. Miller was the hottest player in golf with eleven PGA Tour wins in the previous fifteen months. He'd won the 1973 U.S. Open with a 63 in the final round—

the lowest round ever in a major championship. Miller had everything going for him except a Masters title.

And no golfer in the world looked better swinging a club than Tom Weiskopf. In what was still the prime of his career at age thirty-two, Weiskopf's up-and-down struggles with obstacles of his own making, as well as those outside his control, were well known. His eleven career wins, including the 1973 British Open, didn't match the pundits' expectations. But in the preceding weeks, his game had risen once again with strong play and a long-overdue win. Now it was off to his favorite course, and arguably, the most famous golf tournament in the world.

| 1 |

THE MASTERS

As during the previous two decades, Masters week in 1975 started the Sunday before…with a thud. That's when the weighty *Sunday Chronicle-Herald* landed on doorsteps and in newspaper racks across the city. Folded inside was its annual Masters Edition supplement.

The *Augusta Chronicle* was Augusta's morning newspaper. Its masthead proudly boasted: "The South's Oldest Newspaper—Established 1785." It had in fact started as the *Augusta Gazette* 190 years earlier as one of the first newspapers in the country. In 1955, William S. Morris, Jr., bought outright control of the *Chronicle* and also purchased the *Augusta Herald*, the city's afternoon paper. Soon thereafter, the two papers would combine Sunday publication.

Under Morris, the paper began producing this all-encompassing tournament preview in the Sunday edition leading into Masters week. Months went into the planning, selling, writing, design, and editing of the special sections. On April 6, 1975, it tallied forty-eight pages in four different sections for subscribers and anyone putting down thirty-five cents for a copy. Executives at the paper believed it was the largest annual special section dedicated to a sporting event in the world.

Inside, readers found stories touching on each of the seventy-six players in the field, past Masters tournaments, and the course. And there were advertisements. In the Masters Edition alone, there were 202 different display ads with another 119 in a classified directory. On the bottom right of page 10E, Wickes Lumber offered to wood panel an interior twelve-by-twelve-foot room of your house for $31.08. On 2F, Shoney's promoted a curb-and-carry-out special: two of its Big Boy sandwiches for $1. On the bottom right of page 11G, Goodyear advertised their lube and oil change for just $4.44. And in a full page on 12F, Piggly Wiggly of Georgia used clip art images of the Statue of Liberty and a golf ball to announce: "We salute…the Masters Golf Tournament, another great example of the fruits of America's free enterprise system. When a few men can conceive, finance, and build a dream…we all benefit from it."

The newspaper was the one remaining connection that many Augustans had to the tournament. Sure, locals interacted with visitors as they spent money at hotels and restaurants, and there were those who still attended the tournament. But there were no more nights filled with formal balls or concerts or boxing matches. The Masters Parade and Miss Golf Pageant ended in the mid-1960s. Now, the tournament didn't need the promotion, nor the ticket sales. The grand hotels like the Bon Air, in which the Hogans and the Nelsons and the Nicklauses stayed, had shuttered years earlier. Northerners stopped vacationing in Augusta decades ago; Florida was their destination now. Contestants rented private houses for the week (the going rate around $1,000 and up) and spent less time eating out and socializing. The Masters had become so successful that it had outgrown the city, which had given the club $10,000 to help put on the first tournament in 1934.

City officials still used the tournament to recruit businesses, but Augusta had changed as well. Downtown merchants had moved to the suburbs, and the city's population, split almost equally between whites and blacks, was still grappling with the remnants of segregation. Bitterness over court-ordered integration and school busing lingered, as well as wounds from a 1970 riot in which six black men were killed following the death of another black man while in police custody.

"Outside the gates was so horrible, and inside the gates was so perfect," says Ben Wright, an Englishman who had initially covered the Masters as the first golf correspondent for the *Financial Times* in 1966. "It was a total contrast."

When constructed, Augusta National Golf Club was in the country, although only three miles northwest of downtown. To viewers on television, the manicured layout colored in hues of deep green still looked like it was miles from civilization, somewhere deep in the Georgia countryside. In reality, the property had become engulfed by commercial establishments, strip malls, and residential neighborhoods. The course had literally turned into a golfing oasis.

The main thoroughfare outside the club is Georgia Highway 28, commonly referred to as Washington Road. It's named indirectly for the nation's first president as it was the road connecting Augusta to Washington, Georgia. Golf's ultimate pinch-me moment occurs when players turn off of Washington at the main guard gate. Magnolia Lane lies in front of them—330-feet of paved asphalt that runs straight to the front of the clubhouse. Making the drive under a canopy of sixty-one magnolia trees means they've arrived at the game's most hallowed doorstep. The invitation they received in the mail just months earlier has come to life.

IT'S UNFATHOMABLE, but in the beginning players actually turned down invitations to the Masters. Even holding an annual tournament at Augusta National Golf Club wasn't an initial thought in the mind of the legendary figure who founded the club.

Robert Tyre Jones, Jr.—Bob to his friends, Bobby to his legion of fans—was possibly the most famous sportsman in America during his tenure on the links. Throughout the 1920s, radio and newspapers carried the news of his exploits, creating a man of mythical proportions who was universally admired for his humility, integrity, and thoughtfulness.

Jones was America's first golfing prodigy, having picked up the game as a five year old at East Lake Country Club in Atlanta. At age fourteen, he reached the quarterfinals of the U.S. Amateur in 1916. At age twenty-one, he captured his first major at the 1923 U.S. Open, a championship he would win a record-tying four times. He added a record five U.S. Amateur titles, three British Opens, and one British Amateur—all without devoting his complete attention to the game. He was an amateur—a term derived from the Latin word *amare*, meaning love. He played the game not for money but for the love of it. And the public loved him back. He was afforded the rare honor of two ticker tape parades in New York City following returns from British Open triumphs in 1926 and 1930.

Jones left the most improbable accomplishment for last. In a span of 120 days in 1930, he won what were considered the four majors of that period—the British Amateur at St. Andrews, the British Open at Royal Liverpool, the U.S. Open at Interlachen, and then the U.S. Amateur at Merion. It was referred to as the Impregnable Quadrilateral, or the Grand Slam—the greatest feat in golf history. Three months later, he retired from competitive golf at age twenty-eight.

At that time, Jones's efforts to build his own golf club were already underway. He had enlisted a New York investment banker he'd met named Clifford Roberts to help him, and they began scouting parcels in Augusta, Georgia—a town on the eastern side of the state that cozied up to the state line with South Carolina and was at the time Georgia's second largest city.

Founded in 1736 as a trading post on the banks of the Savannah River, Augusta had once been an industrial center of the Confederacy. On his "March to the Sea" in 1864, however, General William Sherman bypassed the city. As one of the few cities in the South with its infrastructure intact following the Civil War, Augusta expanded its canal to the river and became a hub of cotton manufacturing. Its success soon attracted northerners looking for a convenient vacation spot where the winters were mild. Grand hotels and golf courses were constructed, and Augusta was on par with Pinehurst, North Carolina, and nearby Aiken, South Carolina, as holiday destinations after the turn of the century.

Upon seeing a 365-acre site that was once home to Fruitlands Nurseries—one of the largest in the South—Jones knew they had found the spot. "It seems that this land had been lying here for years just waiting for someone to lay a golf course upon it," wrote Jones in his book *Golf Is My Game*. In 1931, the site was purchased, architect Dr. Alister MacKenzie was chosen to design the course (with significant input from Jones), and construction began.

It was absolutely the worse time to build a golf course. When the club formally opened for play in January 1933, the country was coming off its worst year of the Great Depression with 23.6 percent unemployment and a gross national product that fell by 13.4 percent. Roberts had figured selling national memberships to a private club built by the world's most famous golfer would be effortless. Suddenly, even with an initiation fee of $350 and annual dues of $60, he could get few men to join. By 1935, the number of golf courses in the United States had contracted by a third, and Augusta National would dangle on a financial teeter-totter with its survival unsure for years.

For Jones, difficult times didn't dampen lofty goals. He wanted to bring a U.S. Open to his course. America's national championship was his true love. He finished first or second eight times in a nine-year span. With Jones's stature and connections within the United States Golf Association, his dream was to have the championship played in the South for the first time. But the Open was traditionally held in June or July when the club would be closed during the hot Georgia summers, and USGA officials feared that moving the championship up to March or April would create too much of an inconvenience for players and the qualifiers that would have to be held in parts of the country that might still have snow on the ground. And they thought Augusta was too small to support the event.

Jones's disappointment inspired a thought in Roberts. The club could hold its own tournament and make it unique. There would be no qualifying to get in the field. It would be invitation-only.

The intention wasn't for the tournament to become a major championship or a championship of any sort. For Jones, nothing rivaled the U.S. Open. In fact, Jones, Roberts, and Fielding Wallace, the club's first secretary, initially believed conducting a successful event might entice the USGA to bring the Open southward. Instead, their tournament would be a celebration of golf—the great champions, top players of the day, and Bobby Jones. And, everyone with a financial stake hoped the tournament would help sell more memberships.

First, they needed Bob Jones to come out of retirement. He would be the major drawing card. Jones didn't want to play, but he realized the benefits his appearance would bring and eventually relented.

Then, they needed lots of publicity. For that, there was member Grantland Rice, the preeminent sports writer of the time. O.B. Keeler, who had followed Jones's entire career, was also on board. Persuading their fellow scribes of the era to cover the tournament wasn't a problem either. Most of them adored Jones and were delighted to provide good publicity to any endeavor with which he was associated.

Since it was going to be an invitational, players would have to be invited. At the time, telephone usage was expensive, and not only did many people not have one, but those who did often shared a party line with others. The telegraph had been in use for nearly a century, but it was far too informal. Therefore, formal invitations were mailed. It was the least expensive, quickest, and most convenient and reliable form of communication in 1934.

All former champions of the U.S. Open and U.S. Amateur were invited, as well as the top players from the present day. Even with Bobby Jones committed to play, the acceptance rate wasn't 100 percent. In those tough economic times, there were players who couldn't afford to travel and leave their club jobs for a week.

With Jones in the field of seventy-two, the inaugural tournament teed off on March 22, 1934. R.S. Stonehouse struck the opening tee shot on what's now the 10th hole (the nines had been reversed during construction, and they were reversed again prior to the second Masters). Horton Smith, one of the game's young stars who would meet his future wife that week (the daughter of member Alfred S. Bourne), won the tournament. Jones finished a respectable tied for 13th and continued to play in the Masters until 1947.

The following year, Gene Sarazen, the game's top player who wasn't in the field in 1934 because of a previously scheduled tour of South America, entered. He seemingly had no chance to win as he stood in the fairway of the 15th hole—which had been the 6th the previous year. This hole was a downhill par five with water in front of the green. Just 220 yards away, Sarazen decided to go for the green on his second shot. He hit a 4-wood that cleared the water and tracked right into the hole for a double eagle. With one swing, the 15th at Augusta National became one of the most famous holes in golf with the rarest feat in golf mythologized at the typewriters of Rice, Keeler, and others. Sarazen's double eagle spurred him on to tie Craig Wood, who had all but been handed the winner's check. Sarazen won in a playoff the next day.

After only its second year, the Masters achieved star status, but it wasn't officially the Masters. Roberts had originally proposed the event be called the Masters Tournament, and in fact, that's what nearly everyone from club members to press members called it from the very beginning. Jones objected, thinking it too presumptuous, and it was officially the Augusta National Invitation Tournament. By 1939, he relented on this as well.

Jones, Sarazen, and the public relations machine had put the Masters on the front pages of sports sections across America. But it would take the Second World War and a reset for both the country and the club before the tournament would really take off.

Initially, the Masters had been anything but a financial success, but it survived the Depression. Following the War, its commitment to excellence, forward thinking, and the decision to plow money back into the course and tournament were paying off. It had weathered the storm and positioned itself as one of the top tournaments in golf.

The star soon became the course itself with dramatic elevation changes, ingenious green complexes, and memorable risk-reward holes. The goal was a links-style golf course that made players think with many features taken from Jones and MacKenzie's favorite, the Old Course in St. Andrews, Scotland. The layout, with scattered hillocks and mounds, had relatively few bunkers and no rough. It was not particularly long either, but in Jones's opinion it provided "the most interesting test of golf in America." The generous width of the fairways emphasized second shots with preferred angles of attack from certain sides, and the greens were large and undulating. The routing of the holes provided constant change in direction. Owing to the land's history, it became a most esthetically pleasing course with azaleas, dogwoods, and pines lining the corridors.

The players were treated better at Augusta National than at any other stop on the professional circuit. From the beginning, the tournament rounds were contested over four days, at a time when tournaments usually were three-day affairs with 36 holes on a Saturday to skirt blue laws and the Sabbath. The pairings were changed daily, and players were grouped in speedier twosomes for every round. In the late-1940s, scoreboards were placed throughout the course instead of employing standard bearers to walk with each group. In the early-1950s, ropes lined the playing areas of each hole with only contestants and caddies allowed inside them. Annually, the purse was one of the largest in golf, and, unlike other tournaments, there was no entry fee. In 1951, officials paid every single professional in the field, and once a cut was instituted in 1957, they kept paying those who missed it. And of course with its limited invitation-only field, the Masters, as its name implied, developed an air of exclusivity with players treated more like guests instead of competitors.

In addition to the players, there was a commitment to the enjoyment of spectators—or patrons as Roberts preferred to call them. Natural mounding was constructed around greens for better sight-lines. There was a lack of overt commercialization. There was private security. In 1960, the club worked with television to create a new scoring system using numbers in relation to par—red numbers to signify how many strokes under par a player was at that point, green ones representing over par. Prices of food, beverage, and merchandise remained reasonable. By 1975, a ham sandwich cost just sixty-five cents and a Coca-Cola forty cents. "We put some meat into the sandwiches, too, and our Cokes are fourteen ounces," club manager Phil Wahl pointed out. There was no charge for on-site parking in one of 10,000 spaces. Spectator guides with a map of the course, descriptions of the holes, and bios of the players were always complimentary since their first publication in 1949, as were daily pairing sheets. The goal was to provide patrons with an unparalleled experience.

The tournament's reputation was also enhanced when each of the first nine Masters was won by a future World Golf Hall of Famer, a trend that continued with the likes of Sam Snead, Ben Hogan, Jimmy Demaret, and Cary Middlecoff after the war. To the general public, big name winners meant it was a big tournament. And the club got even more attention in the 1950s when one of its members, Dwight D. Eisenhower, was elected President of the United States.

Images of Eisenhower at Augusta were yet another symbol to be ingrained in the minds of the sporting public. There was the iconic logo devised by Jones himself, an outline of the United States with a flagstick and hole cut where Georgia lies. There was the green jacket, initially made for club members to wear. Beginning in 1949, a jacket was awarded to each champion—one of the most distinguished and recognizable awards in sports. And unlike other championships, having the Masters at the same course year-after-year meant the public was intimately familiar with holes such as 15 and 16 and 18.

Finally, the tournament's position on the calendar turned out to be key. In the beginning, a benefit was that sportswriters returning northward from baseball spring training in Florida would stop off to cover the proceedings. But being played before the U.S. Open, PGA, and Western Open, the Masters became the first big event of the year. Everyone looked forward to it with anticipation for months; thus, it was discussed and talked about more than any other. For fans across the country, it marked the start of golf season.

By 1975, the Masters was the biggest event in golf and one of the most preeminent in all of sports. And the man responsible for most of its success was Clifford Roberts.

As Chairman of both the Masters Tournament and Augusta National Golf Club, Roberts's goal was to set the tournament apart from every other sporting event. In his book *The Story of Augusta National Golf Club*, Roberts wrote, "The Masters is operated for the single purpose of benefitting the game itself." He was extremely meticulous, and as far as he was concerned, the word "shortcut" didn't exist. Attention was paid to every detail. At the concession stands, even the paper cups and sandwich wrappers were green in order to blend in with the surroundings if dropped. The yellow pansies in front of the clubhouse received as much care as anything else. By 1975, more than $1 million had been spent on improvements to the tournament and course.

"Mr. Roberts was a perfectionist—110 percent," says Bob Kletcke, a Chicago native who arrived at the club as an assistant professional in 1963 and served as co-head professional from 1967–2004. "He wanted things done the right way, and that's the reason the Masters is what it is today."

As the 1975 Masters approached, Roberts was eighty-one years old, and the club was doing just fine now with close to 300 members and decades removed from financial uncertainty. He had announced his intention of retiring and was in the midst of choosing a successor.

"At least forty of our members are capable of running the Masters Tournament, and they could do it better than I do," he proclaimed during the week of the tournament. The members loved golf and being involved in the twenty-four different committees that ran the tournament, including one called the Tournament Improvements Committee comprised of seven members and ten champions.

Kletcke remembers one profound statement from Roberts: "Bob, when we stop showing the world how to put on a golf tournament, we'll cancel it."

All of it—the nostalgia, beauty, serenity, history, hospitality, and exclusivity—created a mystique around the Masters. When you say "the Masters" to players, they don't think of an answer, they emote one. "It was the whole feeling that came over you when you turned off of Washington Road and went onto Magnolia Lane," says Billy Casper. Those feelings elevated the Masters to a pedestal of importance explained best by Dave Marr: "At my first Masters, I got the feeling that if I didn't play well, I wouldn't go to heaven."

Everything started with that invitation. As Emily Post wrote in 1922, "Good taste or bad is revealed in everything we are, do or have…. Rules of etiquette are nothing more than sign-posts by which we are guided to the goal of good taste."

An invitation to the Masters was a sign of what golfers would experience their first time there. The Masters had become the best-run golf tournament in the world. It was a club you wanted to be a part of, and for young players, their first invitation was a rite of passage into golfhood. It was all quite different from 1934.

"At first, you were invited to a party, a celebration of golf, of Bob Jones," says Johnny Miller. "Augusta was just a Bing Crosby Pro-Am. It used to be just a fun event. The next thing you know, it became this major."

IN EARLY APRIL 1975, Vietnam still lingered on the front pages of American newspapers. U.S. Marines gathered off shore of the country to evacuate 6,000 people from Saigon, which was about to fall. Although it had come and gone, Watergate really hadn't passed in the psyche of the American public. The economy was sputtering. Authorities were still searching for a female fugitive with one of the country's most famous last names: Patricia Hearst. Amid all this, one of the country's favorite distractions became golf.

Alan Shepard famously kicked off the decade by hitting a 6-iron on the moon in 1971. The World Golf Hall of Fame opened in 1974, just a month after another golf-loving U.S. President, Gerald Ford, moved into the White House. As air travel in the 1970s became easier and more convenient, golf in places like Florida, Arizona, and Hawaii grew alongside the spread of the condominium and time-share craze. More courses were being built, and more people were playing them. By 1975, there were more than 12 million golfers in the United States with 11,370 courses—numbers nearly triple and double what they were in 1960 respectively.

In the professional game, big, corporate money was on the brink of entering, but in 1975 tournaments were fronted by A-list celebrities who were avid golfers and arguably the most famous people in America. There was the Bob Hope Desert Classic, the Dean Martin Tucson Open, the Bing Crosby Pro-Am, the Andy Williams San Diego Open, the Glen Campbell Los Angeles Open, the Jackie Gleason Inverrary Classic, the Danny Thomas Memphis Classic, and the Sammy Davis Jr. Greater Hartford Open. All these tournaments contributed millions of dollars to local charities.

Those celebrities didn't put up the sponsorship dollars like MONY, Kemper Insurance, or Eastern Airlines—three of the few title sponsors of events that year. But their high profiles did give the game pizzazz and panache and drew interest from many people who were not inclined to follow golf. In early 1975, only the rain-plagued event in Hawaii suffered a decline in attendance from the previous year. Record crowds had already flocked to a half-dozen tour stops, from 38,000 during the final day at Tucson to 47,100 on a Sunday at Greensboro.

Even though the sport could be expensive to produce on television (upwards of $500,000 at the time, approximately ten times as much as a single ballgame), golf was gaining more exposure. Only a handful of tournaments were televised in the 1960s. In 1975, there would be a record twenty-six. Television ratings were as strong as ever with the Bing Crosby tournament in February seen in more than ten million homes. Golf was front page on most sports sections around the nation.

"Those were the glory days of golf," says Miller.

Still, there was an innocence to the game. Big-time corporate money and sponsorships had yet to flood in. It was a fight to earn good money. "We played golf to win so we had the opportunity to make a living," said Nicklaus. "We didn't make our living on the golf course.... I never used it as a job. I used it as a game. I always thought if I played the game well, my financial rewards would be there, but it came because I played well."

Deane Beman saw things differently. As the new commissioner of the Tournament Players Division (TPD), which had been formed in 1968 when the touring professionals broke away from the PGA of America (it wouldn't be called the PGA Tour until 1976), Beman foresaw the many opportunities awaiting the tour. The marriage of corporate sponsors and television was at hand. The total purses of tournaments in 1975, of which there were forty-two official events and another nine satellite stops, reached nearly $7.9 million. Due to the recession, it was a figure lower than the last two seasons, but purses would increase this year and wouldn't slide again until 1992 because of another economic dip.

One of Beman's initial strikes came during his first Masters week as commissioner, which had become a time for leading officials from golf organizations all over the world to make contacts and conduct business. Beman announced the fledgling Tournament Players Championship would move to March in 1976. In addition, the World Series of Golf held in September, now owned by the TPD and PGA, would be expanded "to serve as a true world championship," according to PGA president Henry Poe. With that event, the Tour was moving it outside the shadow of the PGA Championship, and with the other, it was trying to out-flank the Masters.

"I think this sets the stage for a major tournament," said Beman of the TPC. "Becoming a major tournament requires a test of time. You must have the proper organization. And obviously you have to be accepted by the players, public, and the press." His words were soaked in irony. Augusta National had done this already, and Beman was careful to add, "I don't think anything possibly can take away from this (the Masters) championship."

But the more important the sport became and the more important other events tried to become, the more important the Masters remained. Even as the sport increased in popularity and other entities angled for a piece of the pie, the Masters strengthened its hold within the game.

Under that backdrop, Nicklaus, Miller, and Weiskopf made their way to Augusta, Georgia, in 1975. Right behind them were a slew of talented players, each a future Hall of Famer: Arnold Palmer, Gary Player, Lee Trevino, Billy Casper, Tom Watson, Hale Irwin, Raymond Floyd, Lanny Wadkins, Tom Kite, and Hubert Green. All of these men were born within twenty years of one another, combining for sixty-six major championships and 420 PGA Tour wins by the end of their careers.

"Without a doubt, I know that I was in one of the greatest—if not the greatest—eras of players that this game will ever see," says Weiskopf. "I'm talking shot makers. I'm talking guys who were consistently there every week."

It was quite a field that would make up the thirty-ninth Masters Tournament.

For many Americans, however, something of significance stood out when they saw all of the men listed above. None were black.

Eleven years after passage of the Civil Rights Bill and at a time by which nearly all levels of society and culture had been integrated, black athletes had achieved upper echelon status in almost every sport. In the thirty-eight previous Masters, a total of 574 different men had received invitations from all over the world. Even though Pete Brown and Charlie Sifford had won official PGA Tour tournaments, a black golfer had never been invited to compete.

That was until January 1, 1975, when a tournament secretary stuck a ten-cent stamp on an envelope addressed to 1701 Taylor Street NW, Washington, D.C. 20011. Enclosed was an invitation for Robert Lee Elder.

1975 MASTERS QUALIFICATIONS
FOR INVITATION

1. Masters Tournament Champions. (Lifetime.)
2. U.S. Open Champions. (Honorary, non-competing after 5 years.)
3. U.S. Amateur Champions. (Honorary, non-competing after 2 years.)
4. British Open Champions. (Honorary, non-competing after 5 years.)
5. British Amateur Champions. (Honorary, non-competing after 2 years.)
6. PGA Champions. (Honorary, non-competing after 5 years.)
7. 1973 U.S. Ryder Cup Team.
8. 1974 U.S. World Amateur Team. (Walker Cup Team invited in even-numbered years.)
9. The first 24 players, including ties, in the 1974 Masters Tournament.
10. The first 16 players, including ties, in the 1974 U.S. Open Championship.
11. The first 8 players, including ties, in the 1974 PGA Championship.
12. Semi-Finalists in the 1974 U.S. Amateur Championship.
13. PGA Co-sponsored Tour Tournament winners (classified by the Tournament Players Division as one of its major events) from finish of the 1974 Masters Tournament to start of the 1975 Masters.

| 2 |

MONDAY, APRIL 7

Lee Elder had vowed to himself never to return to the Monsanto Open. Not after the abuse he received there in 1968, his rookie year on the PGA Tour, when he wasn't even allowed in the clubhouse. "I'm tired of being called 'nigger' and 'black boy'," he said of his treatment.

But Elder was a golfer—a black golfer—and the opportunity to play couldn't be passed up, especially for someone yet to win on the big-time circuit. So Elder went back to Pensacola, Florida, every year until April 1974 when he again thought about skipping the tournament. It was just days after another Masters had passed—another Masters without him or any black player in the field. Even after Hank Aaron, a black athlete, had become baseball's new home run king in Atlanta on April 8, Elder still didn't feel motivated. But his wife Rose, who served as his manager but had to stay home for business, encouraged him to go. He had played well at Pensacola Country Club and did enjoy the course, finishing tied for 6th and tied for 10th the previous two years.

So just three days after his friend Gary Player won the Masters, Elder flew down to the Florida panhandle. With just one top-ten on the season, he opened with 67 that Thursday afternoon—his lowest round of the year. Then he shot another subpar round of 69 on Friday and a 71 on Saturday. By Sunday's final round, Elder had made it into the last grouping, just two back—the eleventh time he'd been within two shots of the final-round lead. Here was another chance. A chance for his first win. A chance for a Masters invitation.

The odds had to be in Elder's favor because they were against him for so much of his life.

Elder was born in Dallas, Texas, in 1934 just three-and-a-half months after the inaugural Masters. His father was killed in the Second World War, and his grief-stricken mother passed away soon thereafter. To help support his other nine siblings, Elder began caddying at a local course and became enamored with the sport of golf. As a teen, he dropped out of high school and, instead, honed his golf game and began playing big-money matches under the tutelage and support of legendary hustler Titanic Thompson. Later he refined his game under former Tour player Ray Mangrum and the legendary black golfer Ted Rhodes.

After a stint in the U.S. Army, Elder started on the professional tour—but not the PGA Tour, where a "Caucasian only" rule was enforced until 1961. Elder began competing in the United Golfers Association, which he dominated for nearly a decade, winning four national titles on whatever hardscrabble municipal tracts they could find that were open to minorities.

In 1967, Elder captured more than three-quarters of the UGA events and scraped up enough money to try the Qualifying Tournament for the PGA Tour. "You had to have proof of $20,000, that was the exact number," says Bob Murphy, who had a sponsor and entered the same year. Players such as Elder, who was thirty-three years old and black, didn't have those same opportunities, but Elder made it through on his first try.

The 1974 season was his seventh on the PGA Tour. He had failed to convert three final-round leads into a win. His career record included six runner-up finishes, three third-place finishes, and a load of heartbreak. "I'd be thinking about Augusta rather than taking my time and focusing on winning a golf tournament," he admitted.

At Memphis in 1969, he was the 54-hole co-leader before Dave Hill fired a 65 to pass him. A few weeks later at the Buick Open, using a borrowed putter, he led the field after the second and third rounds, but on the last day he ballooned to an 80, which left him tied for 12th. There was another 54-hole lead squandered at San Diego in 1971. The next year at Hartford, he hung a five-foot birdie putt on the lip at the 72nd hole that would have won, only to have good friend Lee Trevino make one from twelve feet on the last and sixteen feet on the first extra hole to deny Elder again.

The closest call of all had occurred in Elder's rookie season of 1968 at the American Golf Classic where he faced Jack Nicklaus in a sudden-death playoff on national television. The two matched each other for four holes. "I had to make a putt at every one of them to keep it going, and I made them all," recounts Nicklaus. "I think I wore Lee out." Finally on the fifth extra hole, Nicklaus prevailed. Elder may not have won, but it was a victory for black golfers everywhere. "Elder did more for Negro golf in forty-five minutes than everybody else put together had done in forty-five years," said Maxwell Stanford, then president of the UGA.

This time around in Pensacola, Elder entered the final round in 3rd place, trailing another player anxious for his maiden PGA Tour title. Peter Oosterhuis was twenty-five years old—fourteen years Elder's junior—with just eight starts in the United States but a wealth of experience. He had already won eleven times around the world (two of those in duels with Gary Player), led the Order of Merit in Europe three years running, and played on two Ryder Cup teams. He stood out on a golf course as much as Elder did. He was six-feet, five-inches tall. And he was English.

Although his parents played golf, Oosterhuis didn't take to the game until age twelve when he caught the eye of a professional during a clinic for school kids in southeast London. Oosterhuis took divots on his shots when nobody else did. He began spending more time at golf than on his school work as he rose up the amateur ranks. After going to work for an insurance brokerage, visions of a professional career never entered his mind until the 1968 World Amateur Team, when someone asked him if he'd ever thought about turning professional. He hadn't until that moment. Oosterhuis turned pro and took his game around the world, from Europe to Australia to South Africa and back, but the Englishman longed to play in America. He had already played in the Masters, his first invitation coming as a complete surprise to him when it arrived in the winter of 1971 at his parents' home in England while he was in South Africa. They called him with the words, "Peter's got an invitation to the Masters." He even led the Masters going into the final round in 1973 by three shots and was still in it toward the end until a bogey at the par-five 15th left him two shots behind.

"Accurate and steady was the name of Elder's game," says Oosterhuis. "You got a feeling he was pretty determined when he was out there." Oosterhuis wasn't aware of the significance of a possible victory for Elder, but as the afternoon progressed, he remembers many more cheers for the American than the Englishman, no matter the race. "I felt that they were rooting for Lee," recalls Oosterhuis, "the American as opposed to the foreigner." Elder felt the support, saying, "It was a white gallery, and they were pulling for me, a black man. But I felt they were pulling for me as a golfer, not a black man. That's the way I want it."

On the final nine, the tournament became a two-man battle on a layout that suited each. Pensacola Country Club was a flat, short (6,679 yards), tree-lined layout just off Pensacola Bay with small, pushed-up greens. Oosterhuis considered his irons and short game his strengthens, but his driving could be wayward. Off the tees at Pensacola, he could utilize his 1-iron that had brought him so much success elsewhere. Elder was known for his accuracy tee-to-green, and this type of course helped separate him from the field as well. But reading the extremely grainy Bermuda grass greens was a challenge. On Friday alone, Elder had missed six putts inside seven feet.

Oosterhuis's short game shone going down the stretch. He chipped in for birdie on the 11th. He holed out a bunker shot for birdie on the 13th. After rolling in a twelve-foot birdie on the 16th, the Englishman held a two-shot lead with two holes to play. He looked like a winner, so much so that Tour officials were huddling to determine whether or not a win would make him a Tour member and whether or not he'd be eligible for the following week's Tournament of Champions.

Then, Elder hit a 7-iron to three feet for birdie at the 17th hole. One behind on the 18th, he pulled his drive left. Looking forward, there was a path to the green. He hooked a low 6-iron around the trees to four feet. He made the putt to force the playoff.

Pensacola, like a majority of PGA Tour events in the mid-1970s, was not televised. So Rose Elder was kept up to date via telephone from the course courtesy of Hubert Green and his wife.

The playoff began on the 1st hole, where Elder again found trouble off the tee, but the normally sure-footed Oosterhuis missed a two footer for the win. Then on the 2nd hole, Oosterhuis missed a four footer for birdie to win, and followed that with another short birdie miss on the 3rd.

With both players lying two on nearly the same line at the 4th hole, Oosterhuis, just a foot farther out, cozied his putt up to the hole for a certain par. Elder had an eighteen-foot putt for birdie. After seeing his opponent's putt, he struck his on-line, and when it hit the back of the cup and disappeared Elder literally leaped right into the history books.

"One of the happiest things is that now that story, the blacks and the Masters, is done with," said Elder later. "All of this publicity has given them a kind of bad name."

The club, tournament, and Clifford Roberts had taken widespread criticism over the years, with charges of racial discrimination coming from black players, journalists, and even U.S. Congressmen. In June 1971, Roberts announced a series of changes in Masters invitation categories. Beginning for the 1972 tournament, winners of PGA Tour events in the preceding twelve months would earn invitations. The Masters had always said that if a black player qualified under one of the entry criteria, he would be invited. Roberts was true to his word, almost immediately calling Pensacola Country Club. Unable to talk personally with Elder, he passed along his congratulations and told officials that he was delighted Elder would be invited. A statement he later released read: "I believe that the PGA has designated the Monsanto Open as one of its major tournaments. In that case, Lee Elder has earned his invitation and he will receive it. We're pleased that Elder is the representative of his race to qualify here because he has been a fine player for a number of years. He is quite likely to make a good showing."

After years of coming up short, Elder was a PGA Tour winner. Relieved, he told his wife on the phone after the tournament, "It's finally over." But it was only the beginning.

"IT REMINDS ME of the first Masters in 1934," said seventy-year-old Fred Corcoran, a former PGA Tournament Director who was a pioneering organizer and agent in the game. "Then everybody was talking about Bob Jones's return to golf. Now, everybody is talking about Elder." But just days before, his golf game was in shambles before the biggest week of his career. He sat sixty-first on the money list with only $10,313 in earnings. All of the distractions had brought down his game.

After his Monsanto Open victory, Elder returned home the next morning to a large welcoming party at Baltimore-Washington International Airport. He was front page news in that morning's *Washington Post* with a large photo and story just across from another headline that read "President To Reply On Tapes." The next fifty weeks would be quite eventful for both Elder and the country as a whole. Immediately, the Elders' phone was besieged with dozen of interview and media requests and kept ringing for twelve months: *Sports Illustrated, Golf Digest, Golf Magazine, People, Ebony, Jet,* the *New York Times,* and *The Flip Wilson Show* just to name a few.

In addition to the constant media queries, Elder sat through countless meetings for his scholarship fund and attended to endless sponsorship obligations. Of course, there were death threats. Some said watch out when you get to Augusta. Others said you'll never make it to Augusta. He had to endure political and social pressures from both outside and inside his camp. There were whites who didn't want him to play and blacks who thought he wasn't black enough and that Charlie Sifford deserved to be the first. Some thought he should boycott as a protest. "As hard as I've tried to get there, how can I run away?" he said.

The pressures even came from his inner circle. "They used to have a virtual entourage around them and with them all the time," says Murphy. "I always felt there were people trying to get him to do something for them all the time. That's distracting."

The attention increased beginning on August 8, 1974, when President Richard Nixon resigned and Vice President Gerald Ford became president. Ford was a terrific athlete growing up and star football player at the University of Michigan; yet he didn't start playing golf seriously until the mid-1960s. Ford soon played golf religiously and enjoyed his time around professional golfers. He was hooked on golf and on Elder as well. They played a casual round on October 20, and, on December 1, Ford attended a dinner in honor of Elder at the Washington Hilton to raise money for his scholarship fund. Ford told the attendees, "People won't remember 1975 as the first full year of Gerald Ford's presidency; they'll remember it as the year Lee Elder first played in the Masters."

Elder must have felt like he was running for political office, as every move he made was followed and dissected. Even normally innocent practice rounds like the one he played on October 28 became national news. That's when Roberts took the proactive step of arranging a trip to Augusta National for Elder. He would play with Deane Beman; Jim Gabrielsen, a standout amateur from Atlanta; and their host member, J. Paul Austin, president, CEO, and chairman of the board of Coca-Cola and chairman of the TPD policy board. Roberts sent a chauffeured-driven limousine to pick them up at nearby Daniel Field. Roberts also invited CBS News and the Augusta newspapers to cover the occasion. Elder hit his first tee shot into the right trees. Everyone took a mulligan, but Elder couldn't break par, shooting a two-over 74.

Being under a magnifying glass took its toll. "I was tight," said Elder. "I never had that much attention, where all eyes are on you and every place you turn someone is talking to you. It certainly weighs pretty heavy." Elder didn't have the time to put as much work into his golf game. He put on weight. A chronic back condition flared up. He began having knee pains.

His outlook remained bleak until April 6. In one day, Elder's mood changed with a final-round 69 at the Greater Greensboro Open. The round included a double eagle on the par-five 14th, holing a 5-iron from 181 yards—the first on Tour in one year. The 12th-place finish was his best result in more than six months.

Elder's original goal at the Masters was to finish in the top-twenty-four, which earned invitations for the next year. His result in Greensboro elevated his optimism. "I'm thinking along the lines of winning," he said. "I feel I have a good shot. I'm playing well enough to win perhaps, if the breaks go my way."

Lee Elder arrived at the Augusta National Golf Club for the 1975 Masters around 2:30 p.m. Monday with his wife Rose and longtime friend Dr. Philip Smith, the director of the Martin Luther King Hospital in Los Angeles. Immediately, he was enveloped by members of the press—sportswriters, television and radio reporters, some of whom had been waiting in the parking lot for several hours. Walking from his car to the clubhouse, he said, "I'm not talking. Every time I talk, I get in trouble."

The constant attention had overwhelmed even one of the most accommodating pros. He had already shunned most media requests the previous few weeks. "All he asks is a week to be left alone," said Rose. "He is here to play a tournament. After all, he has been talking for fifty-two weeks." But the demand to hear from Elder was so great that all parties agreed it was best for one more press conference to be staged Tuesday afternoon.

Elder registered at the tournament office—he would be contestant number 68—and was assigned a locker where he changed. He went to hit a few balls on the practice range and then onto the course where he played six holes in the late afternoon. Elder wouldn't talk on this day, but Henry Brown, his caddie, would. A thirty-six-year-old cab driver in Augusta, Brown began caddying at age thirteen and had carried the bags for Pete Cooper, Al Mengert, Art Wall, and Robert De Vicenzo, including the 1968 tournament in which De Vicenzo's signing of an incorrect scorecard—his playing competitor Tommy Aaron had written a "4" on the scorecard under the 17th hole when he actually made a "3"—gave Bob Goalby a one-shot victory instead of a playoff between the two. "I can walk this course backwards," said a confident Brown. "I know every blade of grass on it. I am No. 1." Brown was also an accomplished player with a low-handicap and the same cross-handed swing Elder once employed. "He's a fellow I think probably could beat me," joked Elder, who had already invited him to his celebrity pro-am the following month. "I think I might switch over and carry the bag for him."

Tuesday morning, Elder played a full practice round with John Mahaffey and Lu Liang-Huan of Taiwan. Since his first trip around the course six months earlier, he had put new irons in the bag. "I couldn't get it up in the air," said Elder. "I changed to Lil' David

Slingers, and I also bent my irons so I can get them up in the air."
Slingers were irons marketed more to high handicappers who had
trouble getting the ball aloft. The heads were offset with a thin top
edge and a more rounded, weighty bottom sole. They were also supposed to be shank-proof.

Elder didn't change his game, though. "I still cut the ball. I haven't
changed to a draw," he said. "There are several holes that you must
draw the ball but I felt it would be too great a sacrifice to try to
hook. When I try to hook, I have a tendency to hit over the top of
the ball and duck hook it." That was the miss he dreaded, so much so
that Elder used a double-overlapping grip—two fingers of his right
hand over two fingers of his left hand—to prevent turning his hands
over too much.

Elder reported shooting a 71 in his Tuesday practice round, three-
putting the 18th for bogey. He then ate lunch before his scheduled
3:00 p.m. press conference. At exactly the same time, another significant moment in American sports was occurring 700 miles north
of Augusta.

It was major league baseball's opening day, and when the first
pitch was thrown at 2:00 p.m. inside Cleveland's Municipal Stadium,
another racial barrier in American sports would fall. Frank Robinson
debuted as the Cleveland Indians' player-manager—the first black
manager in baseball history. Like Elder's Masters appearance, the
anticipation for this moment had been building since Robinson was
hired the previous October immediately after the 1974 season. There
was a thirty-minute pre-game ceremony in front of 56,204 fans.
Jackie Robinson's widow Rachel took part in the festivities, saying
she wished her late husband, who died of a heart attack in October
1972, could experience the moment. At age 39, Frank Robinson, the
only player to win the MVP award in both leagues, was just a year
younger than Elder, but already in his twentieth major league season.
Facing the New York Yankees, he penciled himself in the second
spot in the batting order as a designated hitter. In the bottom of the

first inning on a 2–2 count after fouling off three pitches by Doc Medich, Robinson connected on a fastball, sending a low screamer just over the left-field wall for home run number 575 in his career. Elder would love to rise to his occasion in such fashion. Behind a complete game from Gaylord Perry, the Indians won 5–3.

Elder didn't see or desire the comparisons to Frank Robinson, or Hank Aaron, or Arthur Ashe, or Jackie Robinson. Asked about the symbolism of the moment, he proclaimed, "I really don't feel like a great man in history. And that's the way I would like it to be. I don't think they're looking for me to be any kind of saint. I am playing for Lee and Rose Elder and nobody else, just like I always have."

In the packed press center for his question-and-answer session, he was visibly nervous and edgy, leaning forward with arms folded on a table and nursing a cigarette. Normally, he smoked two-plus packs a day but was trying to scale back for this week. Having to answer the same questions which had been posed over and over the previous year didn't help.

"I haven't been playing well," he said in explaining his recent reluctance to grant one-on-one interviews. "I just started to hit the ball well last week, and I wanted to work on my game. This is something I've wanted to do for a long time. I knew that if I stopped and answered questions from each of you, I'd have no chance to practice at all. But if I win Sunday, I'll be here, and I'll be very happy to answer any questions. And I'll give everybody an individual interview."

If Elder felt a circus atmosphere at the course, it wasn't much calmer off the grounds. Elder had dozens of people with him—family, friends (including football great Jim Brown), and colleagues with the Lee Elder Scholarship Fund. He rented two houses and booked five rooms at a local motel, both to accommodate his clan and throw off anyone who wanted to do him harm. He joked that real pressure was finding tickets for friends and associates. "I think they had a graduated scale depending on who you were," says Gary Koch, who never received the opportunity to buy more than eight in any of his years as a competitor. "How well you had performed in the game kind of dictated how many tickets you were allowed." Nicklaus and Palmer got their share. Elder had requested sixty-nine, but the club allowed him to purchase only twenty-five, still far more than the club usually gave players. But Elder felt the pressure. "I have to play well to keep from embarrassing other people by embarrassing myself," he said.

To those within the inner circle of the professional golf tour, Lee Elder's trip to Augusta National may not have seemed that big a deal. They had all played with him, changed shoes in the locker room with him, eaten dinner with him, and traded stories with him. He had been a presence on Tour for eight years and had played in nine major championships. For those outside the golf beltway, his opening tee shot on Thursday had become a very big deal.

THE FIELD OF seventy-six for the 1975 Masters was the smallest in seven years. It was supposed to be seventy-seven, but Donald Swaelens, from Belgium, withdrew prior to coming to the tournament after being diagnosed with pancreatic cancer. A veteran of the European professional circuit, the thirty-nine-year-old was set to make his first Masters appearance after finishing tied for 7th at the 1974 British Open. Instead, Swaelens's condition worsened, and he passed away two weeks later in Brussels.

In all, competing were fifty-three American professionals, seven American amateurs, and sixteen foreign professionals. The Masters Tournament made a distinction between Americans and non-Americans at the time. Even foreign players who didn't meet one of the thirteen qualification criteria could be invited at the club's discretion. Eight different countries outside the United States were represented—South Africa (four), Australia (three), England (three), Japan (two), Argentina (one), Mexico (one), New Zealand (one), and Taiwan (one). Every foreign professional would be paired with an American in the opening round.

"It may be the most prestigious tournament," said Trevino, "but it has the weakest field of any tournament we play in this country. With all those old Masters champions and foreign players invited every year, there aren't as many strong contenders."

That made experience even more important. Because it's played at the same venue every year, experience outweighed almost every other factor. Outside the first and second Masters, no one had ever won in his first attempt. Even the greats had only modest success: Byron Nelson tied for 9th in 1935, Sam Snead 18th in 1937, Ben Hogan tied for 25th in 1938, Arnold Palmer tied for 10th in 1955, Gary Player tied for 24th in 1957, and Jack Nicklaus missed the cut in 1959. Since the inaugural Masters in 1934, only twelve players had ever finished in the top-five in their first appearance. This year fifteen players were competing in their first Masters, including Lee Elder, who at age forty was the oldest among them.

Because of those pre-requisites, the same names tended to pop up on the Masters leaderboard. For the better players, it may have been the easiest major to win. For almost the previous decade and a half, the three most frequent names were Nicklaus, Palmer, and Player. They had played the golf course enough and figured out how to adapt their games. The trio had won ten of the previous seventeen Masters. They had been labeled the Big Three.

Palmer wasn't necessarily a high-ball hitter, but he attacked the golf course with such venom that it didn't matter. Now forty-five, the last of his four Masters wins had come eleven years earlier. He hadn't won on Tour in more than two years. Possibly due to a renewed effort to give up smoking in January, a light had instead been lit in his game. A bogey on the 71st hole at Hawaii cost him a shot at a victory (he finished 3rd) as did a poor final round at Jacksonville. Four days before the start of the Masters, he fired a 66 in Greensboro—the lowest round of the day in windy weather and on fast greens. "I've had putting troubles the last couple of years," said Palmer. "Right now, I can say that my tee-to-green game is the best it has been in some time. How well I do this week depends on my putting."

Palmer flew down to Augusta late Sunday afternoon in his private plane. On Monday, he enjoyed a steak sandwich and ginger ale in the grill room before starting his first practice round of the week by himself. Eventually joined by Bert Yancey, Palmer bogeyed the 1st hole, but consecutive birdies at the 2nd and the 3rd had the patrons cheering before the tournament had even started. Was it possible Palmer had one more charge left in him? "The Masters has always had a special meaning for me. Winning this year would mean a great deal to me," he said.

Player wasn't a high-ball hitter either, but his grit, determination, course management, and self-belief were an ideal combination for the major championships. The South African was the first international champion of the Masters in 1961. In 1974, Player was one behind Dave Stockton after 54 holes, but birdies at the 6th and 9th gave him a two-shot lead with nine to play. The likes of Nicklaus, Weiskopf, Irwin, and Stockton put pressure on him, but each made crucial mistakes on the closing nine. Player hit a 9-iron to within inches on the 71st hole for birdie and wrapped up his eighth major title with a par on the 18th. "Gary's game was designed around majors," says Johnny Miller. "He normally didn't have the horsepower to beat me or Nicklaus or Weiskopf on a normal course—the top players who were on. But on pressure-packed major courses, he could win. Other guys would get nervous. He was bull doggy and never gave up."

"My goal is to become recognized as the No. 1 player in the world," said Player. "I feel it will be measured by your performance in the major tournaments." That meant de-throning Jack Nicklaus. Back-to-back Masters titles would help his case. Only one man had accomplished that: Jack Nicklaus.

Tuesday, Player suffered an allergic reaction to some shrimp he ate at the turn and had to retire after eleven holes due to swelling and a rash on the right side of his body. A cortisone shot from a doctor on-site helped, but of more concern to Player was his lack of competitive golf. He did not come to the United States until two weeks earlier after having taken two months off from tournament golf. "I can't put golf before my family," said Player. "I don't regret the nice long holiday." He planned three trips to the States in 1975—all around the majors—and never spent more than five weeks away from home. He would have preferred two more starts before Masters week, and now he was forced to take the rest of the day off.

While Nicklaus and other experienced champions were favored, truth be told any number of players had their chances. Recent winners in odd-numbered years had been Gay Brewer (1967), George Archer (1969), Charles Coody (1971), and Tommy Aaron (1973)—all accomplished veteran players but none considered a contender at the beginning of those weeks.

In fact, the last eight Masters had been won by eight different players. Would someone like Miller or Weiskopf be the ninth?

| 3 |

TUESDAY, APRIL 8

As a young boy growing up in southeastern Virginia, Curtis Strange didn't need the Sunday edition of the *Augusta Chronicle-Herald* to learn about the Masters. He had already been educated by his Granddaddy, Clarence Ball, who had attended the tournament many times and always brought back a trinket and a story. Later, images from Augusta mesmerized him on the small black-and-white television in the golf shop his father Tom owned. "Who didn't watch it as a kid?" says Strange. "Especially back then when golf wasn't on TV that much. When it came on, people stopped in the golf shop and watched it."

Tom Strange was a very good golfer, good enough to win five Virginia State Opens and qualify for six U.S. Opens. Just as it was for Bobby Jones and most other American golfers born in the first half of the twentieth century, the U.S. Open was the most important title to win. Still, when Tom Strange played in the championship, his dream was to finish in the top sixteen—that would earn him a Masters invitation. It never came.

Tom Strange died of cancer in 1969. He was just thirty-nine years old; Curtis was fourteen. It took a long time for his passion for golf to return, but eventually it did. Strange earned a golf scholarship to Wake Forest University, and as a freshman at the 1974 NCAA Championship at Carlton Oaks Country Club in San Diego, Strange found himself in the last group with Florida's Gary Koch. On the par-five 18th hole, Wake Forest and Florida were tied for the team championship, and Strange trailed Koch by one for the individual championship. Strange coolly hit a 1-iron to seven feet and made the eagle putt, clinching both titles.

In the U.S. Amateur later that summer at Ridgewood (New Jersey) Country Club, Strange made it to the quarterfinals where he faced Jerry Courville of Connecticut. "I was so nervous because I knew the winner was going to the Masters," says Strange, who was fully aware that the Masters was trimming the number of players it invited from the previous year's U.S. Amateur from the eight quarterfinalists to the four semifinalists. Strange beat Courville, 2 and 1, to ensure his trip to the land of his father's dreams. When the invitation came, Strange wasted no time in writing his reply to Mr. Roberts. Soon thereafter, the invitation was framed by his mother Elizabeth.

The week before the 1975 Masters, Strange teed it up in his first PGA Tour event after receiving a sponsor's exemption to the Greater Greensboro Open, just thirty miles from the Wake Forest campus. In foul weather, Strange shot 83-75 to miss the cut by eight strokes. It wasn't all disappointing as his mind had been drifting southward. Strange went back to Winston-Salem, stuffed his clothes and clubs in his yellow Chevy Nova, and made the three-hour drive to Augusta Saturday morning. "It was all such a blur," says Strange, age twenty at the time. "It's hard to put into words when you're a college kid driving by yourself. You get in the gate, you're driving down this lane that isn't that long, and you pull right up at the clubhouse."

Once in the club's parking lot, he unloaded his bags and took them into the clubhouse. A few weeks after receiving the invitation, Strange and the other six amateurs received more correspondence from the club—a letter offering them residence in the Crow's Nest, just as Nicklaus and Miller had experienced.

The Crow's Nest is a thirty-by-forty-foot room on the third floor of the clubhouse where the club allows amateurs to stay during the tournament. It was a Spartan setting. Partitions and dividers separated the twin beds in the room, and there was one common bathroom. It was like a youth hostel in golf heaven. In the mornings, the boys would climb up a ladder that led to the cupola. There, they could see the surroundings out all four sides. If it was windy or rainy, they could go back to bed. If not, they would rush to go play.

"They couldn't provide stuff for nothing for the amateurs," says Koch, who drove up from Gainesville, Florida, and was staying in the Crow's Nest for the second year in a row. "They were charging $1 for breakfast, $1 for lunch, and $3 for dinner. You have complete run of the clubhouse. You can order anything you want, and you'll get a bill. The room was like $5 a day, so like $10 a day to live there."

In his day, Jack Nicklaus took advantage of the run of the club, particularly in the dining room where he treated it like an all-you-can-eat buffet. "After four days, they clamped down on Phil Rodgers and me, and wouldn't let us order two steaks apiece at dinner," says Nicklaus, "but we were still allowed a double shrimp cocktail."

Although the accommodations and decor had hardly changed from the days when Nicklaus stayed there, for college kids living in ratty apartments and dorms, the Crow's Nest was a step up. The club welcomed them beginning on Saturday. Strange and Koch would be joined by Craig Stadler, the 1973 U.S. Amateur champion, and Jerry Pate, the 1974 U.S. Amateur champion. "It was such a special thing to get to do, we all felt like we needed to mind our p's and q's so we don't screw this thing up," says Koch.

"I got my money's worth down there," says Strange, not in the realm of extra steaks, but atmosphere. Most nights Strange would sneak downstairs to the library. "When the lights went off, I went looking at books and old pictures," he says. Like many former guests of the Crow's Nest, Strange absconded with his own pieces of memorabilia—a white towel and an orange juice canister with the club logo, which served as his penny jar for the next three decades.

Later that Sunday, Strange was on the golf course for the first time ever at Augusta National.

FIRST TIMERS at Augusta National were immediately struck by two things. Upon walking out the back of the clubhouse, they noticed the property's scale and its significant elevation change. From the high point at the 1st green to the low point at the 11th green along Rae's Creek, there was a drop of more than 150 feet. The slope was dramatic in places. Secondly, they took in the sheer beauty of the grounds and its immaculate conditioning, much of it accomplished through sheer manpower at the time. "There wasn't a weed anywhere," says Ben Wright. On the course, tees were cut to 7/32 of an inch. Fairways were cut to 5/16 of an inch. Greens were cut to 1/8 of an inch. There was no rough and relatively few bunkers compared to other courses with just forty-four.

In 1975, a look at the scorecard revealed that the course played to a par of 72, at 7,020 yards in length—only 320 yards longer than when it opened. The card included a numerical oddity that the yardage of each nine was the same (3,510). There were four par three holes, four par five holes, and ten par four holes.

AUGUSTA NATIONAL GOLF CLUB

HOLE	1	2	3	4	5	6	7	8	9	OUT
PAR	4	5	4	3	4	3	4	5	4	36
YARDS	400	555	360	220	450	190	365	530	440	3,510

HOLE	10	11	12	13	14	15	16	17	18	IN
PAR	4	4	3	5	4	5	3	4	4	36
YARDS	485	445	155	475	420	520	190	400	420	3,510

From there, rookies had to learn the subtleties of the course that weren't so obvious. The course didn't play as long as the total yardage indicated, but it did play differently from the original intent. Every hole had undergone significant changes from its original design. MacKenzie, who died just two and a half months before the first Masters and never saw the completed course, wouldn't have recognized the game.

MacKenzie and Jones originally wanted a links-style course, but the design was outdated almost as soon as it opened. Bobby Jones played his entire career with hickory-shafted clubs, and photographs show him hitting shots with them to fairway locations and green sites during construction of Augusta National. In 1924, steel shafts in clubs were legalized by the USGA, and slowly they became the shaft of choice. Steel shafts were more durable, but they also changed the way the game was played. To maximize performance of hickory shafts, swings were slower, flatter, and handsier—the players had to wait for the clubhead to catch up with their hands at impact. This sweeping action produced lower shots, usually draws, that ran more. Steel shafts allowed players to swing harder and more upright—producing higher shots that flew farther and performed more consistently.

Many of the holes at Augusta had been laid out with the ball flight of hickory-shafted clubs in mind, and Jones's preferred ball flight off the tee happened to be a draw. That was part of the reason so many holes moved right-to-left off the tee. Nine of the fourteen par-fours and fives at Augusta favored a draw: holes 2, 5, 9, 10, 11, 13, 14, 15, and 17. Some players, like Johnny Miller, felt not one fade was required anywhere off the tee at Augusta.

"You needed to hit a draw to give yourself access to the golf course," says Bob Murphy, who would be playing in his seventh Masters. Draws not only got the ball around the corner on those holes, but they also found speed slots on certain holes like the 2nd, 10th, and 13th where the balls could get twenty, thirty-five, even fifty yards extra roll. That left players the advantage of hitting significantly less club going into the greens.

When he arrived for his first Masters in 1971, Jerry Heard faded the ball. "When I got there, they were asking, 'Heardie, how you gonna play it this week, you gonna cut it or hook it?'" he says. "I said, 'I'm going to cut it.' So I play my first practice round, and they said, 'Now what are you going to do?' And I say, 'I'm going to hook it'."

Bobby Nichols, teeing up in his eleventh Masters in 1975, remembers someone asking Jimmy Demaret how he ever won three times at Augusta National considering Demaret predominately played a fade. Demaret replied, "Well, if I was a hooker I'd have won six."

Off the tee, the course didn't so much favor longer hitters as it disenfranchised the shorter ones. With all four par fives being reachable, long hitters like Dewitt Weaver, Larry Ziegler, Weiskopf, Nicklaus, and Miller had an edge. Short hitters couldn't reach the plateaus on some of the fairways and were hitting into the hills instead of carrying them. But at Augusta, short hitters had their advantage taken away as well. Long hitters as a group are less accurate, but wayward tee shots weren't punished as much at Augusta. Bobby Jones, a long hitter himself, wanted no long rough on the course. Because of that, missing the fairways wasn't punished like it was at a U.S. Open.

While length could help, first timers learned it wasn't nearly the advantage that hitting the ball high was. "It's not the length of the course," said the rookie Pate. "It's the hardness of the greens."

The greens were grassed with Tifton 328 hybrid Bermuda, a strain of warm-season grass that thrives in the South with a wide blade and deep-root structure. But Bermuda goes dormant and turns brown after the first freeze. It doesn't begin growing again until high temperatures reach the mid 70s. So the greens were overseeded in the fall with perennial ryegrass, a cool-season grass. April was a shoulder month, and it was always a balancing act to keep those two different grasses in harmony during a transition period. In 1975, the Bermuda was stronger as Augusta had enjoyed a warm, wet spring thus far. Sometimes that wasn't the case. Tough winters could kill the Bermuda and come tournament time the rye could be dying out due to weather or tournament conditions, causing the greens to quicken with sparse grass coverage (and higher scores). In warm years, though, the Bermuda could be strong enough for the grain of the grass to affect putts.

Under the right conditions, the greens, with their Bermuda base and Georgia red clay, could also get extremely firm. Balls would spin, but players were usually hitting approach shots from uneven or inconsistent lies. When dry, balls could bounce as high as six feet in the air when they hit greens. In those circumstances, the course almost played like a links, just the intent of Jones and MacKenzie, who said, "Most American greens are overwatered, and it is hoped that we will not make this mistake at Augusta."

"The approach shots to me were very difficult," says Koch. Most of the players in the field couldn't carry the ball to the back hole location on the 18th, or carry it over the false fronts on the 5th or 14th holes and make their ball stop. "That's why guys like Weiskopf, Nicklaus, and a handful of others did so well," says Koch. "The ability to hit the ball way up in the air was a huge, huge advantage back then at that golf course."

The fairways were also overseeded, with fescue grass being used starting in 1973. The transition period could produce inconsistent conditions that favored high-ball hitters as well. "You could have fairways that were pretty thin," says John Mahaffey, who made his second Masters start in 1975. "It would benefit a guy like a Watson or a Nicklaus who hit the ball high and picked it. They could count on the height of the ball to stop it, not the spin."

Once on the greens, newbies had to decipher their beguiling contours. With the overseed and time of the year, the grain of the

Bermuda grass and the effect it had on pulling balls was not as prevalent. Players tried to stay aware of the lowest point on the course, the 11th green—local knowledge that Gary Koch's caddie imparted to him during his first start in 1974. Koch, a putting maestro growing up who was called "Drain" by other players, recalls his caddie reading the break on one putt that left him flabbergasted. "I said, 'What, are you kidding me?' Sure enough, it did what he said," says Koch.

Along with the breaks, speed was also a big issue. Although nowhere near as fast as they would become decades later, for standards at the time, the greens were very quick. While downhill putts would run out, uphill putts could be really slow. "I can't overstate how intimidating those surfaces are your first couple times there," says Strange. Under the right conditions and if on top of their games, short hitters, low-ball hitters, and faders could all win at Augusta National. But bad putters never stood a chance.

This is the course Strange and the other first timers played as much as they could while experiencing the traditions of the club and tournament. It was hard enough for seasoned professionals to follow their normal weekly routine at the Masters. For a Tour stop, they usually arrived on a Tuesday and played a pro-am on Wednesday, followed by the event. For the Masters, however, even the pros came in Sunday or Monday, played multiple rounds, and hit more balls on the range than they normally would. Young amateurs had no chance. "By Thursday, my body had figured out something was going on here," says Koch. "This must be way more important."

As tradition dictated, all of the amateurs were to be paired with Masters champions. It was the hospitable thing to do—having players who know the course chaperone the youngsters around. Just as Nicklaus and Miller played with Jimmy Demaret in their first Masters rounds, each of the seven amateurs would be paired with one of the twelve Masters champions in the field. Complete first-round tee times were released Wednesday, but tournament officials publicized eight featured pairings the day before with marquee names such as Palmer, Trevino, Player, and Weiskopf.

"Somebody asked me, 'Have you seen the pairings?' I said, 'No'," recalls Strange. He had been drawn with Jack Nicklaus. "I was a basket case until I teed off Thursday."

NEARLY TWO DOZEN players were already on the grounds Sunday, and the rest of them arrived Monday. Gates opened for the first time at 8:00 a.m. Monday. Tickets were no longer available at King's Way Pharmacy or Bill's Barber Shop. The Masters was now one of the toughest tickets in sports. For the tenth consecutive year, tickets for the Masters were sold out. Series badges, as they were called, allowed patrons admission to the tournament rounds only, Thursday–Sunday, and, if necessary, to an 18-hole playoff on Monday. Since 1966, these tickets for the tournament rounds proper had been sold out on a priority basis to established customers, a list that numbered around 30,000. The high demand and increased numbers of people on the grounds—everyone who applied was once sold a ticket—forced the club to close this list in 1972. A waiting list was then established. In 1975, there were five times as many requests as tickets. Soon, even the waiting list was closed. "I'm still most unhappy about the fact that we can only take care of about one-fifth of the people that would like to attend the Masters Tournament," said Clifford Roberts.

Season badges were not good for practice days, so Monday, Tuesday, or Wednesday, people could walk right up to the gate and buy a daily ticket for $5. They were unlimited. Practice round patrons could walk the course, take photographs, film with movie cameras, get autographs, and see all the best players. All except the favorite, Jack Nicklaus.

The pudgy kid from Columbus had figured out a lot since his first trip to Augusta sixteen years earlier. Gone were the long car rides and side-trips to other Tour stops. It was now a private plane and regimented schedule. Nicklaus planned the first three-and-a-half months of the year around the Masters, and for a half-dozen years it was unchanged—roughly three events on the West Coast and then three events in the South.

"I always started in January picking the tournaments that I wanted to play that would give me the competition that I wanted and maybe give me similar conditions that I wanted, give me the opportunity to play shots that I wanted to play, that I thought that I might play (at Augusta)," says Nicklaus. "I avoided a lot of tournaments two or three weeks before the Masters simply because you knew you were going to hit a ton of wind and you were going to be playing a lot of knock down shots and stuff like that. Occasionally, I would play some of those, but most of the time, not. I like to play the courses where you needed to fly your ball in the air."

Another custom that continued just as it had the previous ten years: Jack Nicklaus traveled to Augusta for his practice rounds the week before the 1975 Masters. It was a routine he continued at the other majors as well with lots of success. "I always believed in being prepared," says Nicklaus.

Fate also played a part. In 1963, bursitis in his left hip caused him to shuffle his schedule. Instead of playing the week before, he went to Augusta for some practice. And he won his first Masters. The next year, he played the Greater Greensboro Open, a tournament that had been moved to the week before the Masters that season and would stay that way on the calendar for twenty-five years. "I went to Greensboro in 1964 (finishing 4th) and didn't win the Masters (tied for 2nd). That was my last time at Greensboro," says Nicklaus, who then won the following two Masters.

"Nothing against Greensboro, I felt my preparation was far better going to Augusta than playing a tournament," he says. "I enjoyed going to Augusta—the peaceful quiet of nobody else there. Going out and playing and enjoying the golf course.

"Would I rather win Greensboro or the Masters? Duh."

But Nicklaus, who wasn't without superstitions, admits, "If I had played well at Greensboro and won the Masters, I probably would have said my preparation was playing the week before the tournament."

Golfers such as Weiskopf, Player, and Trevino preferred to play their way in. While they and others such as Miller and Palmer were in the Piedmont of North Carolina, on Wednesday, April 2, Nicklaus flew up from his home in the Lost Tree Village development of North Palm Beach, Florida, where he moved his family in 1965. Rising at 5:30 a.m., he made a stop in Atlanta for two morning business meetings before landing in Augusta that afternoon. He ate a bowl of oyster stew in the clubhouse before getting to work.

Nicklaus liked to play at least four rounds on these sojourns. Sometimes he'd play nine in the morning, have lunch, then play the other nine in the afternoon. Other times, he would take his time and stay out all day—just he and caddie Willie Peterson, who had seen enough practice rounds to know whether Nicklaus was ready or not.

Usually, he played by himself, but there were times he'd play with good friend and fellow tour pro Gardner Dickinson or maybe one of Augusta National's two head professionals, Dave Spencer or Bob Kletcke, who had taken $4 off Nicklaus during a practice round at the 1956 U.S. Junior Amateur. Nicklaus never forgot it, but Kletcke always refused to let him play for those $4 back. Kletcke recalls one such pre-tournament round in which Nicklaus was a long way back on the par-five 13th. Even though he couldn't see the green around the dogleg, he chose a 1-iron for the shot that demanded a high, towering hook. "I looked at Gardner, and he looked at me. And I shook my head 'no,' and he shook his head 'yes'," says Kletcke. It drew thirty yards, but fell just short of the green. Kletcke questioned Nicklaus, who responded by hitting the shot again, this time to ten feet. "That's one of the greatest golf shots I've ever seen," says Kletcke. "I never will forget it."

Hampered by one-and-a-quarter inches of rain on Thursday, Nicklaus got in just three rounds this time. He played his final practice round with amateur George Burns on Saturday and struck the ball well from tee to green, shooting a 70. Peterson pronounced that his boss was in great form.

"If I shot 276 or 277, I knew that I'd played fairly well to be able to do that. Generally speaking that was going to win the next week," says Nicklaus. "I had a good week of preparation. Now I can enjoy my weekend and get away from the game, then come back. I've got all my preparation I need out of the way. I can just go play."

Nicklaus returned home Saturday evening, enjoyed some family time, and flew back up to Augusta Tuesday morning. So for him, the actual week of the Masters would almost follow the routine of a normal tournament.

When asked if he was surprised no one consistently copied his routine of preparation for the majors, Nicklaus says slyly, "That was great." Nicklaus was never going to be less prepared than anyone else. This gave him an added psychological advantage. "He almost thought he deserved to win," says Johnny Miller.

The trip in 1975 also gave Nicklaus the opportunity to test out a couple of new sticks around Augusta National. Nicklaus had been playing MacGregor golf clubs since age eleven and had the same set of VIP irons by Nicklaus—he had consulted on their design—in his bag since 1967. The set included a 1-iron through a pitching wedge—all with lead tape on the back and black leather grips with gold lacing. He had even used the same MacGregor Tommy Armour 3-wood since 1958. Prior to this Masters, though, two significant changes had been made in the Nicklaus bag.

When Nicklaus had turned professional, the MacGregor Tommy Armour driver he used may have been his favorite club. His ability to hit it long and straight set up his entire game. On a trip to South Africa in early 1966, however, the driver broke, and Nicklaus struggled to find a suitable replacement in the following years.

Before the days of equipment trucks and scientific fitting, players obtained clubs in more rudimentary ways. "We used to pass clubs around," says Weiskopf. "That's how we got clubs. That was our club fitting." In late 1974, Dickinson broke his driver and Nicklaus loaned him his spare. Needing a new spare to carry with him, Nicklaus found an old driver head lying around that David Graham had once given him. Nicklaus attached a shaft and grip. This MacGregor Tommy Armour 693 driver was anything but new. The style of the head and markings indicated that it was probably from 1948. The late-1940s had been the heyday of MacGregor's drivers. The vintage driver was nearly an antique.

Nicklaus took the new club with him, and during a tournament in Japan it got passed to youngster Eddie Pearce. Upon returning it, Pearce raved about the driver. Nicklaus hit some balls with it and liked it. He stuck with his normal driver at the start of 1975, but soon began tinkering with the spare again. He put in a different shaft, but that cost him twenty yards in distance. Then he kinked the shaft to take some of the loft off the club until he was satisfied with the effect.

The ever-plotting Nicklaus waited until the Doral Open in March to debut the driver, due to the course's spaciousness and lack of out-of-bounds. The tournament couldn't come soon enough. The week before in Fort Lauderdale, he let a three-shot lead with seven holes to play slip away with a double bogey and two bogeys—a very un-Nicklaus like finish. He thought his game was on schedule, but admitted, "Well, maybe I'm one day, one round behind schedule." At Doral, though, the driver eased his concerns. Nicklaus shot all four rounds under par in Miami and holed a twenty-foot birdie putt on the final hole to cap off his first win in more than six months.

"I lose a little distance with this driver," said Nicklaus, "but I control the ball better with it." He was pleased his game was rounding into shape. "I think winning here is indicative of the way I feel I'll play at Augusta. I'm very pleased," he told the press.

Nicklaus took the following week off, and during a practice round at the Jupiter Hills Club near his home, he made another discovery.

Three years earlier, he had been forced to retire the sand wedge he'd used since turning professional. As with the driver, he had been scrounging around looking for another he liked before Jupiter Hills head professional Phil Greenwald loaned him an original Wilson R-90 sand wedge. The club was from the mid-1930s, just a few years after they were mass marketed from Gene Sarazen's invention. Instead of grooves, the worn face was hand-punched with dots—186 of them aligned in eleven vertical rows. "The ones with dots sold for $5, those with lines for $6," said Nicklaus. He loved the club and took it home. With his steep swing plane, Nicklaus wasn't considered a great bunker player. The sand wedge would be useful on holes like the par-five 2nd, where a majority of second shot attempts into that green ended up in one of two front bunkers.

The next week, he took his driver and sand wedge to compete in his final event before the Masters. On the opening day at the Heritage Classic on Hilton Head Island, South Carolina, Nicklaus shot 66. Then on the second day, he fired a course-record 8-under-par 63. Nicklaus considered Harbour Town Golf Links, with its narrow, tree-lined fairways and small greens, tougher to score on than Augusta National. Although challenged by Tom Weiskopf down the stretch, Nicklaus led wire-to-wire for his fifty-sixth PGA Tour win and a new tournament record of 271, 13 under par.

With two consecutive victories and two new clubs in his bag that were a combined seventy years old, he flew the 500 miles back up to Augusta Tuesday morning. He promptly registered and was given number 76—the next-to-last man to sign in (Terry Diehl was the last). That number would be on Peterson's caddie overalls and the light blue colored player contestant pin that was Nicklaus's badge for the week. He got back on the course in mid-afternoon and walked up the 18th at dinner time. According to Peterson, he shot another 70. Afterward, Nicklaus showered, changed, and went to the Masters Club Dinner, the annual Tuesday night gathering of Masters champions (with Roberts the only non-golfer who attended).

The affair began in 1952 after being suggested by Ben Hogan, who was the only one of the twenty-two living champions not present in 1975.

On Wednesday morning, Nicklaus played nine holes before his pre-tournament press conference. As was usually the case during that period, he would skip that afternoon's Par Three Contest. Nicklaus avoided another tiring round and seeing another set of greens he didn't need. Instead, he would just hit a few practice balls. His goal was to be prepared for Thursday.

There was a different air to Nicklaus's confidence this year. "I honestly played pretty good the last six weeks. I didn't have to work on any particular part of my game when I came here," said Nicklaus. "I'm better prepared than I've been in several years."

"There were fifteen or twenty of us who could beat him," says Murphy. "We did not beat him when he was on. You could get close, but you didn't quite get it done. But if he wasn't playing his best, then we could sneak in and get him."

Jack Nicklaus had been the favorite in virtually every Masters for the last decade. With his record and stellar play the previous month, he was the odds-makers favorite again in 1975 and the overwhelming choice of local professionals and sports writers in the *Augusta Chronicle's* pre-tournament poll. The players sensed it and most all of them agreed with Gary Player: "If anybody beats Jack Nicklaus this week, he'll win the golf tournament."

| 4 |

WEDNESDAY, APRIL 9

"**I** was a twenty-three-year-old rookie on Tour in 1975, and I made the cut in my very first start ever at Phoenix," recalls Roger Maltbie, who had seen Johnny Miller, four years older than him, play junior golf in the northern California area. "That got me in Tucson the next week, where I made the cut again. I was on Tour and making money ($929 in those two events). I thought I was doing great. Then I realized Johnny beat me those two weeks by sixty strokes. What I thought was good didn't mesh with reality. A lot of people felt that way with Johnny at that time."

From the outside, 1975 appeared to start just as 1974 had for Johnny Miller, the game's hottest—and winningest—player the previous year and a half. But a swing thought Miller had gleaned from his rivals meant his game was even better.

"What changed in '75 was I started compressing the ball a little more," says Miller, the unanimous player of the year in 1974 with eight wins on Tour. "I was watching Nicklaus and Weiskopf, and I noticed the way their hip action worked. They weren't sliding as much as I was. And they were turning their left hip like there was a knife against it. They would just cut the pant, but they wouldn't stab themselves. I was sagging my hip into the knife blade. So I started to turn my hips a little more and snap—a little more speed in the hips. And I started hitting down on it more."

Miller, who never hit the ball well on the practice range, was now striping it all the time. "In '75 I played absolutely the best golf of my life," he says. "Everyone thinks that it was '74, but it was really '75."

After some significant time off, Miller began each year invigorated, and 1975 was no different. The first full week of January in Phoenix, Miller consistently hit his approach shots so close to the hole that he was actually upset at the end of the tournament that he hadn't holed an iron shot. He shot a course-record 61 in the second round and coasted to a fourteen-shot win with a then-record 24 under par total. The "Desert Fox", as he had been nicknamed, traveled down Interstate 10 the next week and produced another near-flawless performance, shooting a 61 in the final round at Tucson National for a nine-shot win at 25 under par. "I went out and birdied six of the first seven holes that Sunday, and I'd lost a shot to him," says John Mahaffey of that final round. "He was awesome." After finishing tied for 6th in defense of his title at Pebble Beach, Miller returned to desert golf and dominated the field at the Bob Hope Classic in early February, winning by three over Bob Murphy. At the end of that evening's NBC Nightly News, Tom Snyder sarcastically pointed out, "He's now played in four tournaments this year, and he has only won three."

"I don't know that you can play any better than he played," says Murphy. "He was just incredible." Miller refused to let up either. The further under par he got, the more he attacked.

"When Johnny Miller got to hitting it at the flag—'flagging it' is what we called it—no one hit it closer to the hole," says Tom Weiskopf. "It didn't matter what club it was—3-wood, 2-iron, wedge, 6-iron. Hole after hole, he was straight at the flag."

"I had a good run of putting, and I was the best ball-striker on Tour," says Miller. "If I was on at all I could pretty much blow away fields. I was not afraid of anything in 1975."

Miller's sudden success made him one of the hottest properties in sports. *Newsweek* magazine splashed Miller across the cover of its February 3, 1975, issue with the headline "Golf's New Golden Boy." "Best in game," claimed *Golf Digest* in its 1975 Masters preview issue, installing him as the favorite. The week before the tournament, *Golf World* magazine superimposed him walking on water at Augusta National's 16th hole with the title: "Will the Miller Magic Work at Augusta?"

For a cover story in February 1974, *The Sporting News* had asked, "The New Nicklaus?" By 1975, that headline wasn't a question.

"In '74, I was sort of a sensation winning the first three tournaments, but I wasn't the favorite over Nicklaus in anything," says Miller, who went into the 1975 Masters having recorded eleven PGA Tour wins in the last fifteen months against Nicklaus's four. "A lot of the announcers were saying I was better than Nicklaus by then."

The prospect of a Nicklaus–Miller duel at the Masters to settle the world golfing order had media and fans alike salivating. It was a long way from the first time the two blonde-haired golfers had met during the 1966 U.S. Open, when Nicklaus was the young gun dominating golf and Miller was a scrawny nineteen-year-old amateur.

Through Johnny Swanson, an Olympic Club member and a mutual friend, Nicklaus and Miller played a practice round together that Tuesday at the Olympic Club. The naïve Miller, who used such days for quick light-hearted play, was shocked at what he witnessed. "What I couldn't understand was how serious he was on every shot," says Miller. "Every shot was like he was playing in the dang U.S. Open on Sunday. I'd never seen anybody put so much effort into every shot in a practice round. He was intense in his concentration. Everything had a purpose." It took Miller many years before he correlated the benefits of practicing like you play.

Another surprise greeted Miller the following day when Nicklaus asked him to join in another practice round—not at the Olympic Club but instead at nearby San Francisco Golf Club. He couldn't believe they were playing another course the day before the U.S. Open, and he never asked Nicklaus why. But Nicklaus had never played there and figured he'd had enough preparation at Olympic. Nicklaus remembers Miller's play, though. "He didn't carry it 180 yards, little skinny kid just bunted it along the ground, but he chipped and putted fantastic," says Nicklaus. "I just didn't think he had enough strength." They came to the par-five 18th hole, one Miller had never reached in two shots. "[Nicklaus] took out this 3-wood—must have been about 260 yards into the wind—and flew it on the green," says Miller. "That was a shot I'd never seen before."

In the championship, fate intervened and paired Miller and Nicklaus together for the third round. Both were tied for 5th, but in reality it wasn't a good break for Miller. "In his mind, I was like his little brother or something. There was an affection there that he sort of guided me along," says Miller. On national television, he shot 74 that day to Nicklaus's 69. After the round, Nicklaus complimented him on his temperament and observed that he'd hit it farther when he filled out. Miller would finish tied for 8th and low amateur. Nicklaus would shoot a 74 in the final round and finish in 3rd place, seven shots out of a playoff between Billy Casper and Arnold Palmer.

They wouldn't play together in the limelight again for six years, and by then Miller was a different specimen. "Once he grew up, he grew up to be a big strong guy," says Nicklaus. In primetime on the East Coast after most of the country had watched Roger Staubach and the Dallas Cowboys defeat the Miami Dolphins in that afternoon's Super Bowl, the two battled one another in the final round of the 1972 Crosby Pro-Am. A Nielsen rating of 13.1 made it one of the highest rated golf broadcasts ever, and all those people watched NBC as Miller, tied for the lead, faced a sidehill lie for his approach shot in the 16th fairway at Pebble Beach. He proceeded to hit a dead shank into the gallery on the right—a golfer's most dreaded miss. Nicklaus eventually defeated Miller in a playoff with a birdie on the first extra hole, but Miller, and many watching at home, never forgot that shot on the 16th. It lingered in the back of his mind for the rest of his career. Whenever he encountered a similar scenario, he always asked himself: "Am I going to shank this?"

Three years later, Miller had become known more for his sound-bites than shanks. "I was sort of outspoken when I talked about Jack," says Miller, "I said, 'Hey, I can beat Jack.' I said, 'I might be the best player in the world.' It was a little bit hearsay I guess. But at the time I really thought that every time I play with Jack I do well, and I was winning a lot of events."

Leading into the Masters, Miller had said: "Jack has been on top so long people are beginning to look for someone to beat him. Now people are starting to say, 'Maybe, right now, Johnny Miller is better.' Right now, I might be."

Inadvertently, Miller had stirred the conversation, and the Nick-laus–Miller showdown was all anyone wanted to talk about and see. By the 1975 Masters, Nicklaus and Miller had received seven differ-ent propositions from promoters wanting to stage a winner-take-all televised match. Two of them offered $1 million to the victor at a time when the average first-place winner's check on Tour was a mere $35,000. Nicklaus declined. He thought such a match shouldn't line the pockets of those outside the game and questioned what such a spectacle would prove. Miller thought why not.

For weeks leading into the tournament, Miller was asked noth-ing but questions about Jack Nicklaus and displacing him as the game's preeminent player. Nicklaus heard nothing but questions about Johnny Miller and his three wins on the year.

At Doral, Nicklaus responded to a question about Miller by say-ing, "Yeah, how about him? He's obviously a very fine player. He's won a lot of golf tournaments in the last year or so and he'll win a lot more."

Nicklaus, who always gave honest and thoughtful answers to any question, wasn't upset by Miller's mouth as much as his position above him on the leaderboards. "I never try to beat one man. I try to beat the field," he said. "Of course, you can always figure that if you're beating Arnold or Gary or Lee or Miller or Weiskopf, you're going to be right up there. I'm no more aware of him than I am any good player. I'm aware of him if he gets on the leaderboard. Any player who is on the leaderboard obviously is playing well and is a challenge, a player to be reckoned with. But really, I look at numbers not names."

As for Johnny Miller, Nicklaus said: "I read the papers just like everyone else. He has shot some fantastic scores. But I think it's good for me and good for the game to have someone playing well. It's probably good for you to have someone beating your brains out once in a while."

Once at Augusta, Nicklaus didn't sugarcoat his view of Miller's standing in the game. "I think Gary (Player) and Lee (Trevino) are better golfers than Johnny," he said during his pre-tournament press conference. "As far as I am concerned, winning the major tournaments are the real test. Gary's won eight, Lee five, and Johnny only one.

"For sheer ability, Miller and Tom Weiskopf probably have more going for them than anybody out there today, but neither of them approaches what Player or Trevino have done."

Miller counters, "He knew that Weiskopf had the horsepower and I had the horsepower to beat him at times. We were more of a threat because Billy (Casper) and Gary and Lee were short hitters."

Miller had loads of respect for Nicklaus and found himself acquiescing to Nicklaus's position as the Masters drew near. "Jack Nicklaus is better than I am," he said at Doral. "He has more capability and more experience. You're not going to catch me low-rating a guy who's won twelve major tournaments. If Jack were at his best I wouldn't want to play him every day. I've been the best for a spell, now, because I have these streaks where I can do anything. But right now the variance in Nicklaus's game is smaller than the variance in mine. His bad tournaments are better than my bad tournaments. When he plays well, he wins. When he plays badly, he finishes second. When he plays terrible, he finishes third."

At Augusta, Miller compared his fire-at-the-flag style of golf to that of Nicklaus's disciplined approach. "I play differently than he does," he said. "When he's playing well, he's consistent. I may go crazy and beat him, but he's a better player. He's stronger, and he has more experience. Ever since I was a little kid, I've played hot and cold, but I'd rather do that than play cold all the time."

So far in 1975, Nicklaus had had a Jack Frost effect on Miller, who hadn't finished ahead of Nicklaus in any of the four events they had both played: the Crosby Pro-Am, L.A. Open, Doral Open, and Heritage Classic. In fact, Miller had bettered him in only three of the last eighteen events that they'd played. Miller's sudden struggles were more pronounced against Nicklaus, none more so than the first round at Hilton Head when Miller shot a 78 to Nicklaus's 66. After missing the cut for the first time in two years, Miller added Greensboro to his schedule at the last minute. "Jack's going in as a winner," said Miller. "I don't want to go in as a loser." He finished tied for 6th there and pronounced himself ready: "With me, playing good is about 90 percent inspiration. There's no problem getting inspired about the Masters."

After arriving in Augusta Sunday evening, Miller played eighteen holes each day. His practice round partners included Jerry Heard, Sam Snead, J.C. Snead, Grier Jones, Lee Trevino, and Billy Casper, who had taught Miller his strategy for playing much of the course. He played with Casper Monday and was so relaxed that upon coming across a baby turtle by the 11th green, Miller decided to pick it up and take it home for his kids to see.

Surprisingly, Miller was not included in the feature pairings released Tuesday. He was on NBC that night, receiving an award for best men's golfer from Bob Hope during the Gillette Cavalcade of Champions 1974 that had been taped earlier in the year.

With three victories heading into the year's first major, Miller had been the clear Masters favorite a month earlier. Now with his hot streak in March, Nicklaus had taken that honor, and by the day before the opening round of the Masters, bookmakers in Las Vegas had moved another player's odds lower than Miller's as well.

MILLER HAD FLOWN down from Greensboro Sunday night on a private plane with Tom Weiskopf. While Miller hadn't planned on playing competitively the week before, Weiskopf had. He didn't follow the Nicklaus prescription, preferring to play his way into Augusta. Only once had he come a week early. That was in 1974 because he was playing so poorly and felt he needed the practice. This year following Hilton Head, he did sneak in one day of practice at Augusta before hiring a helicopter to transport him the 250 miles northeast to Greensboro.

Weiskopf's year in 1975 had gotten off to as slow a start as Miller's had quickly. He missed the cut in the season's first two events at Phoenix and Tucson and broke 70 only twice in his first five starts. His game gradually rounded into form, and at the Greater Greensboro Open everything clicked. He opened with a bogey-free round of seven-under-par 64 at Sedgefield Country Club—the low round of the day by three shots in blustery conditions that produced twenty-three rounds in the 80s.

"That 64 by Weiskopf at Greensboro in the wind may be one of the greatest rounds ever," said Jim Colbert. Weiskopf agreed the next day, "I really think it was the best round I've ever played. A lot of players told me they think it's better than Miller's 61 (at Tucson)." Arnold Palmer and others felt the greens were running as fast as those at Augusta National. "The fastest I can remember on the tour," said Weiskopf.

The weather remained chilly and breezy all week, but Weiskopf continued his stellar play, leading wire to wire. In the final round, he eagled the par-five 9th by making a fifty-foot putt and cruised home for the title. "There's nothing like a win to boost your confidence," said Weiskopf of his first victory anywhere in fifteen months. "I really played as good for four rounds from tee to green as I have ever played. There wasn't a single part of my game that I felt was weak.

"It has taken me three hard months of work to get my swing back to where it was in 1973. I'm hitting the same type of shots. I'm pretty satisfied with my mental attitude. I'm patient, and my concentration is excellent."

Only Art Wall had followed a win with another the next week in the Masters, having done so in 1959 at the Azalea Open, but Weiskopf was undeterred. "There's no reason I can't go into that final hole at Augusta with a chance to win," he said. "I've got a good chance to win at Augusta and a better chance than 90 percent of the field. I'm confident it will happen some year. It's just a matter of time until I do."

Suddenly, Weiskopf was back and interloping in the Nicklaus–Miller conversation. "We surely weren't enemies," says Miller of his relationship with Weiskopf. "We were interesting rivals. He was so in love with Jack Nicklaus. He actually didn't like me because I was threatening Jack Nicklaus. To him that was like, 'What are you kidding me? How many majors have you won? You don't deserve to be on the same golf course with Jack Nicklaus.' He was sort of a tough guy. I liked Tom, but he really didn't like me."

The dynamic between Weiskopf and Nicklaus was a little different. Miller had been hearing the "next Nicklaus" talk for a year. Weiskopf, who was from the same state as Nicklaus, went to the same university, and lived in his hometown, had been hearing it for more than ten years.

Nearly three years younger than Nicklaus, Weiskopf grew up in northern Ohio. He enrolled at Ohio State in August 1960 and remembers seeing Nicklaus there for the first time. Although never teammates with him because freshmen were ineligible to play varsity sports until 1972, Weiskopf went to the range and saw the team's junior star warming up. "I wasn't even that good then," says Weiskopf, who was seventeen at the time. "I thought, 'I'd like to play like that guy'." Weiskopf never met Nicklaus that day. He just watched.

A few years later, he was playing like that guy. A long hitter who could blast majestic, controlled shots, Weiskopf quickly drew comparisons to his fellow Buckeye whose footsteps were in front of him.

Usually being the first is an accomplishment, but for Weiskopf, being the first "next Jack Nicklaus" was a cross to bear.

"Kaye Kessler and Paul Hornung—two writers from the Columbus area—they really kind of started that," says Weiskopf of the sports writers of the *Citizen-Journal* and *Evening Dispatch*, respectively. "That became a little suffocating."

Rarely did a story or column or television mention of Weiskopf come without a "Nicklaus" reference. It was perpetuated by everyone. Even when the press needed a different angle, it followed the same path: "The man to succeed Arnold Palmer," wrote *Golf Digest* in 1968. Even if Weiskopf didn't read the papers and magazines, he had to field the questions and hear the fans and that festered in his mind. "I didn't want to be compared to him," he says. "I didn't have the same makeup."

Weiskopf, like Miller, didn't play golf as Nicklaus did. After all, his instruction book written in 1969 was titled *Go For The Flag*. He also lacked essential traits Nicklaus possessed: patience, course management, and a calmness when things went wrong. Weiskopf was a perfectionist with a long memory and short temper.

"I lacked the two most important things that he had over me," says Weiskopf. "His motivation to be the greatest and the concentration that he could keep. We're different. I didn't have the same motivation. I didn't have the concentration all the time."

Every player in the early- and mid-1970s lived in the shadow of Jack Nicklaus. But for guys like Gary Player and Lee Trevino, their games really didn't compare when it came to the eye test. Tom Weiskopf's grade on the eye test was A+, so the comparisons to

Nicklaus were more pronounced as were the criticisms as to why he couldn't produce similar results.

"Again, they don't know me," Weiskopf says. "They only look at the way I hit a golf ball. I had the power he had. He never could outdrive me. I had the long-iron game that he had. The games were very similar."

Although they never wound up fraternizing at Ohio State, the two developed a friendship on Tour. They played practice rounds together. They went hunting together. "They were friends and Tom truly admired Jack," says Maltbie. Indeed, Weiskopf thought the world of Nicklaus.

"Jack is the record book," said Weiskopf. "Jack is what every golfer wants to be." Nearly four decades later, Weiskopf feels the same: "He's an icon. He's a role model. He's the greatest."

Their relationship came to resemble that of big brother-little brother: Weiskopf, the little brother, admiring Nicklaus and placing him upon a pedestal. When little brother couldn't climb alongside, however, there could be anger and hurt feelings.

"Jack respected him. Tom respected Jack," says Kaye Kessler. "But Jack was a thorn in Tom's side his whole career. It bugged the hell out of Tom."

"I remember him saying to me that Jack always seems to find a way to beat me," says Ben Wright, who became good friends with Weiskopf in the 1970s.

Weiskopf had gotten the best of Nicklaus once in the inaugural Inverrary Classic in 1972. But his eleven wins at the time were overshadowed by eighteen runner-up finishes on Tour—three of them to Nicklaus coming at the 1972 Masters, 1973 Atlanta Classic, and 1975 Heritage Classic. "Everywhere we went, the talk was that Weiskopf can't beat Nicklaus," says Murphy.

"I think, in truth, Tom Weiskopf did not believe that he could beat Jack in a major championship on Sunday," adds Murphy. "I don't know that there were any of us who didn't feel that same thing.

You had no right to believe it, especially if it was a major. He was going to get you."

Weiskopf witnessed their differences during one day at the 1973 Ryder Cup at Muirfield in Scotland, when they both played on the United States team.

In the morning, he and Nicklaus partnered in a foursome (alternate-shot) match against the Great Britain and Ireland side of Brian Barnes and Peter Butler. Weiskopf remembers one hole where Nicklaus asked him to read a putt for him. Weiskopf said, "Split the hole on the left." "That's exactly what I thought it was going to do," said Nicklaus. The ball went down in the hole and came out. Nicklaus stared at the ball and the hole. Weiskopf said, "I can't believe that didn't go in the hole, Jack." Nicklaus replied, "I MADE IT. It just didn't go in." In his mind, he made it. It wasn't his fault it didn't go in.

"That defines him perfectly," says Weiskopf. "That is what Jack Nicklaus is all about. That is the way he thinks."

After winning that match 1 up, in the afternoon they were together again, this time in a four-ball match against Clive Clark and Eddie Polland. Nicklaus told his wife Barbara to wait at the turn and just walk the last couple of holes as the match would end soon thereafter. Nicklaus was determined to beat Clark, Polland, and, it appeared, Weiskopf. On one green near the conclusion of the match, Weiskopf's ball was about ten feet from the hole for birdie, Nicklaus's just outside him on nearly the same line. "I said, 'Which way do you want me to move this?'" recalls Weiskopf. "He said, 'Nah, pick it up.' I said, 'What?' He said, 'Pick up your coin. Don't worry, I'll make this'." He did. They would win, 3 and 2. He not only put it to the other team, but he put it to Weiskopf who was enjoying the best year of his career. "It was the only time I rooted against him," he says.

"I wasn't afraid of Jack, and Jack knew that" says Miller. "Tom Weiskopf probably had the horsepower also to beat Jack and the game to beat Jack, but he was so in awe of Jack that he just couldn't imagine beating Jack Nicklaus. He put him in such high esteem, mentally, the way he prepared for tournaments, how well he played under pressure, how he hit the ball. He was just so impressed with Jack—which you probably should be—but so impressed that he just couldn't beat him."

Nicklaus noticed it as well: "I just believe that he didn't believe he could beat me... And if you think that way, you're not going to beat somebody."

From Weiskopf's side, it was a love-hate relationship that flipped back and forth regularly. "They had one hell of a rivalry," says Kessler. "Jack would just piss Tom off. He really got his goat. But Tom loved Jack."

"There was a whole inferiority complex about Nicklaus," says Wright. One time after a few drinks, Wright recalls Weiskopf telling him, "You know, I get so mad. Everybody says Nicklaus and Weiskopf are great friends. I hate him. I've always hated him.

"Nicklaus did in Weiskopf. No question, he destroyed him because he got that bug in his head."

In the end, it goes back to Columbus. "It would've been different (had Nicklaus not been from Ohio and gone to OSU)," admits Weiskopf. "You just get tired of reading that stuff all the time. Of being reminded."

With Weiskopf's resurgent play, he would hear it again this week.

On Monday, Weiskopf played a practice round with Ed Sneed, Tony Jacklin, and Maurice Bembridge. On Tuesday, he joined Arnold Palmer. On Wednesday, there was another round. "I played a lot of holes when I played practice rounds. I was a 36- or 45-hole guy a lot. There wasn't enough time in the day," says Weiskopf. "It never bothered me. I was in shape."

Even with his renewed game, Weiskopf admitted who the favorite was. "If I was a betting man and I was told I could pick only one man out of the field that man would be Jack Nicklaus," he said. "Jack is just a phenomenal man."

The day before the tournament's start, Nevada oddsmakers listed Nicklaus as the favorite at 3/1. Weiskopf was next at 6/1, followed at 8/1 by Miller along with Player and Hale Irwin, the reigning U.S. Open champion. "I would say Weiskopf's odds are as good as anybody's," said Miller, who on Monday played Jimmy "the Greek" Snyder and rated himself at 6/1.

No matter the order or the odds, Nicklaus, Miller, and Weiskopf were definitely the three overwhelming favorites. Not only were they the three most gifted players, they were the three hottest. But with so many variables and other talented players on Tour, pretournament storylines didn't always pan out. Golf isn't like the Miss America contest. The prettiest swings and best players rarely play well the same week. Even Nicklaus had won only 20 percent of the time he teed it up in his career as a professional on Tour. The likelihood of that trio all playing well and in contention late Sunday afternoon was very remote.

THE BUILD UP to the Masters Tournament ended Wednesday afternoon with the Par Three Contest, another Roberts creation. In the very first Masters of 1934, a driving contest and iron contest had been staged during the tournament, and such extra-curricular activities became an annual staple. In 1958, the club hired George Cobb to design a nine-hole par-three course on the east side of the property. In 1960, they inaugurated a par three competition to be played the day before the start of the tournament, replacing another driving and putting contest. Any player could participate, and non-competing invitees joined in as well. Miller and Weiskopf chose to play, Nicklaus did not.

The competition began at 1:00 p.m. Twelve holes-in-one had been made in the contest's history, but none would be added on this day. Lee Elder took home one of the nine closest-to-the-pin trophies after hitting it to nineteen inches on the 2nd. For the first time, a four-way sudden-death playoff took place with Isao Aoki,

Bobby Cole, Peter Oosterhuis, and Sam Snead, the defending champion, after they tied with scores of 23, which was four under par. Aoki won on the second playoff hole. The thirty-four-year-old Japanese star, who played almost exclusively in his home country, was appearing in his second Masters and only event of the year on the U.S. mainland. No player had won the Par Three Contest and Masters Tournament in the same year.

The weather had been delightful for the three practice days: clear and temperate with highs reaching 70 every day. Thanks to a mild winter, course conditions had been pristine. "It's as good as it has been in some time," said Nicklaus. Weiskopf agreed: "Just perfect. It's in the best shape I've seen it." But change was on the way overnight with rain forecasted Thursday. "If it rains, then they'll eat it up, and I'm talking about players like Weiskopf and Nicklaus," said Lee Trevino.

"Jack Nicklaus against Johnny Miller, Lee Elder's debut as the first black in the Masters, the resurgence of Tom Weiskopf, Lee Trevino's return, and the title defense of Gary Player have made this one of the most talked-about weeks in tournament history," wrote Robert Eubanks on the front page of Thursday's *Augusta Chronicle*.

Which story would be the headline on Monday morning?

| 5 |

THURSDAY, APRIL 10

For the twenty-second consecutive year, the first player to tee off in the Masters would be one without a chance of winning. Fred McLeod, after all, was ninety-two years old. Beginning in 1954, officials moved he and Jock Hutchison to the earliest tee time because of their speedy pace of play. There they stayed. Both natives of Scotland, McLeod emigrated from North Berwick at age twenty, and Hutchison from St. Andrews at age twenty-one. The two old pros had helped establish golf in the United States of America. McLeod, who didn't reach five and a half feet in spikes and barely weighed more than 100 pounds, captured the 1908 U.S. Open and two North & South Open titles. Hutchison found even more success, winning the 1920 PGA Championship, two Western Opens, a North & South, and the 1921 British Open in a return to his birthplace. And although they would never win a Masters, each had won at Augusta National. The club hosted the first two Senior PGA Championships—the only event to be contested there other than the Maters. The respective champions in 1937 and 1938 were Hutchison and McLeod.

Their pairing and tee shots became ceremonial in 1963 when the growing number in the field (there were a record 110 starters in

1962) forced officials to make Hutchison, McLeod, and others honorary invitees. With this new non-competing category, past champions of the other three majors and U.S. Amateurs could attend the tournament, play practice rounds, and participate in the Par Three Contest. Still, the two Scots frequently kept playing after their tee shots, routinely scooting around nine holes in ninety minutes.

Hutchison hadn't participated in the opening tee shot since 1973 and was unable to attend at all this year. So for the second year McLeod had the honors to himself. Still spry, McLeod didn't retire from his position as head professional at Columbia Country Club in Maryland until age eighty-four after fifty-five years of service. Resplendent in his Tartan pants, white dress shirt, and tartan tie underneath a Christmas-red cardigan, McLeod stood over the ball and took the club halfway back. Under low clouds that seemed to touch the ground and resemble his homeland of Scotland, he poked the ball through the mist. At 9:20 a.m., the thirty-ninth Masters Tournament was underway.

There is no organization, association, or club in the sporting world that has done more to foster the connection to their game's past than the Augusta National Golf Club. McLeod embodied this link—the oldest living U.S. Open champion and one of scores of professional emigrants from the links of Scotland and England who helped spread the game in the United States. But on this day, the focus at Augusta National was its break from the past.

THIRTY-EIGHT GROUPS of twos would go off on Thursday. First at 9:30 a.m. were Bob Menne and Lou Graham. The last would be nearly five hours later, Gary Groh and Terry Dill at 2:24 p.m. Everyone started on the 1st tee, situated just a few yards from the clubhouse. Players wanted to avoid the bunker on the right side of the fairway on this 400-yard par four. "The opening tee shot was a piece of cake," says Tom Weiskopf of the hole at the time. "It's just being on the first tee. You're getting going. The nerves. The anxiety."

As play commenced, a light rain began to fall. Not ideal weather for the patrons, but good for scoring. The first player to take advantage was in the fifth group off. His name was Miller. Allen Miller.

"The Masters is like an actor going on stage. It's a real production," said the twenty-six-year-old from Pensacola, Florida, who was commonly referred to by the press as "the other Miller." The moniker didn't bother Allen, who at the time was known more inside golf circles for his columns in *Golf World* magazine. He had been one of the nation's leading amateurs in the late-1960s and early-1970s. An All-American just up the road at the University of Georgia, he played in three Masters as an amateur, finishing tied for 42nd in 1971. This Masters was his first as a professional after earning his invitation with a win at the Tallahassee Open in April 1974, the same week Johnny Miller won the Tournament of Champions. "I haven't been as good as a pro because my game isn't as good as it was then (as an amateur)," said Miller, in his fourth full season on Tour. He admitted to making a common mistake—trying to change his game for the Tour. In an attempt to hit it farther, he lost his swing and confidence.

As so many players at the Masters did, Miller entered the week full of hope, although he had been struggling mightily with his game. In the previous month, he ran out of golf balls during practice rounds in both Jacksonville and Hilton Head. Just seventy-fourth on the money list and with a scoring average of 74.6 in his last two starts, golf was work, not fun as it was when he was a hot-shot amateur. For help, he called Bob Toski, and Monday on the practice range something clicked. Miller rolled in a twenty-five footer for birdie on the 1st hole, which after the round he claimed, "I don't remember playing it, I was so nervous." But it was a bunker save on the downhill, par-three 6th hole that was the real spur to his round. Thanks to Clifford Roberts.

Normally, balls landing in wet sand would plug. This wasn't ordinary sand anymore at Augusta National. Following the 1974

Masters, the local quarry where the club's sand came from ran dry. In the meantime, Roberts had become enamored with the sand at Grandfather Golf & Country Club in the northwest mountains of North Carolina where he spent a majority of his summers.

Roberts called his pro Bob Kletcke, who also happened to be the head professional at Grandfather during the summer season. Kletcke knew all about the sand and the man in charge. "You get a hold of him and see if he wants to sell us some sand," said Roberts, who called back three times that day to see if Kletcke had gotten hold of him. "He's working, Mr. Roberts, he'll call me tonight," Kletcke told him. That evening, Kletcke talked with his friend who owned the quarry in nearby Spruce Pine. Little did they know that their conversation would create the most famous bunker sand in the world.

Only it wasn't sand. It was a byproduct of feldspar mining. Feldspar is a major ingredient in the manufacturing of many types of glass and ceramics. The majority of it is mined in a section of the North Carolina mountains. The byproduct is basically ground-up rock, so it can't adhere to itself. When dry, it doesn't stay together, and because of that, the material tended to disperse when balls hit. Therefore, balls wouldn't bury as much as they had before. Roberts loved it because it was plentiful, easy to get, and had a distinctive bright white color. He had all of the bunker sand at Augusta National replaced. After the 1975 Masters, calls to Spruce Pine for the new sand came from around the world.

Allen used the momentum from that sand save on the 6th to birdie five of his next seven holes. A missed eight footer for par on the 18th didn't dampen his outlook as he grabbed the early lead in the clubhouse. In a matter of four hours, he went from contemplating a layoff from the Tour to shooting a 68—his first sub-70 round in more than two months.

One by one, players teed off. The starting times continued to click by until the time of 11:15 a.m. and the fifteenth pairing of the day. After 354 days, the most anticipated first-round tee time in Masters history was here.

LEE ELDER CLAIMED he had a peaceful night's sleep. "I went to sleep at midnight and slept until 8:00 a.m.," he said. "I've been trying to keep the people around me from getting too nervous all week." But Elder later admitted that he had not slept well.

Making the walk to the 1st tee with Elder would be forty-four-year-old Gene Littler, the 1961 U.S. Open champion and veteran of twenty Masters, who lost to Billy Casper in a playoff for the 1970 tournament. Elder hadn't found out his pairing until Wednesday morning. Many had thought Elder's tee time would have been announced as a marquee pairing a day earlier.

In addition to being one of the most successful players of his era, Littler was known as one of the nicest guys on Tour. The pairing wasn't circumstance. He was a cancer survivor, having had a malignant melanoma tumor in a lymph gland under his left arm removed during extensive surgery the week of the 1972 Masters. Littler came back six months later with great success, and in 1975 captured the Bing Crosby National Pro-Am for his twenty-sixth PGA Tour title, a win that earned him a Masters invitation. On Wednesday night, the Golf Writers Association of America presented him the Charles Bartlett Award for contributions to society.

Officials hoped that Littler's steady, comforting nature would rub off on Elder, but it hadn't helped before the start of their round. As Elder was readying himself in the locker room, he placed his golf balls in his locker and his watch in his pants pocket—instead of the other way around. "I was shaking so bad, I didn't think I was ever going to be able to relax," said Elder.

Wearing green pants and a green sweater over a green golf shirt—all different shades mind you—Elder strode nervously to the first tee in the light drizzle and low overcast conditions, the sun trying mightily to peak through. Even though the club had provided extra security, he knew it took only one person to slip through the gates unnoticed to take away his moment—or his life.

On the 400-yard opening hole that moved gently to the right, Littler hit first—a low drive pulled left off the fairway. Then, it was Elder's turn, twenty-eight years to the day that Jackie Robinson's contract was purchased by the Brooklyn Dodgers, making him the first black major league baseball player. "Lee Elder now driving, fore please," announced club member Phil Harison, who had served as the starter since 1948. Elder pushed his tee into the Georgia soil and placed his ball on top of it for the most pressure-filled opening tee shot in history of the game.

In front of several hundred people, Elder addressed the ball. He took a quick look down the fairway, then waggled the club. Again, a peak and a waggle. The only sound was the soft pitapat of rain as Elder took the club back. He struck his tee shot down the center of the fairway. The spectators clapped politely, their applause muted only because most were holding umbrellas. A relieved Elder picked up his tee, having not embarrassed himself, his entourage, or his race. The first black competitor in the Masters had officially teed off.

Followed by a legion of friends and family, most wearing "Good Luck Lee" buttons, Elder walked with his chest out briskly down the hill on the 1st hole and then back up to the fairway. He hit his approach shot fifteen feet behind the hole and barely missed his birdie putt, leaving it inches short. On the dogleg left par-five 2nd, he hit a wedge to fifteen feet for a birdie to get to one under. It would be the only time Elder would be in red figures for the tournament. Once he got going, Elder claimed most of the nerves went away. "Gene talked to me quite a bit and really helped," Elder said. "The gallery was fantastic. They applauded me on the greens. I couldn't ask for any more."

But the distractions that had infected Elder's game remained with him. He drove the ball well enough but his iron play wasn't sharp. Under ideal conditions for scoring, he bogeyed the par-three 4th after missing the green; the par-five 8th after missing a four-foot putt; the par-five 15th after a poor wedge shot; and par-three 16th after a three putt. A birdie at the 17th from twelve feet helped him salvage a 74, the same score he shot in his first trip around the layout six months earlier.

Elder wasn't as much disappointed as he was relieved. "I'm glad the first round is over," Elder said. "Now the people around me don't have to worry about me shooting an 85."

TWO PAIRINGS in front of Lee Elder was the player always just above "Nicklaus" on the alphabetical field list. Bobby Nichols, one of the most popular players on Tour, had won eleven times in a sixteen-year career. Of all the competitors Nicklaus would not be happy to look up at on the leaderboard, it was Bobby Nichols.

It started twelve years earlier in Houston. Nicklaus was a rookie on the circuit, looking for his first win when Nichols edged him and Dan Sikes in a playoff. Two months later when Nicklaus finally did get his maiden victory at the U.S. Open, Nichols tried to spoil things again. He was tied for the lead with four holes to play before bogey-ing Oakmont's 15th and 18th holes to finish tied for 3rd, two shots behind.

Then, there was the 1964 PGA Championship at Columbus (Ohio) Country Club. It would be the only major championship Nicklaus would ever play in his hometown, and Bobby Nichols took it away from him. The omens were in Nichols's favor all week. On the way to the course for the first round, the tire on his car went flat. He flagged down someone who gave him a ride to the club, arriving just before his starting time. He went right out and shot a championship-record 64. Nichols never looked back, even though he seemingly hit it everywhere. After holing approximately eighty feet worth of putts on the final four holes, he won wire-to-wire by three shots to earn, at the time, a lifetime exemption on Tour. His total of 271 stood as a tournament record for thirty years. Nicklaus closed with a 64 himself, just missing a thirty-foot eagle putt on the final hole for

63, which would have been the first ever in a major. Nicklaus tied for 2nd with Arnold Palmer, his playing competitor that day, who shot all four rounds in the 60s.

Born in Louisville, Nichols had begun caddying as a nine-year-old at Audubon Country Club. Toting bags was made even more enjoyable by a club member who took a liking for him—Pee Wee Reese, the Brooklyn Dodger shortstop who played there regularly in the off-season.

Nichols was a good athlete in high school, a standout in both football and basketball. But life changed for the junior early one September evening in 1952 as he sat in the front passenger seat of his good friend's car, riding along with three others. The time was just after 8:00 in the evening when Nichols told his friend, "Jimmy, I got to get home, football practice is tomorrow morning." Soon, the car picked up the pace, as Nichols says Jimmy "had a tendency to get a little heavy on the pedal." In the blink of an eye, the car veered off the road and struck a post. When the police looked inside what was left of the vehicle, the speedometer was stuck on 107 miles per hour.

"When I look at the pictures, I think how did anyone get out of that thing alive?" says Nichols, the most seriously injured of the group. In the minutes, hours, and days following the accident, that question wasn't asked. The crash threw Nichols from the car, puncturing his spine, shattering his pelvis, and causing severe internal injuries to his kidneys and lungs, as well as a brain concussion. "They gave me my last rites," says Nichols. "They put a sheet over me actually."

But Nichols fought. They took him to the hospital where he remained unconscious for thirteen days. He stayed in traction for a total of ninety-six days. Miraculously, Nichols suffered no long-term ill effects. His football days were over, though; golf would be his sport once he started playing again the following May.

While in the hospital, Nichols received a letter from Ben Hogan, who had been in a near-fatal crash himself nearly four years earlier. "It was pretty inspirational," says Nichols, of the encouragement and direction the letter gave him. Years later, Nichols would get to know Hogan and thank him personally. As fate would have it, Hogan was Nichols's playing competitor in the final group of the 1964 PGA Championship. The following month, they got paired together again at the Carling World Open at Oakland Hills outside Detroit where Hogan won the 1951 U.S. Open, and Nichols won again. When the two ran into each other checking out of the hotel the next morning, Hogan looked at Nichols and said, "You ought to pay me to play with you."

Nichols's high school football coach was also looking out for him. Johnny Meihaus had played for Bear Bryant at the University of Kentucky. Now at Texas A&M, Bryant heard Nichols's story and told him to come down to College Station, Texas—he'd give him a football scholarship, even though he would never put on a helmet. "That meant so much," says Nichols. "I had no money. In those days, there were only half-scholarships for spring sports. The only time you could get a full ride was for football or basketball."

Nichols hung around the team and took in the practices and games. "I admired his success and watched how he treated players," he says. Bryant's pre-season workouts at A&M were legendary. Nichols recalls there being ninety-nine guys on scholarship, and ten days later, only twenty-nine were left. It wasn't until after Bryant left A&M for Alabama in 1958 that the coach began playing golf. Over the years, he and Nichols played together a lot. Bryant always requested to play with him in pro-ams. "In my lifetime, I've had two or three people who have stood out and helped me along in my career," says Nichols, "and he was one of those. Just a special individual."

After making the most of playing golf on a football scholarship, Nichols took a job as an assistant professional at Midland Country Club in Texas. The members and staff there put up the money to get him started on Tour in 1960. Nichols made his first appearance at the Masters in 1963 and always enjoyed playing there since it was around his birthday, April 14. In fact, Bryant, who came to the Masters for a period in the late-1960s and early-1970s, would buy a birthday cake for Nichols, bring it to the course, and set it on a table just outside the clubhouse for other players to enjoy.

But Nichols, a husky six feet, two inches and 195 pounds, also liked the way Augusta National set up for his game. "I never was a real accurate driver of the ball," he says. "I could hit it quite a long ways, and I could hit it fairly high." He felt the strength of his game was his middle irons, and although he wasn't the best at turning the ball over right-to-left, he hit it long enough and high enough to more than off-set that deficiency.

Nichols used his smooth swing to nearly win the green jacket in 1967, when he engaged in a final-round duel with fellow Kentuckian Gay Brewer, a good friend since childhood who should've won the previous year had he not three-putted the 72nd hole to fall into a playoff with Nicklaus that he subsequently lost. Brewer was another player who could hit the ball high thanks to a Nicklaus-like takeaway—straight back with a flying elbow—and really spin the ball. Trailing by one on the final hole, Nichols hit a 9-iron fifteen feet right of the pin. "It looked like the putt's got to go right," he says, "but it stayed straight."

Nichols didn't record another top-ten at Augusta until a tie for 7th in 1974. That year turned out to be one of the best years of his career, winning twice (San Diego and Canadian Open) and earning a career-best $124,747. His success was even more remarkable because Nichols was one of the few PGA Tour players who also held a job as a head club professional. Since 1968, he had served in that capacity at Firestone Country Club in Akron, Ohio. His workload at the club meant Nichols rarely played or practiced when not on the road.

"I was pretty pumped up after '74 and with the couple of wins I felt confident," says Nichols, who lost on the first-hole of playoff to J.C. Snead at San Diego at the beginning of the 1975 season. But coming into the Masters, he had mediocre feelings about his game. "I feel that I play well enough at times to be in the Jack Nicklaus,

Johnny Miller category," said Nichols, "but I just can't play good every week like Jack and Johnny."

With his hometown PowerBilt clubs and Titleist balls, Nichols used his length to take advantage of the par fives. He chipped his third shot up to tap-in range on the 8th. He hit a 3-iron second shot to the 13th and two-putted for birdie. He holed a downhill birdie putt on the 15th. He also holed a fifteen-foot birdie putt on the 220-yard par-three 4th hole and an eight footer on the par-four 10th after hitting a 4-iron in. Nichols hit thirteen greens in regulation and got up-and-in on the other five holes. The bogey-free 67 was his lowest round ever in the Masters.

"These were the best scoring conditions I've ever seen at the Masters," said Nichols, who also fired a warning, "I don't play good all the time, but when I am playing good, I usually keep on playing good for a while. When I get a good start, I begin to feel good about my swing, and I play within myself."

The 67 would hold up, and Bobby Nichols would be the first-round leader in the Masters. It was only the second time that he had the outright lead after 18 holes on Tour. The other was that 1964 PGA.

This year, April 14 fell on a Monday, the day after the final round. He would turn forty. Only Ben Hogan at forty in 1953 and Sam Snead at forty-one in 1954 had won the Masters at a more advanced age. It would be a pretty impressive feat for the man *Los Angeles Times* columnist Jim Murray once called: "The best (golfer) who ever died."

FOR THE REMAINDER of the day, temperatures never got out of the mid 60s. Only a tenth of an inch of rain fell officially in Augusta, but the intermittent showers were just enough to soften the course.

"The course was really the best that I've seen it, set up the best for scoring," said defending champion Gary Player, who shot 72, only one stroke higher than his opening round the previous year.

The numbers reflected Player's sentiment. The average score for the day was 73.7—the third lowest opening round average at the time. Sixteen subpar rounds were recorded with only three in the 80s. The only two factors that prevented scores from being even lower were slow greens and hole locations. "The toughest pins were always in round one," says Johnny Miller.

Conditions were a bonus for the longer hitters, who took advantage of the par fives. But the softer greens also allowed the lower-ball hitters to hold the greens, even though some of the shorter hitters were hitting two to four clubs more into some holes. No one took advantage more than Bob Murphy and Lee Trevino, the players right behind Miller, Nicklaus, and Weiskopf on the season's money list.

Murphy, fourth in earnings with $77,970, didn't take up golf seriously until a shoulder injury ended a promising baseball career at the University of Florida. Three years later he won the 1965 U.S. Amateur and then the NCAA the following year. "I was playing really well then," says Murphy of 1975 after missing a significant portion of 1974 with a thumb injury. In February, he finished runner-up at the Bob Hope Classic, three shots behind Miller. Then in front of his mom, dad, and brothers, and while playing with Nicklaus and Palmer in the final round, he won the Jackie Gleason Inverrary Classic near his home in Delray Beach, Florida. The victory was his first in nearly five years and earned him the final invitation into the Masters field just six weeks before the tournament.

Right behind Murphy on the money list was Lee Trevino in fifth place with $71,983. Trevino had won the last major—the 1974 PGA Championship at Tanglewood Park in North Carolina, besting Nicklaus by a single shot. Trevino won his twentieth Tour title at the Citrus Open in Orlando five weeks earlier and had come to Augusta off a 4th-place finish at Greensboro.

But neither Murphy nor Trevino had ever recorded a top-ten finish in the Masters and weren't on anybody's list of favorites.

"The only time I played well at Augusta—and Trevino the same—is when the weather was crap," says Murphy. The two players had four things going against them: their lack of length, their left-to-right-ball direction, their low ball flight, and their attitude.

"It was wide open, and we wanted it to be twenty-four yards wide," says Murphy, whose strength was accuracy. The lack of rough and virtual absence of fairway bunkers—only six holes had them—negated their strengths. Neither could take advantage of the par fives—they had to lay up on most of them, where as Jack, John, and Tom regularly reached all of them in two shots.

"It was set up for the guys who hit it long," he says. "And those were the guys who won."

"My swing was built around a fade," says Murphy, who admits he even thought about leaving his driver out of the bag that week. "Of all the courses I played anywhere, Augusta was as close to an unfavorite as I had."

Murphy tried to compensate: "I used to start four of five weeks ahead, I'd change 3-woods, drivers—all kinds of different ideas. I just didn't have those shots. And even if I had been able to put the ball down farther, I still would've been at a disadvantage because my iron shots were too low going into those greens."

Augusta National was particularly frustrating for Trevino, the 1971 Player of the Year, who at that moment was the one golfer who had proven he could go head-to-head with Nicklaus in majors and beat him. Trevino's toughness and determination were born from golf's ultimate rags-to-riches story. He grew up in Dallas, was raised by his grandfather, dropped out of school at age eight, and spent four years in the U.S. Marines. He worked as an assistant professional in El Paso, Texas, playing big money games when he sent in an entry fee for the 1966 U.S. Open. Two years later he won the championship with Nicklaus finishing 2nd. He beat Nicklaus in a playoff at the 1971 U.S. Open. Again over Nicklaus, he won the 1972 British Open and the 1974 PGA, the most recent major just eight months earlier on a course with thick, damp rough and tee shots that required more fades than draws. Four times Trevino resigned Nicklaus to runner-up finishes in majors, yet he felt he just couldn't compete against him at the Masters. "Trevino was awesome," says Miller. "Somehow he convinced himself he couldn't win there."

Trevino concurred, saying the Masters was "a perfect example of my talking too much and then psyching myself out." He even skipped the Masters in 1970, 1971, and 1974. "That was the greatest mistake I've made in my career," said Trevino years later.

"Lee didn't handle well the pomp and circumstance that is Augusta," says Murphy. Both Trevino and Murphy were street-wise, self-made players who could be cantankerous at times.

Some of the protocol didn't sit well with the two of them. In 1971 when near the lead after each of the first two days, a cart was brought up behind the 18th to take Murphy to the press center. "I slid over and tapped the seat for Gayle (his wife) to get in, and the guy told me they don't have women in golf carts here," says Murphy. "We walked."

The little slights, either real or perceived, bothered Trevino as well and his run-ins became front-page news. Early in the week of the 1972 tournament, Trevino nearly walked out after a security guard on the 8th hole tried to kick out his friend and regular Tour caddie Neal Harvey for wearing a tournament badge instead of a practice round ticket. Trevino regularly changed his shoes in the parking lot, although he claimed it was because the range was closer to his car than the clubhouse. Next to the lack of a black competitor in the tournament prior to 1975, his actions had been public relations problem number one for the club.

"Lee mocked Augusta National. The guys were rich, had everything, and were maybe a little arrogant," says Murphy. "He didn't have any use for those people."

On the course, Augusta National just didn't play to his strength and that unique swing he developed on the public courses in Texas. Utilizing a strong right hand grip, he got ahead of the ball on the downswing and held on. The result was a low, push-cut that he could always hit solidly with complete control of the trajectory. "Lee Trevino developed a system for hitting a golf ball that worked for Lee Trevino," says Roger Maltbie. "If you had to get the ball in the fairway on the last hole for the whole world, he'd be the guy I'd pick." Nicklaus said the two best ball strikers he ever saw were Hogan and Trevino. But Trevino couldn't hit the ball high, and he couldn't hit it long.

Trevino claimed he didn't consider going back to Augusta until August 1974 when he won his first PGA Championship. He now had captured three of the four professional majors. "A career grand slam is very much on my mind," said Trevino of the feat only four players had accomplished—Gene Sarazen, Ben Hogan, Gary Player, and Jack Nicklaus. "That is why the Masters is so important to me; it's the only one I haven't won."

"Trevino often said, 'Had it not been the Masters, Murph, you and I would have never played there'," says Murphy. "But being Augusta, you went."

Trevino began the opening round paired with his friend Jerry Heard. At the Citrus Open in 1972, Heard was in the fairway needing par on the 72nd hole to win. He was playing with Trevino, who knew that the youngster was pumping adrenaline, so Trevino told him, "Whatever club you think you're going to hit, hit one less Heardie." So instead of hitting a 6-iron from 162 yards, Heard took a 7-iron and flew it just past the flagstick. "If he hadn't said that, I might not have won the tournament," admits Heard.

Trevino's attitude was slightly different on this day. "He was ranting and raving," says Heard. "I remember we got up to that first tee, and you're always a little nervous. But he was really nervous. I was wondering why he's so nervous today. He was way worse than me." The nerves helped Trevino focus. He birdied three of the first four holes, prompting scoring officials to put his name up on the large leaderboards around the course—a rare sight for patrons. Even going out in 33 did little to pump up his self-belief.

"All he did was talk about how he couldn't play this course," says Heard. On the dogleg left 10th hole, he hung his tee shot out to the right, leaving him on top of the hill and a long way from the hole. He then hit a beautiful high cut with a long iron onto the green. Heard turned to him and said, "Would you get out of here, you can play this golf course." Trevino kept chattering himself out of it. "It was all b.s., he could play as good as anybody else," says Heard.

Nicklaus had also been trying to convince Trevino that he could perform well at Augusta National, and Trevino was slightly more confident this time after the addition of one weapon to his arsenal. "I learned the hook about six months ago," he said. "I used it in the PGA and at Firestone (both wins for him). The hook gets away from you a lot more than the fade, but it gives me confidence in cold weather and at Augusta."

Trevino was going along at three under par until bogeys on the 16th and 18th holes resigned him to an opening round 71. Still, it was only his fourth subpar score in seventeen rounds at Augusta National. "Today it was just like any other tournament," said Trevino. "The greens were slow and holding."

For Murphy, an eagle on the 13th—one of a record seven there on the day—offset a double bogey on the par-four 11th. Four birdies and two bogeys gave him a 70.

And Murphy did it in style too. Every year he had seven custom-made pants—britches as he calls them—tailor-made just for Augusta. "It was the ticket," he says.

MURPHY AND TREVINO weren't the only ones who took advantage of the excellent scoring conditions.

Making his presence known was Sam Snead, the oldest player in the field, just a month shy of turning sixty-three. Snead was a three-time Masters winner and the all-time victory leader on the PGA Tour. "If television would have come along earlier," says Miller, "Sam Snead would've been Arnold Palmer."

Snead was one of twelve champions in the field—that being a life-time category—but his appearance wasn't ceremonial. Eight months earlier at the most recent major, Snead finished tied for 3rd at the PGA Championship, challenging Trevino and Nicklaus for the title. At age sixty-two, he became the oldest player in the history of the game to finish in the top-five of a major championship.

Snead's graceful swing was considered the prettiest in golf. On this day, he went off paired with Peter Oosterhuis, the man Lee Elder had defeated at Pensacola. "It was so smooth and so rhythmic—a great shoulder turn," said Oosterhuis, who played with Snead for the first time that day. "He made it look so easy."

Snead, who had played in every Masters but the first three, quickly got to two under par. Employing a distinctive side-saddle putting stroke, his name appeared on the leaderboards after birdies at 13 and 14 moved him to three under before bogeying two of the last three holes. Oosterhuis remembers Snead's playful manner. "I think he enjoyed messing with me," he recalls. Indeed, Snead got the last laugh. His score of 71 bettered Oosterhuis—thirty-six years his junior—by eight shots.

Even with a 71, Snead wasn't low Snead for the day. His nephew J.C. shot 69, one of six sub-70 scores on the day. The younger Snead finished runner-up to Tommy Aaron in the 1973 Masters and was coming off the best year of his career; however, he had missed the cut in his last three starts—a problem he blamed on having played and practiced too much since the start of the year. Wet weather kept his trademark panama hat in the locker room on this day. Snead nearly made an ace on the 16th when his tee shot hit the flagstick. He arrived at the 18th without a bogey before pushing his drive right to drop a shot.

Arnold Palmer came in with 69, as did Tom Weiskopf. His momentum from Greensboro continuing, Weiskopf took advantage of the par fives, birdying all of them. He two-putted the 2nd from twenty feet after hitting the green in two shots with a 4-iron, pitched to six feet on the 8th, chipped to seven feet on the 13th, and two-putted the 15th from twenty feet after reaching it in two with another 4-iron. In his career, Weiskopf was 56 under par on the par fives, an impressive total considering in 116 attempts he'd made only one eagle.

Weiskopf was without a bogey on his card until he came to the 18th, the 420-yard dogleg right par four that rose seventy feet from the tee to the green. In March, nineteen pine saplings had been planted along the left corner of the dogleg, just before the two bunkers that were added in 1966 as a response to Jack Nicklaus's prodigious drives up the left side of the fairway the previous year. Those bunkers narrowed the fairway width to just thirty yards and took the driver out of the longer players' hands. The new trees made the tee shot on the hole even tougher, eliminating the option of bailing out to the left and still having a clear shot to the green.

The hole was giving players fits today, yielding just three birdies and playing almost a quarter-shot over par. Among the players with under-par rounds, Palmer, J.C. Snead, Sam Snead, Larry Ziegler, and Allen Miller all made five on the hole. Weiskopf committed to never using a driver off the 18th tee. On this day, it was his approach shot that caused him trouble when he over-shot the green and failed to get up-and-down for par.

Still, it was Weiskopf's best start at a Masters and his first opening round in the 60s. To Weiskopf, it could have been better. He placed the blame for any poor shots on fliers due to the wet conditions. And like Palmer and Trevino, Weiskopf's instincts couldn't totally adjust to the slower greens. Weiskopf counted seven birdie putts between ten and fifteen feet that he failed to convert. "Even though I knew that the greens were slow today, I would leave them short," he confessed. After some of the fastest greens of the year at Greensboro the week before, Weiskopf predicted, "The greens will never get fast this week."

Murphy was tied for 7th with his 70, along with two of the best putters in the game: forty-three-year-old Billy Casper, the 1970 winner, and a twenty-five-year-old Kansan named Tom Watson.

Only eleven first-round leaders had gone on to win the thirty-eight previous Masters, but the highest opening round ever by a champion was 74. As the axiom went, a player couldn't win the Masters on Thursday, but he could lose it. It appeared one player had done just that.

AS FOR THE more famous Miller, Johnny got nervous for only two tournaments a year: the U.S. Open and the Masters.

"Jack obviously sold the world on how important majors are," says Miller. "I didn't grow up with that kind of thinking. That was a problem for me. I didn't dream of winning a bunch of majors. I just wanted to win tournaments. I didn't really care what they were.

"I loved to play aggressive golf and the majors really didn't pattern into my game."

He admitted that he had been suffering from "Masters fever" for a month, envisioning every shot he'd face and working on his draw. Miller felt no fades were required off any tee at Augusta, but a right-to-left ball flight was mandatory on holes such as 2, 5, 9, 10, 11, 13, 14, 15, and 17.

During a practice round earlier in the week, a voice had told him to do something he'd never tried: copy George Knudson. The veteran from Canada was recognized as a great ball striker who drew his shots. With more of a closed stance, Miller shifted all of his weight to the back right heel on his backswing, instead of being centered over his foot. On the downswing, he moved his weight to his left toes, which promoted an inside-out swing plane. The move produced a high, soft draw Miller could use on the holes that swung to the left and to any hole locations that were on the left side of greens. "It was something I'd never done before—the only time I'd ever used it," says Miller. "I just started hitting it so consistently that way."

By now, Miller knew the course. This was his sixth Masters. But controlling his emotions remained a problem. "I was over amped," he says. "I was over my comfort zone even before the tournament started. Even though I loved the Masters tournament, I just wanted to win it too badly."

Never getting over the opening round hump frustrated Miller. Struggling with his putting in 1972, he changed putters but still had nine three-putt greens in 36 holes. He shot matching rounds of 76 to miss the cut. Thinking the course placed too much of an emphasis on putting, he said they should rename it the "Augusta Spring Putting Contest." In 1973, he opened with a 75, but came back with a 69 and 71 the following two days to stand four back going into the final round. A Sunday 73 though, left him tied for 6th. By the 1974 Masters, Miller had already won four events on the year and was number one on the money list—only Sam Snead had won more times before the Masters with five in 1950. But Miller's forthright nature did him in. In a *People* magazine article published the day before the tournament, he was quoted as saying, "If I don't win the Masters, I'll be surprised." Miller meant that he thought he would win it sometime, but his remarks were interpreted as that week. The article rocked Miller. Not used to the spotlight's glare, he opened with a 72 and then a 74. Miller managed to shoot under par scores of 69–70 on the weekend to salvage a tie for 15th. "I played fantastically well in 1974 and could not putt at all," says Miller. "I was just choking so bad on my putting.

"By then I knew how to play Augusta, it was just a matter of fighting my nerves with the putter. In majors I got more nervous and that would show up in my putting."

The added attention in 1975 didn't ease Miller's stress level either: "Everyone wanted to know what I was doing, why I was winning everything. I couldn't hardly get from the parking lot to the clubhouse and the clubhouse back through all the people to the driving range, and the driving range back to the clubhouse, and then somehow from the clubhouse to the putting green. Then the putting green to the first tee. It was such a crazy thing starting on Monday, Tuesday, Wednesday..."

Miller was trying his best to accommodate everyone but found it wasn't easy. He had created a monster for himself. "They were in control of me," he says. "It would take so long to get everywhere. It was a crazy time in my life."

Miller came up with an unorthodox thought to lessen the madness.

"I just decided I wasn't going to hit any practice balls all week," says Miller, who began the routine, or lack thereof, on Monday. "Part of me was saying, 'Are you crazy? You have to warm up.' But I was playing so well in the practice rounds," he says.

Beside the putting green, Miller would take fifteen to twenty practice swings to loosen up, stroke some practice putts, and walk directly to the opening tee.

"Every day of the tournament I was semi-freaking out on the first tee," says Miller. "Standing up there with all those people, and I haven't hit a warm-up shot." Miller felt good, though, and began the tournament by hitting his opening shot down the fairway with enough power to easily clear the bunker at the crest of the hill on the right. He would hit the fairway on the 1st hole every day. "Sometimes when you're not real sure it makes you focus even more," he says.

Miller's channeling of George Knudson yielded magical results tee-to-green. If only he could channel his friend Billy Casper on the greens. On that 1st hole, he missed a five-foot putt for par. After a five on the par-five 2nd hole, he couldn't convert a three footer for par on the 3rd hole. Then on the 4th hole, he missed another four-foot par putt. He was three over after four holes.

Miller was a quick player, and being paired with Bruce Crampton, who had the reputation as a slow one, added to Miller's antsiness. His other misses included a six footer at the 7th, a five footer at the 12th, and a fifteen footer at the 17th after a poor greenside bunker shot. The Tour's birdie machine managed to make only two this day: a six footer at the 6th and another at the 8th.

"I was so amped up," says Miller. "I played just fine. It was all putting."

He hit fifteen greens in regulation on a day where he felt he was in-between yardages with his irons on almost every shot, but he didn't make a putt longer than six feet all day. "I'm longer than I ever have been here," he added. "With an average putting round I could have had a 71 today, with good putting, maybe 68 or 69."

Miller had hoped for a different start this time. "Give me a good spurt to be up there with the leaders and I can win," he said. "I don't choke anymore." With five bogeys and two birdies, Miller faced reality. "I played terrible," he said, "and I'll be lucky to be here this weekend."

"I kept putting myself behind the eight ball," says Miller. "That was the problem those first couple of rounds. I was just too dang nervous."

Once again, Miller had failed to break par in the opening round for the sixth time in six Masters. A score of 75 left him in a tie for 47th. He trailed by eight shots. "Maybe it's all my good luck averaging out," he admitted. "If I keep putting like this tomorrow, I'll be back in California by Saturday."

BY THURSDAY, Curtis Strange's entire family had made it down to Augusta, including his grandfather, his mother, and his identical twin brother, Allan. They were all present around the first tee for his 12:04 p.m. starting time. The hundreds of other patrons around the teeing ground were there to see Jack Nicklaus.

Strange had actually met Nicklaus for the first time Saturday as Nicklaus was leaving and again on Wednesday. "He couldn't have been nicer," said Strange. He wasn't as big in stature as Strange thought he'd be, nor were his hands big when he shook them. But that didn't settle the nerves. "I was so intimidated just running across him the two times before earlier in the week," he says. "Jack's just an intimidating figure and person."

As with all of the amateur pairings in the opening round, the Masters champion in the group teed off first. Nicklaus sent a towering drive that split the middle of the fairway. Strange says he somehow got the tee in the ground and the ball to stay on it. He ripped his drive hard down the right side with enough power to clear the bunker, though just off the fairway. "I was very much relieved," he says of his first shot in a Masters.

Strange's nerves calmed down after that. He hit a 9-iron into the opening green, about twenty-two feet behind the hole. Strange then struck what he thought was a pretty good putt. It just missed but kept rolling, and rolling, and rolling. The ball eventually stopped eight feet past the hole. Nicklaus turned toward Strange. "He looked at me and said, 'Welcome to Thursday at Augusta'," recalls Strange. "They were quicker."

There was a good reason, and not necessarily because the club was trying to play tricks on the players. The warm-weather Bermuda grass, which was dormant over the winter, was just beginning to re-emerge. The cool-season ryegrass used to overseed the greens in the autumn was barely hanging on. "If you cut the ryegrass too low for any length of time, it's going to die on you," says Bob Kletcke, especially when they were not watered. This was the reason the greens weren't cut lower until Thursday, but it fooled inexperienced players who had grown accustomed to one speed during practice rounds. The last thing officials wanted during the weekend were brown greens. The fact you never got a true practice round was one of the major complaints at that time. Nicklaus new this and adjusted accordingly.

Strange made the comebacker for par.

What stood out about Nicklaus's game? "Everything. Absolutely everything," replies Strange. "He was long, straight, un-emotional, and went about his business." There wasn't a lot of conversation, but Nicklaus initiated what there was and always in a complimentary tone. Strange felt comfortable the rest of the round and was impressed by his gracious nature and "the overall package" of Nicklaus's game.

With his new driver, Nicklaus didn't hit the ball as far as before. Strange, who was a very long hitter at the time, kept up with him most of the day. Strange used a long swing, upright plane, and strong grip—all characteristics of his game that would later change. The wide fairways helped keep some of his erratic tee shots in play.

Meanwhile, Strange watched Nicklaus hit every green in regulation and hit all four par-five greens in two. Nicklaus two-putted for birdie on the 2nd from twenty-five feet (after a 2-iron), the 13th from thirty feet (3-wood, 4-iron), and 15th from thirty feet (after a 1-iron). He only made par at the 8th, misreading a three footer after hitting his 3-wood seventy feet past hole. His only miss-hit of the day came on the 18th tee, where he switched from a driver to a 3-wood and hit it left of the newly planted trees. Lying 195 yards out, he recovered by hitting a 4-iron to the front of the green and two-putting from sixty feet for par. He had begun with a bogey-free, and stress-free, 68.

"He played absolute perfect golf," says Strange. "One of the greatest rounds I have ever seen in my life. I don't know if he remembers the round or not, but I'd be anxious to know if he does."

Three-and-a-half decades later, Nicklaus doesn't. His response upon hearing of the ball-striking statistics and the score: "I must have really putted awful."

Nicklaus knew that at Augusta a ball in the middle of the green on every hole wouldn't leave a difficult putt. On most greens, they would be manageable uphill putts twenty to thirty feet from the hole. It may not be a makeable birdie putt, but percentages for a two-putt par were pretty good. His experience told him to always protect the short side of the green. Plus the moisture on the ground and balls factored into his caution. "When it is wet, you have to be careful," said Nicklaus. "You can't spin the ball. You can hit some wild looking golf shots."

"I couldn't ask for a better start," Nicklaus admitted at the time. "When you have thirty-six putts and shoot a 68 at Augusta, you've played a pretty good round of golf."

"I relived his round as much as mine that night," says Strange, who felt he hit the ball reasonably well. But his inexperience in dealing with the fast undulating greens, difficult chips and putts, large galleries, and all the other intricacies of the golf course plagued him. Bogeys on three of his last five holes gave him a 75. Only one of the seven amateurs broke par—Jerry Pate with a 71. "I couldn't imagine if I have to play that well to play the Tour," he says. "I've got a long ways to go."

"I wouldn't have traded that experience (of playing with Nicklaus) for the world," says Strange, who had seen up close what the pinnacle of the sport looked like. "I played with him when he was absolutely in his prime. I realized that this guy is the best of all-time."

Nicklaus's score was a foreshadower of bad news for the field. In the other four Masters in which Nicklaus had opened with a 68 or lower, he had won three of them. Nicklaus was conditioned more for distance and endurance than for speed, so a fast start boded poorly for everyone else. As Roger Maltbie figured, "He knew the longer we played, the less chance you had."

LEADERBOARD AFTER 18 HOLES

1.	Bobby Nichols	67	−5
2.	Jack Nicklaus	68	−4
	Allen Miller	68	−4
4.	Tom Weiskopf	69	−3
	Arnold Palmer	69	−3
	J.C. Snead	69	−3
7.	Billy Casper	70	−2
	Bob Murphy	70	−2
	Tom Watson	70	−2
T-39.	Lee Elder	74	+2
T-48.	Johnny Miller	75	+3

| 6 |

NICKLAUS

"Yes sir, Mr. Jones," the clubhouse attendant said, opening the front door to the Scioto Country Club. From a distance, the young man approaching may have borne some resemblance to Mr. Jones with his stout build, his pleated knickers, and his hair parted down the middle. But this fellow was not the Robert Tyre Jones, Jr. The boy, eleven years younger than Jones, seized the opportunity, flashed a smile at the attendant, and walked right in without a clubhouse pass. An innocent case of misidentification that would change golf years later.

That story was a favorite of Charlie Nicklaus's. It occurred during the 1931 Ryder Cup. Although Jones wasn't competing, he came up from Atlanta to attend the matches. Nicklaus liked to say that from that point on, Bobby Jones was his favorite golfer. But his fascination with him had begun even earlier.

The 1926 U.S. Open had also been contested at Scioto, and twelve-year-old Charlie was there, his ticket courtesy of Fred "Doc" Mebs, the pharmacist he worked for after school. Jones was coming off of his first victory in the British Open two weeks earlier and traveled directly from Liverpool, England, to Columbus, Ohio. The long journey by boat and train left Jones weary, and with a 79 in the second round, he looked as if he'd shot himself out of the championship. Following a 71 the next morning, Jones was three shots behind Joe Turnesa going into the final round, and Turnesa retained a sizable lead until bogeying five of his last seven holes. His stumbling finish gave Jones an opportunity to win with a birdie on the par-five 18th hole. After a drive measured at more than 300 yards, Jones laced a mashie just past the flagstick. Two putts later, he was the national champion again and the first person ever to win both the U.S. Open and the British Open in the same year. Little Charlie had watched virtually all 293 of his shots that week.

When Nicklaus's son Jack took up the sport as an impressionable ten-year-old, two-and-a-half decades later, all he heard about was Bob Jones. The family now had membership at Scioto, and every day, Jones stared at him from pictures around the clubhouse. Jack listened to countless stories about Jones and his exploits from his father and other club members, including Stanley Crooks who had befriended him.

He heard about how Jones played the short par-three 9th at Scioto in four over par that week. He heard about the 480-yard par-five 8th, one of Jones's favorite holes on the course, where he made an eagle three in the first round. And of course, he heard about the manner in which Jones played the 72nd hole to ensure victory. Nicklaus took those images and used them for inspiration when he played the course that had changed very little in the previous three decades.

He was schooled on Jones's accomplishments as a teenager, his thirteen major championships, his Grand Slam, and his retirement when at the top of the game.

As much as Jones's golfing prowess, it was his public persona that endeared him to Charlie Nicklaus and the rest of the nation—his sportsmanship, his conduct, his charm, his gentlemanly manners. Even though Jack Nicklaus would never see him hit a golf shot in person, this legendary figure—his accomplishments and character—would become his benchmark.

Imagine their nervousness when in 1955, the Nicklauses first met Bob Jones. Just fifteen, Jack qualified for the United States Amateur in Richmond, Virginia. As it was the twenty-fifth anniversary of his final win at the 1930 Amateur, Jones agreed to come up and speak at the players' dinner. During a practice round, Jones sat in a golf cart watching players come home on the long par-four finishing hole. Jones was already feeling the effects of syringomyelia, a spinal disease he was diagnosed with in 1948. He had not played a round of golf since. He inquired about the only player he saw reach the green in two shots. When told the player was a mere fifteen, Jones was doubly impressed. He asked to meet him.

"This session with Jones was a tremendous thrill for me," said Jack, who always referred to him as "Bob Jones" and addressed him as "Mr. Jones" in person, "but I am sure it meant twice as much to my dad." They talked for twenty minutes, and Jones said he'd be watching for more of him. In his first round match against Bob Gardner, Nicklaus was 1 up after the 10th hole when he saw Jones sitting in a cart at the next tee. The pressure of impressing Jones got to Nicklaus. He went bogey-double bogey-bogey. Feeling his presence was causing the boy to try too hard, Jones left. Nicklaus did recover, although he lost the match on the 18th hole. The Nicklauses saw Jones again at the 1957 Jaycee Tournament in Columbus won by Jack, and for a third time at the 1959 Masters during the annual Wednesday night dinner held for amateurs.

This bond with Jones was the main reason his first invitation to the Masters in 1959 was so meaningful.

"Because of my admiration for Bob Jones, the Masters—the tournament he created, played on the course he helped design—has always been something unbelievably special for me," admitted Nicklaus in 1969. "When I have been fortunate enough to win it, I have treasured not only the victory itself but the generous things he has said about my play at the presentation ceremony. When Bob says something about your golf, you know there is substance and sincerity in it. Above and beyond this, you always feel that he understands what you are all about as a man as well as a golfer. This gives everything a deeper meaning, and it sticks to your bones."

Jones would send letters of congratulations after Nicklaus's significant wins. Each year at the Masters, Nicklaus and his father would visit Jones in his cabin, talking golf and replaying shots Jones had played at Scioto in 1926 (he was a remarkable nine under on the par fives there).

Jones even penned the foreword for Nicklaus's 1969 autobiography, *The Greatest Game of All: My Life in Golf*, in which Jones was effusive in his praise. He wrote, "I do think it is completely safe to say that there has not yet been a more effective golfer than Jack Nicklaus."

Nicklaus doesn't know why Jones took such a liking to him. "Maybe he saw in me some of himself as a young lad and that maybe I could follow a little bit along in the footsteps of what he had started," says Nicklaus, "and that's what he had alluded to me many times in staying an amateur."

By the time Jones passed away on December 18, 1971, Nicklaus had become more like Bobby Jones than any golfer since. His spirit remained with Nicklaus, whose accomplishments and character were now respected and admired as much as Jones's nearly a half century earlier.

Nicklaus was keenly aware how lucky he'd been to have developed this connection to Jones that began through his father and Scioto and its members. "I have learned an awful lot from him," said Nicklaus of Jones.

If not for the pedestal that Bobby Jones sat upon, it's possible Jack Nicklaus's aspirations would have turned to something other than golf.

LIKE MANY BOYS, Jack Nicklaus grew up with childhood dreams of sports stardom. He was supposed to be a star for the Ohio State University Buckeyes football team, sprinting out into the Horseshoe of Ohio Stadium on Saturday fall afternoons in his hometown of

Columbus behind legendary head coach Woody Hayes. For thirteen years, he attended every home football game.

Nicklaus played several sports growing up—baseball, basketball, tennis, track—but football was his favorite. Quarterback, linebacker, and placekicker were a few of the positions he played. His love for all sports came directly from his father Charlie.

Like Bob Jones, Nicklaus was fortunate to be raised in a hard-working, hard-playing, upper-middle class environment. The Nicklaus clan came to the United States from Germany, and Charlie was a third-generation Columbus resident. Growing up, he had continued to work at Mebs Pharmacy, where he fell in love with pharmacy and golf. The first clubs he ever purchased were a used set from Mebs.

But as life moved forward, golf stayed behind. Charlie got his pharmacy degree and license. He married Helen Schoener in 1937, and their first child, Jack William, was born January 21, 1940. They were living the upwardly mobile American dream. Nicklaus opened his own pharmacy in 1942, and by 1960 he had four. Before Jack went off to college, the family would move around town five times until reaching the Upper Arlington home where his first Masters invitation would arrive.

Suburban Columbus provided a good life. The only major incident growing up for Jackie was a brief bout of polio when he was thirteen. It turned out to be mild, and he recovered quickly. His sister Marilyn, three years younger and the Nicklaus's only other child, suffered a more severe case. It took two years for her to fully regain use of one of her legs.

Charlie did everything with his son and became his best friend. He passed on a burning, competitive desire tempered by respect for the game. Charlie taught him to lose graciously. Sportsmanship was important. Congratulate your opponent. Credit him. Mean it. "Charlie gave Jack the presence to learn how to behave on the golf course," says Kaye Kessler. As a kid, Nicklaus won more than he lost, but in the semifinals of the Columbus District Amateur at age thirteen, he lost a

match and walked away. Charlie grabbed Jack and told him to walk back and shake hands. "Charlie said, 'You ever do that again, you're through with golf'," adds Kessler. You're not going to win all the time. When you lose, lose the right way.

With Nicklaus enjoying so many sports as a kid, it took two breaks to get him into golf—one of them literally.

Charlie Nicklaus regaled whomever would listen to his story of how his son began playing golf. It became referred to as "the ankle story." His father had originally strained his right ankle while playing volleyball in 1944. Over the years, the ankle gave him more discomfort until he found out that there had been a small chip on the bone. After surgery to fuse the ankle and a few months in a cast, the doctor instructed him to get as much movement as possible. In the spring of 1950, Nicklaus decided he would rediscover golf since the family had just joined Scioto Country Club. He found he could play only a few holes at a time before needing a rest, so he decided to have his son come along, giving him a cut-down set of Hillerich & Bradsby clubs. Little Jack loved it.

SITTING AT HIS DESK at the *Columbus Citizen-Journal* later that same spring, sportswriter Kaye Kessler received a call from Jack Grout. Just a few months earlier, Kessler had written a story on Grout, who had just been hired as the new head golf professional at Scioto in December. A native of Oklahoma, Grout had been a good player with more than a dozen top-ten finishes as a touring pro, although never an official win. He started his career in 1930 as an assistant pro under his brother at Glen Garden Golf and Country Club in Fort Worth, Texas, the same club where Ben Hogan and Byron Nelson were learning the game as caddies and later as professionals. Grout moved on to Hershey Country Club in Pennsylvania, where he was an assistant to Henry Picard, the 1938 Masters champion. Now forty, Grout, tall with rimless glasses and jet black hair, was anxious to pass on his enthusiastic thoughts about the golf swing.

He wanted to let Kessler know that he was setting up a weekly, two-hour class every Friday morning for juniors. So Kessler and photographer Dick Garrett went out and took a picture of around thirty kids, mostly ages eight, nine, and ten. The picture ran, promoting the clinic without identifying any of the children.

A few months later, Grout again rang Kessler. Their first nine-hole tournament had concluded and one of the boys in the photo shot a 51 the first time ever playing nine holes. "I said, 'You're kidding me, I'm giving up golf'," says Kessler. "Nine holes at Scioto, and he shoots 51?" So Kessler ventured back out to the club and wrote a little blurb about ten-year-old Jackie Nicklaus, who Grout had invited to the clinics after seeing him tag along with his father. Since then there isn't a name that has filled the columns of that paper's sports section more often.

By the end of his first year playing, Nicklaus, who supplemented the classes with a private lesson every couple of weeks, had shot 95 for 18 holes and recorded his first win in the club juvenile championship with a score of 121 for 18 holes. The next year, his best was an 81, and he had become the star pupil of the weekly classes. He was the teacher's pet, for Grout saw something in Nicklaus he had seen in few others. The talent was present, but so was a blend of determination, commitment, and intellect. Through Nicklaus, Grout could impart the swing theories he had conjured up over the last two decades. He hammered it into Nicklaus using three main points.

The first was keeping the head still, just behind the ball. This was the center of balance, and Nicklaus learned the hard way. Grout's assistant Larry Glosser would grab Nicklaus's hair and hold it during the swing. He could soon hold his head still with the hardest of swings.

The second was foot work, instilling in Nicklaus that rolling the ankles was the proper way to ensure a good swing. Nicklaus led with his legs and derived much of his power from them.

The third was to make as full a shoulder turn as possible on the backswing with the widest arc. Grout wanted Nicklaus to extend those muscles while he was young and hit the ball as hard and far as he could. To accomplish this, Nicklaus rotated his chin to the right and allowed his right elbow to move off his body. Grout saw power as an advantage and a skill that was difficult to ingrain when older. "Control can come later," he said. This wasn't a conventional thought at the time.

"He was so soft-spoken and so insightful," says Kessler about Grout. "He would just tell Jack one little thing and that's all he'd need. He had a marvelous calm about him, and I think that was infectious to Jack."

Grout had his swing theories, but he was adaptable to students. For someone his size, Nicklaus had relatively small hands, and his father had initially instructed him to use an interlocking grip in which the pinkie on the right hand wraps around the left forefinger. Grout suggested he change to the Vardon grip in which the two fingers overlapped, but Nicklaus had problems with his hands slipping. So he stuck with the interlocking grip and never changed.

Nicklaus spent more and more time at the club. Even bad weather didn't deter him since Grout had erected a Quonset hut. Named for its place of manufacturing in Quonset Point, Rhode Island, the moveable 16-by-36 foot hut was a prefabricated covering of lightweight, corrugated steel that the U.S. Navy designed for use in World War II. More than 150,000 were made, and the surplus was sold to the public after 1945. Nicklaus spent countless hours hitting balls from underneath it.

Grout was also a fan of Bobby Jones, but it was Nicklaus's visits with Jones during the Masters that connected their philosophies.

"Jones said Stewart Maiden taught him how to manage and be responsible for his own game—his own actions on the golf course—so when he had problems he could correct them himself on the practice tee or during the round," says Nicklaus.

A bell rang in Nicklaus's head. Grout had strived to bestow him with complete knowledge of the golf swing. But he had been returning to Grout whenever something was amiss. Nicklaus figured, like

Jones, that he needed to be able to self-diagnose his flaws and fix them himself. He surmised, "It may be the biggest factor of all in shaping success or failure in the crucible of competition."

This gave Nicklaus two advantages. First, he knew his own swing more than anyone in the game. Second, he was able to salvage rounds others couldn't.

Grout traveled to the Masters nearly every year with Nicklaus, but never stepped foot on the practice range. He followed Jones's maxim and let Nicklaus figure it out for himself. If he was really stuck with mechanics, Grout was available to talk it over with him, but Nicklaus would be a better golfer if he could self-diagnose his faults.

Nicklaus had also been fortunate to grow up playing a Donald Ross design that was one of the top courses in the country. When Bob Kletcke played Scioto for the first time, he immediately realized why Nicklaus learned to hit the ball so high. "They have real small greens there, and it's quite hilly," says Kletcke. "You had to hit the ball real high to keep it on the greens." Right after Nicklaus began playing golf, the professionals returned to Scioto for another major championship, the 1950 PGA. Autograph book in hand, Nicklaus took in the sights and sounds of that week.

The more Nicklaus played, the better he became. By year three, his best score was 74. Then in his fourth year, it was a 69. Members now wandered down to the Quonset hut to watch the long-hitting phenom. "I liked it the best of all the sports I played because I felt I had a reasonable chance of achieving something worthwhile in it," said Nicklaus. As his feats grew, Nicklaus's fate was sealed by the head football coach at Ohio State himself, Woody Hayes. As a friend of the family, Hayes offered some parental advice to Charlie: "Football is a great game, but I know the talents of your son in golf. Keep him as far away from my game as you can."

WITH THESE THREE pillars—Jones, his father, and Grout— Nicklaus burst on the national scene. After his first Masters in 1959, he won the prestigious North & South Amateur at Pinehurst No. 2 the very next week.

Later that summer, it was on to the U.S. Amateur at the Broadmoor in Colorado Springs where Nicklaus drew none other than Robert T. Jones, III in his opening match. But Bob Jones was nowhere to be seen. According to his son, once his father had discovered who he was playing, he changed his mind about coming out to Colorado to watch his offspring play only one match. Indeed, Nicklaus prevailed comfortably, 7 and 6, and kept on winning all the way to the final with Charlie Coe. After trailing in the match for most of the day, Nicklaus birdied the 36th hole to win the title.

The following June, he nearly won the U.S. Open at Cherry Hills in Denver. As a twenty-year-old amateur playing the final two rounds with forty-eight-year-old Ben Hogan, who was the closest thing Nicklaus had to a hero next to Jones. By then, Hogan played only sparingly and was well past his prime. Yet there wasn't anyone out there who controlled his swing better than Hogan. Nicklaus suddenly was in the lead by himself with six holes to play when he faced a twelve-foot birdie putt on the 13th. After running his first attempt a few feet by, Nicklaus was too nervous to ask Hogan about fixing a pitch mark between his ball and the hole. He missed the putt. After the round, Hogan, who had seen his shot at a record fifth U.S. Open drown after sucking back a wedge shot into the water while playing to a front-hole location on the 71st hole, said, "I played with a kid today who if he had a brain would've won."

After the 1960 U.S. Open, Nicklaus didn't see Hogan again until the following Masters ten months later. Hogan walked into the locker room, saw Nicklaus and said, "Hey fella. You got a game." It was the nicest compliment Nicklaus had ever received. Just like Jones, Hogan saw something in Nicklaus that led him to befriend him—as friendly as Hogan could be. Hogan sought out Nicklaus for practice rounds from then on at the Masters. The usual game was a five dollar Nassau. "I don't have to tell you, there are easier ways of making money," said

Nicklaus, who enjoyed the honor of playing with Hogan. "He is the best shotmaker I've ever seen."

But Nicklaus was also able to see how one of the greatest strategists plotted his way around Augusta National. "Hogan wanted to keep everything underneath the hole," says John Mahaffey. "If you could do that and have that kind of control of your golf ball, you'd always have a chance to make birdie."

Nicklaus won the U.S. Amateur again in 1961 and was well on his way to becoming the "next Bobby Jones." Selling insurance and working for a slacks company, he made $24,000 in 1961. His first house cost only $22,000. The comfortable life did not satisfy Nicklaus.

"The chance to make money was not a factor in my decision to turn pro, because I already had enough money," he said. "All I ever wanted to do was play competitive golf against the best players in the world."

The game had changed since the 1920s and 1930s. He concluded that he couldn't become the greatest golfer of all time as an amateur. So in November 1961, Nicklaus did something Bob Jones never did. He sent a letter to the USGA announcing he would turn professional.

MORE THAN ANYTHING, the Jones legacy affected Nicklaus in the following way: the major championships were the highest priorities. To be the best, one must beat the best in the biggest tournaments. Everything else was a sideshow and preparatory work. The four professional majors were the Masters, the United States Open, the British Open, and the PGA Championship. Nicklaus looked at golf through these major-tinted spectacles.

"Jack made majors so much bigger than anything else," says Johnny Miller. "It used to be that a major was a little bit bigger than say a Western Open or a L.A. Open or a Colonial. But they weren't that much bigger. Jack made them like the majors were the only thing, then everybody really started separating the majors from everything else."

Everything Nicklaus did, from his schedule to his practice, was designed around the majors. His affliction was "majoritis" as Miller calls it. "Jack put a premium on major championships," says Billy Casper. "He trained himself to play in major championships."

The Masters, however, was not the most important major to Nicklaus. Being a limited-field invitational event, it may have been the least. Like Jones, the U.S. Open sat number one on Nicklaus's list. That was, after all, the national championship of American golf.

On the other hand, no tournament pulled on Nicklaus's emotions more than the Masters. It may not have been the most important major, but it was his favorite to play. From the first time he stepped on the grounds there in 1959, he and Augusta National were a perfect match.

Of course, there weren't many courses that didn't favor Nicklaus, but there his strengths were accentuated: his prodigious drives; his high, towering iron shots with a slight fade; and his putting. Longer drives equaled shorter irons. Shorter irons equaled loftier clubs for a higher ball flight. A 9-iron for Nicklaus may have been an 8- or 7-iron for someone else.

"While length helps a bit more perhaps than it does at some other courses, to win there takes sound all-round golf," he said. "You must really be in command of your irons to bring the ball in on the proper side of the flag, and you must be a very good putter to cope with the breaks, contours, and the subtle little rolls on the huge greens."

Nicklaus admits to being a good putter, but he thought there were a lot of good putters at the time. It was his strength that separated him from them. "I had more of an advantage than most people because of the ability to eliminate some of the hazards on the golf course from power," he says. "I suppose my power gave me more opportunities to be in that position (to make putts) under pressure."

Nicklaus realized that chipping and putting were key, but since scrambling and short game weren't his strong suits, managing one's way around the greens became more important. He could overpower the course, but he chose to dissect it.

"His style of play was somewhat conservative," says Ed Sneed, another Ohio State golfer who lived in Columbus while winning four times on the Tour. "He went for par fives because it was in his game." Nicklaus didn't need to take unnecessary risks at Augusta National because nearly everything the layout asked of a golfer was already in his game. "The course was just built for Jack," says Miller. "His iron game with that high stopping shot and as good as he was on those par fives. He could just pick his spots."

After that missed cut in his first Masters, he recorded top-twenty finishes in his next three appearances—tied for 13th in 1960 and tied for 7th in 1961 as an amateur and then tied for 15th in his first attempt as a professional in 1962, which was a disappointment to him. "It's not an easy place to learn," said Nicklaus of Augusta. But he developed some axioms. "The secret here is not to make any mistakes on the short holes and get your birdies on the par fives," he said.

In just his second full year as a professional in 1963, Nicklaus arrived wounded and worried. He had been suffering from bursitis in his hip, which had limited his play. But the injury had a silver lining that helped Nicklaus going forward.

"I hurt my hip and couldn't hit it left to right. I was forced to learn how to hit it right to left," says Nicklaus, who felt that was a big key for him on holes 2, 5, 9, 10, 11, 13, 14, and 17. "It really helped. It gave you an advantage." Even so, he did not become preoccupied with hitting a draw. "I never went to Augusta trying to hit right to left shots, unless it was a situation with wind and conditions that I thought I needed to do it," says Nicklaus. "But I had the ability to do it when I wanted it."

"They can say what they want about Nicklaus playing a fade," says Bob Murphy. "He didn't play a fade at Augusta."

In just his fifth Masters, Nicklaus had enough talent, experience, and confidence to handle the tricks and turns that the course could throw up. At age twenty-three, he became the youngest Masters champion. During the presentation ceremony Nicklaus proudly handed his winning golf ball to Jones himself. It would be his only professional major victory without his wife Barbara by his side. She was back home in Columbus pregnant with their second child. Four days later, Nicklaus would be there to welcome son Steve into the world, although he didn't handle that moment as well. He would faint during the births of four of his five children.

After finishing tied for 2nd in 1964, Nicklaus was in contention again in 1965, tied with Arnold Palmer and Gary Player after 36 holes in what looked like a battle of the big three. With little breeze and a lightness in the air, Nicklaus fired a bogey-free 64 in the third round, equaling the course record set a quarter-century earlier by Lloyd Mangrum. He didn't have a score higher than four on his card, hitting every green in regulation but one and birdying all four of the par fives and three of the four par threes. Nicklaus didn't hit a club longer than a 6-iron into any par four, and he went at both par fives on the back in two with 5-irons.

In slightly tougher conditions Sunday, Nicklaus again shot the low round of the day, a 69, to win by a record nine shots at 17-under-par 271. It was the lowest score to par ever in a major and broke Hogan's tournament mark of 274.

"I still say that was the easiest golf tournament I ever played from the standpoint of ease on me because it was just driver, wedge; driver, 9-iron," said Nicklaus. "It was so easy. Everything was easy." Afterward, the superlatives were effusive. Clifford Roberts called it "the finest golf that has ever been exhibited at the Masters and probably the best anywhere." And at the presentation ceremony, Nicklaus's idol Bobby Jones was moved to declare: "Jack is playing an entirely different game—a game I'm not even familiar with." Like Jones at a young age, the twenty-five-year-old Nicklaus was considered the best player in golf.

The next year, Nicklaus returned to create more history in an attempt to become the first to win consecutive titles. Then he nearly didn't play.

Just before bedtime on Wednesday, the night before the tournament, Barbara Nicklaus learned about a plane crash from the local NBC affiliate. Earlier in the day, four friends, Bob and Linda Barton and Jim and Jeretta Long, had taken off from Columbus to fly down to Augusta for the tournament. All were friends of the Nicklaus's, but Bob Barton was especially close having been one of his best friends growing up. Nicklaus was even the best man at his wedding. Barton, an Air Force Reserve pilot with some 4,000 hours flying time, was at the controls of the leased Beach Travelair plane when one of the engines appeared to ice up over mountains in northeast Tennessee. The plane crashed as he attempted an emergency landing near Johnson City. All four were killed instantly.

Nicklaus didn't want to play the next day, but his wife thought he should and convinced him so. Although, he had a hard time concentrating, Nicklaus shot a 68—the low round of the day by three shots.

The weather and course conditions weren't nearly as good in 1966, but Nicklaus remained the man to beat. Playing with Hogan in the final round, Nicklaus pulled a three-and-a-half-foot birdie putt on the 71st hole. It left him tied with Tommy Jacobs and Gay Brewer.

Following the round, he saw highlights running on a television in the clubhouse. Not only was it the first year the Masters was broadcast in color, but it was the first year for CBS's "stop-action" technique, or taped replay as it was later called. Upon watching his putt at the 17th, he immediately noticed his setup. Instead of being directly perpendicular over the ball, his eyes were over the outside of the ball, causing the stroke and ball to go left.

The next day, he didn't hit a bad putt the entire round. He won the 18-hole playoff and literally presented the green jacket to himself.

Then came the Jack-proofing. "They changed the golf course in the mid-1960s because of me," says Nicklaus. "I won the tournament three out of four years, and they put in bunkers and tried to restrict where I could hit the ball." For example, the right fairway bunker on the 1st hole was moved twenty-seven yards closer to the green, and a new bunker was added on the outside of the dogleg on the 2nd hole. None of those alterations changed Nicklaus's attitude. In fact, he believed they helped. "I thought that was great that they made the changes because it forced me to play better golf," he says.

Other players were driving the ball farther now as well. With these changes, Nicklaus had to think even more—which was his strength. More than his physical prowess, Augusta set up well for Nicklaus's mind. With so many risk-reward holes, his calculation of the percentages came down to whether the penalty would be greater than the reward. "I played within myself and what I knew I thought I could do," said Nicklaus, who because of that made fewer poor decisions than anyone.

Nicklaus's success at Augusta National did wane after 1966. In his attempt for three in a row, he missed the cut in 1967. His score of 79 in the second round, in which he bogeyed half of his holes, was his highest competitive round ever at Augusta National.

By the late-1960s, life was changing for Nicklaus. He had a growing family at home and more off-course interests and commitments. He went twelve starts in majors without a title and admits he didn't work as hard as he should have. His professional wake-up call was a personal loss. In February 1970, his father Charlie passed away after a short battle with pancreatic cancer. He was just fifty-six. It was a crushing blow to Nicklaus. His father lived for every tournament, and Nicklaus regretted he hadn't been totally committed the previous few years. So, he rededicated himself. He lost weight and got in shape. Victory in the 1970 British Open at St. Andrews got him back on track.

After finishing joint runner-up in the 1971 Masters, he took control of the 1972 tournament early and led wire-to-wire. Even with some spells of sloppy play—he made three bogeys in the final eight holes—he still won by three shots. Nicklaus finished tied for 3rd in 1973 and tied for 4th in 1974, giving him nine top-five finishes in thirteen Masters starts as a professional.

"Jack Nicklaus was never more comfortable playing any place than he was playing there," says Murphy. "He loved it. He was perfectly comfortable there."

His experience at Augusta and golfing ability gave Nicklaus such a distinct advantage that it allowed him to make statements no one else in the field could. "I could play badly at Augusta and still win," said Nicklaus. "I couldn't play terrible, but I didn't have to play well."

JACK NICKLAUS didn't fist-pump, didn't sword-dance, didn't blow kisses, didn't trash talk, and didn't curse. The closest he got to uttering an on-course expletive was, "Oh, Jack."

But he winked.

It frequently came after a stellar shot and could be sent in the direction of his caddie, his playing competitor, a fan, or a writer. It signaled, "Yes I did it. I'm in control of my game and the situation I'm in." All of his confidence and attitude and bravado were summed up whenever he flashed that wink of an eye.

Ben Wright remembers standing to the side of the tee on the 17th hole during the final round of the 1972 U.S. Open. Nicklaus chose a 1-iron on the hugely difficult par three at Pebble Beach with a stiff wind coming off the ocean. Then a voice that could be heard by everyone on the tee, including Nicklaus, said, "He'll never get there with that." It was the British golf writer Pat Ward-Thomas. Well, Nicklaus rattled the ball off the flagstick and dropped it inches from the hole. He walked off the green, in the direction of Ward-Thomas, looked him in the eye, and without saying a word or breaking his stride, winked at him with a grin. "It was the biggest put-down," says Wright.

Of all the things the wink represented at the golf course, it represented the edge Nicklaus had over everyone else in the game.

"I knew exactly how intimidating I was, and I've got to tell you, it was a tremendous advantage," Nicklaus said. "I knew that many of the other players had the physical skill I had, but I also knew that few of them had the mental skills to use that physical skill properly."

The greats of the game all had a certain edge over their competitors at one point and in varying degrees. Vardon. Hagen. Jones. Nelson. Snead. Hogan. Palmer. To maintain it was sacrosanct. Once the edge was lost, it was never regained. No one knew that better than Ben Hogan.

With a mystique greater than any player in the game's history, Hogan had understood the power of always having an intangible edge over your opponents and felt that his biggest mistake ever was throwing it away at the 1955 U.S. Open at Olympic Club. Before teeing off in an 18-hole playoff with Jack Fleck, a club professional from Iowa who had never won on Tour, Hogan strolled up to him and said, "I see you're playing my clubs, Fleck." By acknowledging Fleck, he had put him at ease and calmed his nerves. The nine-time major champion, maybe the most intimidating figure to ever play the game, had foolishly given away his edge. Later, Hogan believed uttering those seven words allowed Fleck the upset win and prevented him from capturing a record fifth U.S. Open.

The edge Nicklaus held didn't involve any shenanigans that some players would use to try and unnerve or rattle an opponent intentionally. "Gamesmanship was not one of Jack's tactics," says Kessler. Nicklaus claims, "I never worried about an edge. The edge was if I played well I believed I could beat them." His record, performances, and the way he carried himself, however, gave him an edge, even if it was an unspoken psychological one.

"Not in word, but in the way he carried himself, it was very clear who he was and who you were," says Roger Maltbie. "Well earned, and not a hand that he played, but he knew it was there."

His powers were so great that anything he said was taken as a commentary not only on his game, but on yours as well. Maltbie remembers a prime example occurring in the opening round in Memphis, just a month and a half after the 1975 Masters. Victor Regalado, a third-year player on Tour from Mexico, got paired with Nicklaus for one of his first times and kidded with his pals that he couldn't wait to take down "Big Jack." Regalado's bravado held true on the front nine as he was nearly even with Nicklaus and thought he was playing pretty well. Then, on the 10th tee, Nicklaus strode over to Regalado, put his arm around him, and said, "Come on Victor, we got to get going, we're playing like crap." Regalado's spirit sank. Nicklaus birdied 12, 13, 14, 15, and 16 to shoot 31 on the back nine and a 66 for the round. Regalado slumped to a 74 and eventually finished in a tie for 16th at five over while Nicklaus finished tied for 3rd at 11 under. "You think you're giving it all you got, and he's thinking, man I'm missing on four out of six cylinders," says Maltbie.

Nicklaus was in the other players' heads without doing anything. As Tom Weiskopf bluntly puts it, "When you looked at Nicklaus and he looked at you, he knew that you knew that he knew he was going to beat the shit out of you."

That was the case on many Sunday afternoons. Nicklaus didn't even need to play superb golf to win. He would wait for those around him to make mistakes.

"Players would watch the leaderboard, and all of a sudden the Nicklaus name would appear, and they go, uh-oh, here he comes," says John Mahaffey. "All of a sudden, they can't hit it in a ten-acre field, they chili-dip it in the water, and all kinds of stuff happens. Instead of concentrating on your game, you end up watching to see what he's doing."

If Jack Nicklaus lost, that didn't mean his edge was gone. As long as he played well, his edge remained. If someone played better and won, hats off to him.

"Jack was extremely competitive. Jack didn't want to lose. He knew the edge was important," says Sneed. This translated to casual rounds and practice rounds as well. "If he's got a six-foot putt on the

18th hole on Tuesday for $10, Jack knew to step up there and knock it in the middle and look you in the eye. Jack knew what that meant. It wasn't life or death to him, but he didn't want to give anybody a freebie."

Nothing made Nicklaus angrier than when he beat himself, but those occasions did not stick in the minds of his colleagues.

"Ever remember Jack missing one that mattered?" asks Maltbie. "They did happen. They were few and far between. But we all have pictures of all the ones that did go in, that did matter."

EARLY ON, BOB JONES knew Nicklaus possessed everything for extended greatness; but from his own personal experience he concluded that it was possible "providing only that he retains his keenness for competition and his desire to win. It is in these subjective attitudes that the competitive golfer deteriorates long before his physical competence begins to wane."

Jones experienced the phenomenon himself. During his competitive days, Jones played in only a handful of tournaments each year. He juggled getting three degrees from three separate institutions—a Bachelor of Science in Mechanical Engineering from Georgia Tech, a Bachelor of Science in English Literature from Harvard, and a Law degree from Emory. Growing his law practice followed. The pressure and strain of playing well became so great that once Jones won the Grand Slam, he retired.

The fact that his sustained success on the course was under threat wasn't a surprise. Nicklaus was now thirty-five years old, and his life seemed like a multi-exit interstate interchange. He had five children at home. His golf architecture business was beginning to flourish with a dozen projects in some stage of design or construction. He was soon inaugurating his own PGA Tour tournament. There were books and numerous other business ventures and endorsement obligations. Distractions would have affected others. For Nicklaus, all of the off-course responsibilities helped to recharge his golfing batteries.

"I wasn't totally absorbed by the game of golf," says Nicklaus. "I was absorbed more by my family and other things I was doing. That was a blessing to me. I think I would have gone crazy if golf was the only thing I had to think of." The whirlwind kept his senses fresh.

"I wouldn't go on the practice tee for six hours," he says. "I had other things to do. I would go to the practice tee for a couple of hours and I would make sure I got six hours of practice in two hours because I focused on what I was doing."

He practiced because he wanted to, not because he felt like he had to. Pointing to just four events a year helped combat any boredom or mediocrity. "I always built myself up for Augusta and let myself down, and built myself up for the U.S. Open and let myself down," he says. "I did that so that I was always trying to climb a mountain going into a major championship, so that I knew I was focused and working on what I was trying to do." He and Bob Jones were the only players who could raise their games on call and peak for events.

A few months following the 1964 PGA Championship at Columbus Country Club, the champion Bobby Nichols remembers playing with Nicklaus, who said, "We had such tremendous crowds there in Columbus, it got me to thinking this town really needs a golf course." The blueprint was easy.

The Augusta National Golf Club and the Masters inspired Nicklaus to emulate Jones in another way. Back in Columbus on Christmas Eve in 1965, Nicklaus first mentioned his interest in copying the Augusta formula to several hometown friends: Ivor Young, Pandel Savic, and Bob Hoag. The conversation turned more serious one night at the house Nicklaus rented for the 1966 Masters. Nicklaus thought it would be great to have a similar course and event in Columbus. By June, Nicklaus fell in love with a piece of property northwest of the city. But it would be a long journey.

Financing the project proved difficult, even after it was announced in February 1968. Nicklaus bought more land with his own money. Even when it was decided, against his initial desire, that the best way to go forward was to make it a residential development, it remained stalled. By 1973, Nicklaus was on the hook for a lot of money, and options were about to expire that were vital to completing it. "If I ever saw a project that came close to taking someone down the tubes, this was close to it," he said. Finally, a deal was struck with a local securities company and the project, with Nicklaus still in control, moved forward (amazingly with all that going on, he won the 1973 PGA Championship the next week).

He named it Muirfield Village—after the course on the east coast of Scotland where he played his first Walker Cup in 1959 and won his first British Open in 1966. When the course finally opened on Memorial Day 1974, Nicklaus struck the first tee shot. Weiskopf and Putnam Pierman held the scissors at the ribbon cutting ceremony. Two years later, the Memorial Tournament would be inaugurated with Robert Tyre Jones, Jr. as its first Memorial Tournament honoree.

Nineteen Seventy-Four would see Nicklaus release his fifth book, the instructional classic *Golf My Way*. It would see him inducted as part of the inaugural class into the World Golf Hall of Fame in Pinehurst that September. And it would see him continue a remarkable streak of consistent excellence: at least two wins and a top-five position on the money list every season since his rookie year in 1962. But 1974 also served as a kick in the pants for Nicklaus.

He failed to capture a single major championship in 1974—the first time that had happened in five years. "If I have any one goal in golf, it is to try and capture one major championship each year," said Nicklaus during this period. He wasn't getting younger either. Even the game's most popular player, Arnold Palmer, had not won a major championship after age thirty-four. That led Nicklaus to start thinking about the Masters on August 12—the day after the previous year's PGA ended.

"I did not play all that well last year," he said. "Consequently, I have had to work harder on my game. My own game was lousy. I decided that I wanted to play golf for a long time. And that I had to get my game ready."

Nicklaus felt he never had a true break in the early-1970s, which led to him being tired and stale at the start of each year. So he changed his schedule at the end of 1974. Instead of playing until December and raking in money, he played only twice after late September. By taking much of the fall off, he spent time with his five kids, going to games, fishing, hunting, even playing in a recreational basketball league. Nicklaus enjoyed being a homebody (he was always proud that he kept a promise to his wife of never playing more than two weeks in a row his entire career).

The long breaks, he felt, made him much more eager. "That's how I kept myself playing and how I kept myself interested and how I kept kicking myself in the rear end just to get going," he said.

Then Johnny Miller started winning.

"He awakened the wounded bear," accused Miller Barber. "He got Nicklaus mad. When Johnny started tearing up those courses and killing par every round, some guys back home began making noise about Miller taking over as number one man. I tell you this: that Miller thing has Nicklaus in the same frame of mind like he used to be for Palmer when Arnie was number one."

"Don't make Jack mad," said Trevino. "Talk nice to him. Don't wake him up. They woke him up and got him mad in Florida and look what he did to us."

Nicklaus concurred, but without singling out Miller. "Johnny Miller, Sam Spade or whoever it is, my own game was lousy and that was my inspiration and motivation," he said. "Granted when anyone else is playing well, it puts a bug in you. It's a challenge I suppose. Good for me, good for golf.

"Nobody likes to think that he's still not considered the best player in the game."

THE MAJOR-LESS season of 1974 and ascent of Johnny Miller had prodded Nicklaus into focusing even more for this Masters. Yet, there was another unchecked dream. For a man who had accomplished nearly everything in the sport, Nicklaus still longed to reach the ultimate goal that would bring him full-circle with the legacy of Bob Jones: the Grand Slam.

"I have not accomplished all I want in golf," said Nicklaus that Tuesday. "If I could win all four of the majors in a single season, then, perhaps, I would not play the tour as I have played it." Of course, when Jones won his forty-five years earlier, he quit playing competitively. Would Nicklaus do the same?

He had come closest to achieving his quest in 1972. After winning the year's first two majors, the Masters and U.S. Open, he found himself in the lead with three holes to play in the British Open at Muirfield. Harkening back to memories of his triumph there in 1966 when the fairways were narrow and rough deep, Nicklaus had played conservatively on the links course the first three days and stood six shots behind Lee Trevino going into the final round. Changing course, Nicklaus decided to go all out, and by the time he got to the 16th tee he was six under par and leading by one. The spectators had been vocally behind Nicklaus all day as the momentum built. An emotional Nicklaus thought a par-birdie-par finish would win it.

Then, his tee shot on the par-three 16th hopped left into long rough, and he didn't properly read the break on his six footer for par. On the par-five 17th, he hit a drive off-line and couldn't recover for birdie. A par on the last gave him a 66, the low round of the day. "Even though I knew I screwed up coming in a little bit, I still thought that I was going to win the tournament when I finished," said Nicklaus. In trouble virtually the entire way up the 17th having hooked his drive into a bunker, hit his third shot into the rough, and bladed a wedge across the green, Trevino looked dead. Then, he chipped in for par from in back of the green. Trevino made another par on the final hole to edge Nicklaus by one. "I was flattened," said Nicklaus when that happened. "That was a hard, hard loss for me."

"What would he have done had he won all four?" asked Trevino. "There would be nothing left for him to do. He'd have to quit. Thinking back, maybe I should have let him win."

The major season in 1975 set up with layouts Nicklaus thought suited him well: Augusta National, Medinah Country Club outside Chicago, Carnoustie in Scotland, and Firestone Country Club in Akron, Ohio. "They were all good courses for me, and I wanted to get off to the right start," he says.

"So many times playing in the Masters if I didn't win it, I just forgot about the year," confesses Nicklaus. "I wasn't going to win the Grand Slam and that was how it worked."

Whether because of 1974, Johnny Miller, or the Grand Slam, Nicklaus believed he put in more work in preparation for the 1975 majors than he had since he turned professional. Leading into Augusta, the hard work was paying off. He won in each of his previous two starts at Miami and Hilton Head and stated, "I'm probably playing better than I ever have in my life." In fact, Nicklaus was attempting to win three consecutive starts on the PGA Tour for the first time in his career.

With his opening round 68 at Augusta National, Nicklaus was on his way to finding out definitively if this was the best golf of his life. On his way to cementing his place on top of the golf mountain. On his way to emulating Jones—maybe with his own Grand Slam. On his way to having fun.

| 7 |

FRIDAY, APRIL 11

"**M**r. Roberts would like to meet you," said the voice on the other end of the telephone. Vin Scully was already nervous. This call did nothing to alleviate his anxiety.

At age forty-seven, Scully was already a legendary baseball broadcaster. He joined the Brooklyn Dodgers radio team at age twenty-two, just a year after graduating from Fordham University, and then followed the team to Los Angeles in 1958. After a quarter-century in the business, Scully was one of the most revered and respected announcers in all of radio or television. In 1975, he had just been hired by the Columbia Broadcasting System to call NFL games, host tennis, and anchor its golf coverage. That meant he was going to be the lead commentator at the Masters, taking over for Ray Scott, who had called the action from beside the 18th green the previous five years. When Roberts was told of the change, he responded, "You mean the baseball fella?"

The request to meet with Mr. Roberts came on short notice. Even with his new CBS contract, Scully still called Dodgers games, and he and the team were already in Cincinnati to face the Reds in the opening series of the year. He wasn't supposed to travel down for the

Masters until later in the week. It was the CBS golf producer, Frank Chirkinian, on the other end of the line. Scully told him there was no way he could travel to Augusta and make it back in time for the game that night. Chirkinian replied that he'd call back, and a few minutes later he did. "Arnold Palmer's plane is being serviced in Indianapolis. It will swing by, pick you up at Lumpkin Airport so that you can have the morning meeting, and then you can fly back commercially and do the game," he said. The irony of his maiden voyage to the Masters wasn't lost on Scully. "So this left-handed hacker got off in Augusta arriving in Arnold Palmer's jet," he says.

"Even though I had been in the business a long time, I certainly arrived as I would at Notre Dame Cathedral," says Scully. "I was in awe of the history of the place as well as those who were going to play in the tournament. It has quite an effect on you no matter how many baseball games and how many football games and even how many other golf tournaments you had done."

Scully walked into Roberts's office aware of his strictness. He had heard of Jack Whitaker, an esteemed sportscaster who had sat atop the 18th hole perch in the mid-1960s but was taken off the Masters broadcast because he was deemed insufficient in that role. Of Ben Wright, who had to pass a thirty-second test of Roberts's ability to understand his British accent before being approved. "All he wanted to do was just meet me," says Scully, as the two chatted about the weather and Scully's feelings about announcing the Masters. "It was very charming, very, very sweet," he remembers fondly. Scully was relieved to make his flight back to Cincinnati in plenty of time for the game, but he was still wary of what lay ahead on the weekend.

"It was frightening for me," says Scully, whose Masters viewing had been limited over the years. Afternoons on the second Sunday in April had always been taken up by baseball games. "I was afraid that I would make some gigantic mistake during the tournament." So Scully worked extra hard to prepare for the Masters, immersing himself in the lore of Augusta National, researching its history, and compiling notes on present day players, in particular the trio of Nicklaus, Miller, and Weiskopf. Facts on those players became entrenched in Scully's mind.

Scully realized how important the Masters broadcast was. More than anything, television had taken the reins of the Masters and pulled it into the psyche of the nation by way of living rooms and clubhouses. It was first broadcast on CBS in 1956 and capitalized on being one of the few golf events on television. "Back then, it seemed like it was the only golf on TV," says Gary Koch, who remembers watching his first Masters at age ten.

What Koch and others saw was determined by Chirkinian, the network's brilliant, yet autocratic, producer who would be at the controls for CBS's live weekend broadcasts for the 18th consecutive year. For the indomitable forty-eight-year-old, the Masters wasn't sports as much as unscripted theatre.

In no sport does a producer have more impact on what the viewer sees at home than golf. At Augusta National, the playing field is the size of approximately 200 football fields and nearly four miles in length. Dozens of shots are played, or about to be played, at the same time, scattered about on tees, fairways, greens, and from trees and bunkers. Timing and sequence of all those shots are tough to balance, as is a team of announcers throwing back and forth to one another under the direction of a lone voice in their ears.

It's debatable as to what Chirkinian invented and what he just perfected, but there's no question what he innovated. He was present the first time videotape was used and was the person to bring it to golf. He invented the program interrupt system, where the producer/director could talk directly to each announcer in the field. He built scaffolding behind greens to put cameras on. He had the inside of the cups painted white. He placed microphones on the tees and beside the greens. He used boom mikes to capture on-course conversations between players and caddies. He utilized split screen images to perfection at Augusta.

And either he or Roberts or both conceived the idea of over-par/ under-par scoring, which simplified how players stood in relation to one another. It revolutionized golf on television.

"He was always looking for something," says Wright. "He was a genius, an absolute genius." Scully adds, "Frank was a marvelous pro- ducer-director. He understood the game from the grass up."

On Friday, April 11, 1975, there would be no Masters cover- age on television. The local CBS affiliate Channel 12 (WRDW) had a late afternoon line-up of *Match Game*, *Tattle Tales*, *Gomer Pyle*, and *Bonanza*. There weren't even any local highlight shows or specials. It would be another four years before a start-up called ESPN hit the air, and viewers at home would have to wait seven years until the CBS team produced the first live golf on Thursday and Friday at the Masters for USA Network in 1982. The thirty- ninth Masters would be nearly five-eighths finished before any- one at home saw live golf.

The crew wasn't on the air until 4:30 p.m. eastern daylight time Saturday, but their full-ensemble dress rehearsal took place Friday afternoon. They would cover Nicklaus's second nine. Chirkinian had 215 personnel and twenty-two cameras at his disposal and com- mand. All announcers had to be in their towers and on-headset fif- teen minutes before rehearsal. This was his annual masterpiece. And no one would muck it up.

"By jove, it was long," says Wright. "It was longer than the broad- cast quite often. He would have you there until you got it right in his opinion. God bless him, that is exactly what was required. That was why the product was pretty superior in its time. He left no stone unturned. It didn't matter whether it was cameramen at fault or whether it was announcers."

In Chirkinian's mind, the commentators were responsible for voicing the soundtrack. Certain rules applied. "He would excoriate any announcer who stated the obvious," says Wright. Saying a putt had missed would get a "how many million people have seen that miss you dumbass." Chirkinian wanted all his announcers to have both an ego and the ability to suppress it for the good of the team and the broadcast.

One of Chirkinian's innovations was to station an announcer in a tower at each of the final seven holes. Some were golfers, others not. Scully would handle play at the 18th, as well as any action caught at the 9th, 10th, and 11th (even though there were no camera towers on those holes). At the 17th hole sat Frank Glieber, a Dallas-based sportscaster in his eighth Masters who worked a myriad of sports for the network. The legendary British golf writer Henry Longhurst, now sixty-six, took the perch behind the 16th green. Longhurst actually called golf for ABC in the United States, but broadcast this one event a year for CBS. At the 15th hole resided Wright, a veteran English sportswriter whom CBS Sports President Bill McPhail hired over Chirkinian's head for the 1973 season. Beside the 14th was Whitaker, who had returned in 1972 as an emergency fill-in for an ailing Longhurst only to continue on the team. Stationed at the 13th hole was Pat Summerall, the former football player turned sports announcer, who had been at the Masters since 1968. He would also host the green jacket presentation for television. A camera position hadn't been added at the 12th hole until 1973, and calling the play on the par three was Jim Thacker, a local sportscaster in Charlotte who, in addition to the occasional golf tournament, also worked regional ACC basketball games.

Those seven had already sat through the annual television meeting on Thursday up the hill from their compound in Butler Cabin. The meeting was conducted by Bill Kerr, co-chairman of the Television and Radio Committee and retired head of the San Francisco Stock Exchange. The guidelines were the same each year. For example, there should be no mention of prize money. There should be no mention of other tournament names that included sponsors (the Monsanto Open was to be referred to as Pensacola). Many in the room were irked that a man with no working knowledge of sports broadcasting was telling greats like Vin Scully and Henry Longhurst how to do their jobs. "It did surprise me a little that he was lecturing a room full of announcers who had who knows how many years of experience, but it was the Masters so I happily sat there and tried to drink it all in," says Scully. Longhurst, who tended to nod off during the meetings, insisted that he would never have walked on the floor of the exchange and told Kerr how to do his job.

But in reality, this was the club's broadcast as much as anyone's. The event was more-or-less a time buy, which allowed the club to have increased control over the product. There were just two sponsors: the Travelers Insurance Companies and the Cadillac Motor Car Division of General Motors Corporation. As Gene Sarazen would say in the broadcast's taped opening: "You the viewing audience receive top consideration. It is planned to eliminate any interruptions of important tournament action through the limitation of commercial announcements."

For many on the CBS crew, the annual highlight of the week was Wednesday night's annual Calcutta, a pre-tournament party that featured an auction of each player in the field. The winner took home the entire pot, which was always five figures. Wright claims to have won seven Calcuttas. In 1979, he was taken to task for picking a first timer named Fuzzy Zoeller for $50. When Zoeller won, Wright pocketed $26,000. Who had Nicklaus in 1975? "It could have been Summerall, because he tried to buy up everybody," says Wright.

It was about time to get to work.

THE STAGE OF AUGUSTA National was set, but television was nothing unless there was a star to watch. Chirkinian was lucky. During his first year in 1958, a new player didn't just enter stage door left, he kicked it in and commanded the theater. He knocked them dead, picked up the roses thrown at him, and embraced it all. If the Masters was unscripted theatre televised, then its first star was Arnold Palmer.

Palmer loved the camera, and the camera loved him back. Take a poll of members at Augusta National Golf Club of their favorite golfer, and he would have won in a landslide. The viewers at home loved Palmer, too, especially impressionable children who were getting their first look at the game.

"He sort of made the Masters," says Johnny Miller. By 1960, nearly nine out of every ten households owned a television. Kids such as Curtis Strange (his father knew Palmer and played his clubs), Gary Koch, Roger Maltbie, Ed Sneed, and many other Baby Boomers spent their early years watching Palmer swing away on the black-and-white tube and developed an affinity not only for him, but for the course he seemed to own from 1958 to 1964.

"It was always so special to me because Arnold Palmer was my hero as a kid," says Maltbie, who watched it on television in the early-1960s. "It was a place I always wanted to go to."

In the late-1940s, Palmer had desperately wanted to go to the Masters as well. One year, the Wake Forest College golf team he played on was competing in a match in Georgia around the same time as the tournament, and they contacted the club to offer their volunteer services. To Palmer's great disappointment, the boys were turned down. Once Palmer received his own invitation in 1955, getting past the gates would never be an issue the rest of his life.

In 1958, soldiers from nearby Fort Gordon manned the scoreboards, and some made signs that read "Arnie's Army." The moniker stuck, and Augusta National became home base. That year, he won his first professional major at the Masters. He followed with a succession of victories in even-numbered years—1960, 1962, 1964—to become the tournament's first four-time champion.

"Today, I could tell you every shot Arnold hit in 1962," says Sneed, a high school senior at the time.

"There wasn't much not to like about him," says Koch, who became a Palmer fan watching those Masters. "It was the style, the swashbuckler, the whole bit."

Unlike Weiskopf, Miller, or Nicklaus, Palmer didn't so much swing at the ball as attack it, like a machete wielding adventurer off to rescue a damsel in distress. No hands looked better on a golf club than Palmer's. On a plane ride to the Spanish Open in 1975, Jerry Heard asked Palmer, with all his success, what was it he thought about when hitting the ball. Palmer said, "I just grab it real firm with the right hand and hit it as hard as I can." Heard said, "That's it?" Palmer replied, "That's it."

An adventure is what Palmer gave fans. His aggressive style didn't necessarily suit a place like Augusta National and occasionally was his Kryptonite. In 1959, he led by two with seven to play before hitting it in the water on the 12th, bogeying the 17th, and missing a four-foot putt on the 18th. In 1961, he walked off the 18th tee with a one-shot lead, before seeing his friend George Low along the ropes. Palmer strolled closer to say hello, and Low congratulated him on the victory. Suddenly, Palmer was taken out of the moment. He lost his concentration and hit his approach shot into the right bunker. Then, he began playing quickly. His bunker shot ran over green, his chip shot came up well short, and his bogey putt missed. He'd lost by one, and it was down to a mental error.

It spoke to Palmer's mass appeal and charisma that he was so revered. Throughout the blown leads and winless droughts, he remained the fan favorite, even if he hadn't won a major since that 1964 Masters.

Times had been tough on the golf course for Palmer. He had not won on the PGA Tour since the Bob Hope Classic in early 1973. Putting problems dogged him, and he constantly switched putters. With his eye sight deteriorating, he began wearing eye glasses in 1972 and spent the next few years switching between glasses and contact lenses. This year, with the glasses, he had been in position to win at Hawaii, Inverrary, and Jacksonville, only to come undone in the final round each time. The prior week in Greensboro, though, Palmer had his best round of the year on Sunday, a 66.

Still, there was a lack of confidence fans never saw in his heyday. Some felt Palmer had lost his nerve. The day before the 1975 Masters, Palmer said of his next win: "If it doesn't come this year, it may never come."

Palmer had finished well with a final-round 67 in 1974 to place in a tie for 11th, and the momentum had carried over to this year. His opening round of 69 was his best start to the tournament since 1964—his last win. The start was encouraging to Palmer. "The tournament is not going to end just because I broke 70," he said. Palmer birdied holes 2, 6, 13, and 17. He had an opportunity to tie for the lead on the 18th with a birdie before leaving a 3-iron approach wide right and failing to get up and down after missing a fifteen footer. Palmer's round could have been better if not for leaving a few putts short after failing to adjust to slower green speeds. Like Nicklaus, Palmer had been pointing to the Masters since the start of the year. "I've been trying to build my game to a peak," he said. "If it doesn't peak now it may not peak."

Television would have loved Arnie in the second round. Going off at 11:29 a.m., Palmer surged into the lead for a forty-five-minute stretch that had his army on the march. Following a bogey at the 1st, Palmer stuck a pitching wedge to four feet for birdie at the 2nd. He converted an eight-foot birdie putt at the 4th, the longest par three at Augusta National. On the plateaued 7th green guarded by five bunkers, Palmer rolled in a twenty-foot birdie from left of the hole and gave a vigorous fist pump. His caddie sprinted to pick it out of the hole.

The three birdies in his first seven holes vaulted him into the lead at six under. The roars echoed through the course to a level of "ten million decibels" according to playing competitor Tom Watson. There was more excitement on the uphill par-five 8th where, after hitting two shots from the trees on the left, Palmer hit his fourth shot from forty yards to two feet. His charge ended on Amen Corner with back-to-back bogeys at the 11th and 12th and a 4-wood second shot into the water on the 13th. A final birdie on the 15th gave him a one-under 71.

"I had to work a heck of a lot harder to shoot the 71 today than I did yesterday to shoot a 68," he said. It was much more exciting, though. Palmer hit only nine greens in regulation but one-putted eight greens, scrambling for par on holes 5, 6, 8, 9, 10, 13, and 18. It was vintage, retro-Palmer on the greens, hunched over, playing the ball off his left big toe, knees almost touching, draining putt after putt. "In the last seven or eight years or so, my major problem has been getting them up and down. I would just miss the green by a few feet and then take three to get the ball in the hole," he explained.

It had been eleven years since his last major triumph on this course, but now with no one between himself and the leader at the midway point, Arnie's Army had visions of another Augusta conquest. "A lot can happen on this golf course," he said. Maybe even the greatest win of his career.

BY THE END of the day, Palmer's 36-hole score of 140 was matched by two future Hall of Famers—one on the tail end of his career and one just beginning his.

In the Masters, players were repaired after the first round, although not by score. Tee times were made at the committee's discretion. Amateur Craig Stadler played with Palmer on Thursday. Playing alongside Palmer was a thrill for youngsters, but it wasn't something others enjoyed. The pairing was almost like a one-shot penalty a side, not because Palmer wasn't gracious, but because the feverishness of the galleries could spill over the ropes. At least Tom Watson had experience from which to draw.

At age fourteen, Watson had played with Palmer in an exhibition match back in his hometown of Kansas City. "You think I was nervous out there today," said Watson, who was the Kansas City Amateur champion at the time, "but boy was I nervous then." Now twenty-five, Watson was competing in his first Masters as a professional. "Anyone who has ever watched Arnold Palmer play has thought about playing with him in the Masters," he said.

Watson had played in the 1970 tournament as an amateur, but the road back to Augusta had been arduous. He turned professional in

1971 after earning a degree in psychology at Stanford University. He was a high-ball hitter with no fear and a great short game. But Watson soon gained a reputation for squandering leads on Sundays. The most significant occurred at the 1974 U.S. Open, where he led outright after 54 holes only to shoot a 79 in the final round to finish 5th. One week later at the Western Open, Watson started the final round six shots behind and was never in contention until the closing nine. He shot a 69—the only sub-70 round that day—to win his first PGA Tour title.

Instead of being distracted, Watson fed off the feverish atmosphere of a Palmer pairing. On the 13th hole, he lashed a 3-iron second shot to three feet and made the only eagle of the day there. Two birdies and two bogeys coming in gave him a second consecutive round of two-under-par 70 and put him in contention for his first major championship going into the weekend.

Also in at 140 was a man who many saw as the antithesis of Arnold Palmer. Quiet and reserved, Billy Casper kept to himself and his family. He didn't look the part of a golf star, so much so that when he turned professional Hall of Famer Paul Runyan asked him, "Why?"

On the course, Casper was all business. Only five players in the game's history—Snead, Hogan, Palmer, Nicklaus, and Nelson—had won more tournaments. His strengths were on the inside and not easily measured. Unlike most, Casper always had a game plan.

"I got a mental image of each hole in my mind. I would go through each hole and plan where I wanted to hit the ball and places I didn't want to hit the ball, so that when I played each hole I had a pattern that I had established," says Casper. And that never ever changed, no matter his score, the leaders' scores, or conditions.

For many of Palmer's fans, Casper was the man who broke the King's reign. With nine holes to play in the final round of the 1966 U.S. Open, Palmer led by seven shots. By the end of the championship, he and Casper were tied. Casper won in an 18-hole playoff the next day. Palmer had not been the same golfer since.

The self-control and focus displayed by Casper in San Francisco was something he first learned by watching Ben Hogan play a practice round in San Diego for an exhibition years earlier. Hogan would hit balls from all angles to determine the best point of attack on each hole. Casper filed that away. "I knew exactly where I wanted to hit the ball off the tee, and I knew exactly where I wanted to hit the ball on my second shot," he says. Casper employed this discipline during his breakthrough win in the 1959 U.S. Open at Winged Foot when he famously laid up on the par-three 3rd hole all four rounds, then chipped up and one-putted for par each time.

Like Palmer, though, Casper was extremely competitive and had an affinity for Augusta National. "The Open was the tournament that really was the one that you thought more of," says Casper. "Not until I went to Augusta in 1957 did it change. Once I went there I wanted to win the Masters."

Around the greens no one was better than Casper. At age eleven, he began caddying at San Diego Country Club, and at the end of each day, he and his friends would practice putting in the dark. "I feel that's where I developed a very sound touch," says Casper. "You could walk up to see the hole, get the hole in your subconscious, then walk back keeping your eyes on that area where the hole was. It was surprising how close you could get that ball. I did that day after day for a number of years."

Casper felt the most important aspect of putting was reading the greens, especially at Augusta National. "It's a real science to be able to read the greens. I always wanted to know where the highest place was in the area, because that had an effect on the final read of the putt," he says. "I putted with feel. I didn't try to hole putts from any length. I wanted to get the ball next to the hole and get it in from there. If it went in that was a bonus. So consequently, I was a speed putter and always wanted the ball within a two- or three-foot circle when I was any distance away."

To take advantage of his short game at Augusta, Casper worked backward from the hole, always wanting to keep his ball in a position where he could succeed. That strategy gave him confidence that he would succeed. "I always felt that I could win at Augusta," says Casper.

In the 1969 tournament, Casper had been in control from the start but lost the opportunity for victory by playing the first ten holes of the final round in five over. The next year, he found himself in a playoff with fellow San Diegan Gene Littler. After opening with a birdie on the 1st hole, Casper pulled his tee shot left on the 2nd. The ball settled inside a lateral hazard with a stick right behind it. With Littler in the fairway and a branch directly in front of him, the only shot was a 9-iron to get back in play. "It was the most perfect shot I've ever hit in my life," says Casper. "I could have made anything." He made 5; Littler made 6. When he walked off the back of the 18th green as the winner, Cliff Roberts stood waiting for him. They shook hands. "I expected him to say congratulations, but he didn't," says Casper. "He said, 'Thank you, Billy, thank you.' He'd been rooting for me to win and finally I'd won. It made him happy, and of course, what it did for me was unbelievable."

He had come a long way from pulling a trailer from tournament-to-tournament in his first year on Tour. Now forty-three, Casper notched three top-tens on the West Coast, but recently had been spending more time working on his farm than golfing. He had moved into a new home in Mapleton, Utah, just outside Provo. He and wife Shirley were raising eleven children at home, where Casper was also managing an organic orchard of some 6,000 fruit trees, including peaches, pears, and cherries. After five weeks off, he didn't pick up a club until going to Greensboro, where he opened with a 79.

A week later, he was nine shots lower in the opening round of the Masters when Johnny Miller had predicted Casper would do well because he's a "good mudder." "I liked adverse conditions," admits Casper.

On Friday, he finished stronger than anyone. Casper was the only player in the field to birdie the 17th and 18th holes. "It's those holes down around the water—11th, 12th, 13th, 15th, 16th—that scare you to death," he said. Casper made four birdie putts over twelve feet in round two, even though he hit it in the trees on five holes. "The greens are absolutely perfect," he said. "If you can read them right and stroke the ball right, there's no reason you should miss." With another 70 on the scorecard, Casper was in position to win again, this time as the oldest Masters champion.

WITH NO EARLY-ROUND television coverage, the world never saw a live golf shot of Lee Elder in his first Masters. For the second round, he dressed in all cardinal red, with his contestant pin prominently displayed on the front of his visor, which was red.

However, Elder didn't produce any red numbers on his scorecard Friday, failing to record a single birdie. Paired with Miller Barber, Elder's pop stroke resulted in a myriad of three-putt greens, and his iron play was no better than it was the day before.

"Well, you fellows got rid of me," joked Elder. His 78 (40–38) left him at eight over par for the tournament, four shots off the halfway cut line. Elder's Masters, for which he waited 352 days, was over after just two.

"I was too relaxed," he said. In 36 holes, Elder made only two birdies but ten bogeys. "I thought I could do anything and get close to par. I wish I had felt some pressure. Everything I did was incorrect. We were a bunch of choppers, Henry and I."

Indeed, Elder later blamed many of his difficulties on his confident caddie Henry Brown. A year later, he claimed, "My caddie would tell me which club to use for approaches instead of telling me the yardage and letting me make my own club selections. I'd be fifteen or twenty feet beyond the pin. I'm not trying to use him as an excuse, but it happens to be the truth."

"I didn't feel drained after the first round," he admitted. "I did feel relieved. The only pressure was that of keeping the people with me calm. Maybe I should have done something to help keep me calm."

Elder had no regrets about his decision to accept the invitation. "It was worth it, no doubt about it," he said. "Just playing here was worth it. It's everything I thought it would be and more. I expected to play better, and I look forward to playing better next year."

In order to return in 1976, Elder would need a top-sixteen finish in the U.S. Open, a top-eight finish in the PGA, or another win. He hugged and kissed Rose in front of the main scoreboard, posing for photos. For Elder, his exit stayed with him for a long time: "On the way out, after I had finished playing, every black person who worked at the club—caddies, servants, the people who worked in the restaurants—was lined up against the wall, waiting for me, waiting to congratulate me and thank me for what I had done."

In the end, there were no public pickets or threats to the club, disruptions or boycotts. It couldn't have gone smoother as far as the club was concerned, and Elder earned equal amounts of praise. "Elder proved to be some kind of man," wrote Robert Eubanks in the next morning's *Augusta Chronicle*. "He handled the big week with dignity, grace, and poise. Maybe he was on his best behavior just for Augusta. But we don't think so. We think this is par for Lee Elder's course. And Rose Elder, too."

ELDER WAS ONE of thirty in the field of seventy-six who wouldn't make it to the weekend. The 36-hole cut fell at 148. Only the low forty-four players and ties advanced, along with anyone within ten shots of the lead. Four over par matched the lowest cut in Masters history. There hadn't even been a cut in the tournament until 1957 when a record field of 101 necessitated one be made to the lowest forty players. It was changed to low forty-four and ties and ten shots in 1962. The pros who missed still received $1,250.

Among the other notables who missed the cut were Sneed, Mahaffey, and Oosterhuis. Only two of the seven amateurs made the 36-hole cut: twenty-five-year-old George Burns with two rounds of even-par 72, and reigning U.S. Amateur champion Jerry Pate, a twenty-one-year-old senior at Alabama with scores of 71–75, although no birdies Friday. A day after playing with Nicklaus, Curtis Strange shot a 77. With a 74, Gary Koch's mind turned to his wedding two weeks later to his college sweetheart Donna Suarez.

Even with his opening round 71, Sam Snead would not be around for Saturday and Sunday either, but it wasn't because of his score. Snead continued his good play, getting to two under par with a birdie at the 4th. On the 7th hole, however, Snead almost went to the ground. His sciatic nerve was acting up and causing muscle spasms. He proceeded to bogey the 7th, 8th, and 9th holes and, at one over par, decided to withdraw at the turn. Snead would never shoot another subpar round in the Masters.

Allen Miller had been playing with Snead and became a single on the inward nine. A 75 dropped him from tied for 2nd to a tie for 15th. Snead's nephew J.C. was stalled by a shaky driver. He made just one birdie and one bogey for a round of 72 to get in at three under par.

Lee Trevino felt the wet conditions continued to benefit him, allowing him to control his fade and occasional hook better. Trevino birdied the tough par-four 5th, as well as the 7th and 15th holes. He didn't make a bogey until the final hole when he hooked a 4-iron into the front bunker and couldn't get up and down. "I've had great success hooking the ball with my driver. I've been doing it well with my woods, but not so well with my irons," he said. His opening scores of 71–70 marked the first time he shot consecutive rounds under par at the Masters and his best start ever in the tournament.

For opening round leader Bobby Nichols, the toughest part about Friday was Thursday night. "You think about what you want to do the next day, what may happen, what you hope doesn't happen," says Nichols, who had his wife Nancy and three children with him in a rental house. "It's all anxiety, no doubt about it. It's hard to sleep. If you do, you wake up a lot."

Even for someone who had won eleven times, the status of being a leader in the Masters was daunting. "I was a little jittery this morning, and I three-putted the 1st hole," he said. "After that, I had trouble getting the ball to the hole." He seemed to right the ship after a birdie at the 7th, but a missed that two-and-a-half footer at the 8th was backbreaking. "That really shook me up because it was such an easy putt," he said. The second nine wasn't much better with a bogey at the 10th after two hooked shots into the trees and three-putt greens at the 12th and 13th. "I played awful," he said. "I just put too much pressure on my putter." Taking thirty-three putts, he shot 74.

Joining Nichols, Trevino, and Snead at three under were three other players. Pat Fitzsimons, in his first Masters after winning the Los Angeles Open in February, shot a bogey-free 68 to jump twenty-eight places up the leaderboard from a tie for 33rd to a tie for 5th. Homero Blancas, a ten-year veteran with five PGA Tour wins, also got to 141 with a 69, an unexpected score for the Houstonian who had been struggling on Tour until an impromptu swing lesson from 1968 Masters champion Bob Goalby on the range in Jacksonville three weeks earlier helped straighten out his driving.

The sixth player at 141 thought as well as he'd played, that's the worst total he could have shot.

TOM WEISKOPF GOT up early for his 10:26 a.m. tee time at the private house where he, his wife Jeanne, and two young children Heidi, four, and Eric, two, were staying. Weiskopf enjoyed the private lodging. They always ate in because if they went out to restaurants, Weiskopf says, "The fans would just wear you out."

Drizzle early Friday morning gave way to sunshine by afternoon, although temperatures remained cooler than average with highs still in the mid 60s. Balls were still stopping on greens in places they normally wouldn't, and players were still leaving putts short that would usually run out beyond the hole. With the dampness of the course, however, officials hadn't been able to cut the fairways as close as in previous years. The combination of longer grass with the moisture could cause balls to climb up the clubface, meaning shots were more difficult to control and could go farther than intended.

"You really couldn't shoot at the pins, although you know the greens will hold. With the grass being wet, you can't take the chance of knocking the ball over the green or to the right and making bogey or double bogey," said Weiskopf.

Adjustments under different conditions were part of the game, and that's why veterans of Augusta National such as Weiskopf had such an advantage.

Weiskopf played early in the worst conditions of the lingering rain. After birdies at the 2nd and the 6th, Weiskopf climbed into the lead by himself at five under for the tournament. But he caught two bad breaks coming in.

On the dogleg left 13th, his drive went through the fairway and landed in front of a pine cone. He tried to hit a low 2-iron up the fairway, but the ball jumped straight up and hit a tree. Then on the 15th, he hit a long drive down the fairway, but it wound up on one of a series of mounds on the right side. They may not have been hazards, but they could be penal. The mounds had been added in 1969—a move to prevent longer players (like Jack Nicklaus) from blasting it down the slope on that side and having a short second shot (Nicklaus once hit as little as an 8-iron into the green). Officials wanted to make players think off the tee and in the fairway. Even with the uneven lie, Weiskopf decided to go for it, but hit the ball fat and into the middle of the pond. Of all the shots he would hit that week, it was the one he wished he could have back.

"Making two bogeys on two reachable holes is like throwing four shots away, especially when you look at my length," said Weiskopf.

"The thing is that I can reach these holes. I look at the course as a par 70. Two holes, the 8th and 15th, really are par fives because it's hard to hold the 15th green. That makes it a 70."

Weiskopf would have liked to have been holing more putts; otherwise, he was pleased with his game. He hit a 3-wood left on the 18th, but managed to get a 3-iron to the front of the green and two-putt for par. The even-par round of 72 was his sixth consecutive score of par or better at Augusta National.

After he was done, Weiskopf considered his position, which would be a six-way tie for 5th at the end of the day. He referenced Nicklaus, who teed off more than three hours after him, three times in his post-round presser and thought about him once more. He asked, "Right now, what is Jack doing out there?"

MORNING BROKE IN the Nicklaus's rental house that served as their home away from home. The house was shared annually by two other couples: good friends Pandel and Janice Savic and John and Nancy Montgomery. Each morning, Barbara Nicklaus cooked her husband the same meal – a cheese omelet.

This Friday was their son Steve's twelfth birthday, but he wasn't there. Instead, Steve was back in their North Palm Beach, Florida, house. The Nicklauses had five children, the others being: Jackie, age thirteen; Nan, a month away from turning ten; Gary, age six; and Michael, twenty-one months. "We really never took the children to the Masters," says Barbara Nicklaus. "We all knew the word major." The only child with them was their oldest, who was in love with golf and asked to come. Jackie had made his first trip to the Masters at age ten in 1972 and watched his dad win.

Barbara Nicklaus walked every round with her husband. She had her own route around Augusta National, and Jack always knew where she was in the gallery. It had been that way from the beginning, although she initially knew nothing about golf. They met during the first week of school as freshmen at Ohio State. They were engaged on Christmas Eve in 1959. They were married just five weeks after the 1960 U.S. Open during the weekend of the PGA Championship, the one tournament as an amateur he couldn't play.

Barbara held the house together. "That enabled Nicklaus to be the golfer that he was because he had that incredible support," says Wright. "Saint Barbara," as Weiskopf calls her.

"My dad and Jones and Jack Grout and Bob Kepler, my golf coach at Ohio State, all had an influence on how I handled myself and how I handled what success I had," says Nicklaus. "My wife had a lot to do with that. The people I was around all gave me good advice on how to handle yourself and treat other people, which I suppose if you hit me over the head enough times with a two-by-four I'll learn something."

"I'd hate to think what my life would have been had I not married Barbara Bash," he said.

The night before, Jerry Heard had been at his own rental house with his wife Nancy. While they were cooking steaks with friends, a call was placed to the club to see who Heard would be playing with. His friend came back chuckling. "What are you laughing at," said Heard. "Who I got?" "Nicklaus" was the reply. "You gotta be kidding me," said Heard, who had opened with a 71. "Geez, I'm just trying to have a nice little Masters here."

Heard had a while to think about it. They didn't go off until 1:35 p.m., the thirty-second of thirty-eight twosomes. Before they even teed off, Nicklaus had moved up the leaderboard. "I was tied for the lead and had not made a birdie yet," said Nicklaus. "I figured if I could get something going, I would have a good chance of opening up a lead." Nicklaus was one of those who felt the hole locations were easier on this day, but there was a little bit of wind and the wet grass could be tricky. Earlier in the day, Chi Chi Rodriguez had been asked when the rain would stop. He replied, "When Nicklaus tees it up." On cue, the sun came out just as he started.

"You get up on the first tee, and Jiminy Christmas, everybody's out. I remember looking down there, and it was wall to wall," says Heard. "Jack was wonderful to play with."

Even with a solid ball-striking round, Nicklaus's thirty-six putts the previous day hadn't made him happy. He knew how to putt the Augusta National greens, especially with his secret weapon in the bag: the George Low Sportsman Wizard 600 putter.

At the start of his career, Nicklaus used an old-fashioned hickory-shafted putter made for him at the famed Ben Sayers golf shop in North Berwick, Scotland, while he was there for the 1959 Walker Cup at nearby Muirfield. It won him two U.S. Amateurs and an NCAA crown, but at only thirteen ounces in weight, it was too light in Nicklaus's hands for pro tournaments on quicker greens. In his first five starts as a professional on Tour in 1962, he didn't take less than thirty-three putts in any round and his scoring average was a pedestrian 72.0 per round. Worse yet, he hadn't been in contention at all.

Coming off a final-round 75 in Palm Springs, Nicklaus was frustrated as ever and ran into George Low at the Phoenix Open. Low was a former Tour player known for his large size, his humorous banter, and his nomadic existence. Within the inner circle of touring professionals, he was recognized as the world's best putter. In the 1950s, Low contracted with Sportsman's Golf, a company located in Melrose Park, Illinois, and founded in 1948 by four brothers named Hansberger, to design a line of Wizard putters under the Sportsman and Bristol brands. "I understand you're struggling with your putting," Low told Nicklaus. "You can't putt with that old light putter." Low escorted him into the pro shop at Phoenix Country Club, grabbed a Sportsman Wizard 600 autographed model off the rack, and stuck it in Nicklaus's hands.

It was a blade putter, somewhat similar to the head of his Sayers stick, but with a thick flange on the back and much heavier. It had a notch on the top—Nicklaus later added a second for alignment and painted it red. Nicklaus shot a 64 in the following pro-am. The putter just felt right in his hands: thirty-five inches long with a blade three-and-a-half-inches wide. Nicklaus finished tied for 2nd that week in Phoenix and went on to record three wins and sixteen top-tens in the remaining twenty-one starts of his rookie season on Tour.

Over the next four years, Nicklaus rode the putter to victory twenty times, including four majors, but by 1966 he sidelined the Sportsman. He first tried out a Slazenger model, a near duplicate of his Wizard with lead tape on the head for balance. He won the 1966 Masters with that putter. The Sportsman returned briefly, winning the 1966 British Open, before Nicklaus gave a Ping model a run. Then during the week of the 1967 U.S. Open, he developed an attraction for a center-shafted Bullseye putter Deane Beman was using. A friend had the same putter, although it had been painted white to reduce the sun's glare. Nicklaus took it and shot an unheard of 62 in a practice round at Baltusrol Golf Club the next day. "White Fang," as it was nicknamed, won him that Open but stayed in the bag for only a year and a half before the Sportsman was resurrected. Since then, it had notched five more professional majors for Nicklaus.

Nicklaus's style was one in which he hunched over with a slightly open stance to see the line. But his putting prowess wasn't as much technique as it was feel and mental approach.

"When Jack had a huge putt coming up, he'd be standing off to the side, very relaxed," says Bob Murphy. "There was no tension. There was no practicing the putting stroke. It didn't mean anything. What meant something was the mental process when he started into that putt. It was only going in."

"He had unbelievable distance control," says Johnny Miller. "He always left himself a tap-in if it didn't go in." Nicklaus never struck a careless putt, but Miller also had another theory about Nicklaus on the greens: "He was more dangerous from eighteen to twenty-five feet than he was from ten or twelve feet. I think he thought the putts that were eighteen to twenty-five feet, which is where he would hit it a lot playing safe on iron shots, I think he felt more like this is a bonus if I make it where if you knock it eight feet you're supposed to make it. He was lethal on longer putts. He was probably the best ever at making a twenty footer."

Nicklaus, who always kept his golf glove on his left hand when putting—most players, including Miller and Weiskopf, took theirs off for better feel—rolled in a six-foot birdie putt on the par-three 6th followed by a seven-foot birdie putt after hitting the flagstick with his approach shot on the straightaway par-four 7th. He went out in 34.

Then he came to the 11th hole, the beginning of the most famous three-hole stretch in golf. In a *Sports Illustrated* piece in 1958, Herbert Warren Wind had labeled it "Amen Corner" because that's where all the action had taken place that year. Wind took the name from a jazz recording "Shouting at Amen Corner" by a Chicago clarinetist named Milton "Mezz" Mezzrow. Located at the bottom of the course, the three holes presented 1,050 total yards of danger with water in play on every full shot from the fairway at the 11th to the green at the 13th. Just two hours earlier, Palmer had played the trio in two over par. "I always respected the problems you could have with the second shot at 11 and (the tee shot) at 12," says Nicklaus of the pond left of the green on the 11th and Rae's Creek in front of the 12th.

From the fairway of the 445-yard par four, Nicklaus hit a 6-iron to the middle of the green, not challenging the back-right hole location. He then made the uphill twenty-eight footer for birdie—his longest made putt of the week. As the ball was a few feet from curling in the hole, he turned his body and began walking away. Once the ball dropped, his head turned as well and he lifted the Sportsman Wizard high in the air with his right hand—a sign of celebrations to come.

Even though the 12th was the shortest hole on the course at 155 yards, Nicklaus had played it in nine over par in his career—his worst performance on a par three. Hitting to the second smallest green on the course while having to judge the ever-swirling winds that whistled through the pine trees around this hollow, Nicklaus stood by one of his principles: club yourself for safety. On this afternoon, he caught the wind at the right moment, hoisting a 7-iron to the right hole location, hole high just seven feet away. After walking across the Hogan Bridge that spanned Rae's Creek—it had been dedicated in 1958 in honor of Hogan's record 274 in 1953 which Nicklaus broke twelve years later—he made the putt.

Finally on the 475-yard 13th – the shortest par five – he took a 3-wood off the tee, a club Nicklaus and many of the longer professionals usually chose because it was easier to draw around the corner. Nicklaus cut it close to the creek, the ball settling only six feet from it. He hit a 4-iron and liked it immediately, walking after it. The ball finished thirty feet away from the hole on the largest green on the course at 8,400 square feet. A two-putt was never a given on the 13th, but Nicklaus cozied his first attempt up to the hole for an easy birdie. It marked the second time he had accomplished the rare feat of birdying Amen Corner. Nicklaus had previously done it in the first round of his last victory at Augusta in 1972.

Nicklaus, draped in a burgundy cardigan, wasn't stopped after Amen Corner. Although his bid for four birdies in a row was snapped with a missed eight-foot birdie putt at the 14th, he picked back up at the 15th. His driver stopped just barely on the upslope of one of those mounds on the right side of the fairway that cost Weiskopf. Nicklaus didn't have any issues, though. He hit a 2-iron from 220 yards that landed hole high, fifteen feet to the right of the back-center hole location. His eagle putt slid just by, but his sixth birdie in a ten-hole stretch had given him a strangle-hold on the tournament.

He was hitting the ball so well, therefore thirty-one total putts on Friday was okay by him. "If you're knocking the ball on the greens all the time, you're going to have a lot of putts," he said. Following pars on the 16th and 17th holes, Nicklaus came to the 18th as the last player in the field not to make a bogey. It was his longest bogey-free start ever at

Masters—thirty-five holes. The closing hole played as the most difficult in round two, with the northeast wind blowing into the players
and the hole location tucked in the very back of the two-tiered green.
On the uphill approach shot, Nicklaus whipped his 4-iron left of the
green and chipped up. The seven footer for par hit the right edge of the
hole and spun away. He turned his head toward the fairway in dismay.

After the round, a group of writers sought out Jerry Heard in the
locker room. He shot 75, but they were eager to ask him who was
better, Miller or Nicklaus. He was evasive in comparing his friend to
his playing competitor, but about Nicklaus's round he did say, "It was
the easiest 67 you've ever seen. He just did everything you're supposed to do. Hit it on the middle of the greens, knocked it on the
par fives in two, and played very conservative."

By the end of the afternoon, the name of Jack Nicklaus topped the
Masters leaderboard for the first time in three years. Overall, it was
the fourteenth time he'd led after any round. Nicklaus fired the low
round of the day, a 67—good for a glass vase given by the club for the
low score of the round (Nicklaus's ninth such vase)—that was high-
lighted by six birdies and not a single bogey until the last hole. The
round was his lowest second round in the Masters since a 66 in 1963
during his first title. He was the only player in the field with each of
the first two rounds in the 60s. No one had ever shot all four.

His 36-hole total of nine-under-par 135 tied the tournament record, first set by Jack Grout's mentor Henry Picard in 1935 and then
matched by Byron Nelson in 1942 and Ken Venturi as an amateur in
1956. The number left him five shots clear of the field going into the
weekend—matching another Masters record set by Herman Keiser
in 1946.

"One of the great edges he had as a player was when Jack got his
name to the top, you knew it wasn't going to go away," says Maltbie.

After his round, Nicklaus retreated to the press center, which always made him feel right at home. The building was a Quonset hut,
although this one slightly larger than the style he hit balls from at

Scioto. This was a warehouse model, 40-by-100 feet, which since 1953 had housed writers covering the Masters. The 210 typewriters inside would be humming the same headline: "Nicklaus in Control at the Masters."

"I've been trying to get it here all my life," he said to the assembled writers. "I try to prepare my game to reach a certain peak, but that doesn't always work. If it's ever going to be, it should be now. I'm probably playing better than I ever have in my life."

ONE GUY WAS definitely out of it, and a lot of tears weren't shed over him.

Johnny Miller may have been the new golden boy in the eyes of the public, but his blonde hair, upturned collar, squinty eyes, upright gait, cocksure attitude, and shoot-from-the-hip style were not endearing to the rank-and-file in the locker room.

When he went to Tucson in 1975, he was asked about the state of his game. Miller wasn't one to avoid a question, lie, or sugar-coat his answers. So he responded by saying, "I'm going to win." "Nobody says that," says Miller. "It was like what are you doing saying that Miller you cocky son-of-a-gun."

"Johnny was the most outspoken guy you had ever seen in your life," says Heard. "He'd say stuff that came out in the paper, and I'd ask Johnny, 'Why in the heck did you say that?'"

Miller never hit balls after a round at any point during his career. He wasn't into the social scene and didn't drink, smoke, or gallivant with the boys. It led few to understand him.

"He was aloof," says Murphy. "He wasn't that friendly. He wasn't hanging around the locker room, laughing and giggling."

"A lot of guys didn't know Johnny very well. People just never got very close to him," says Heard.

"Johnny used to piss Tom (Weiskopf) off with some of the things he'd say," says Sneed. "Johnny pissed a lot of people off." Players thought, "Who does this guy think he is?"

The Board of Governors

of the

Augusta National Golf Club

cordially invites you to participate in the

Nineteen Hundred and Fifty-Nine

Masters Tournament

to be held at

Augusta, Georgia

the second, third, fourth, and fifth of April

Robert Tyre Jones, Jr.
President

R.S.V.P.

The invitation Jack Nicklaus received to his first Masters in 1959.
(JACK NICKLAUS MUSEUM)

Bobby Jones greets Jack Nicklaus at the 1960 Metropolitan Golf Writers Association dinner in New York City.
(AP PHOTO/MARTY ZIMMERMAN)

Nicklaus hits from a bunker during a practice round at Augusta National in 1975.
(AP PHOTO)

Lee Elder leaps after holing an 18-foot birdie putt to win the 1974 Monsanto Open and earns an invitation to the following year's Masters.
(BETTMANN/CORBIS/ AP IMAGES)

Elder hits his opening tee shot in the 1975 Masters and becomes the first black player to compete in the tournament.
(AP PHOTO)

Arnold Palmer signs autographs for his admirers on Monday of 1975 Masters week.
(AP PHOTO)

Johnny Miller's run at Jack Nicklaus as the world's best golfer began after being teammates at the 1973 World Cup.
(BETTMANN/CORBIS/ AP IMAGES)

Utilizing a weak grip and early set of the wrists, Johnny Miller was able to hit his irons closer to the hole than anyone in the mid-1970s.
(BOB THOMAS/ GETTY IMAGES)

Tom Weiskopf's wide-arc and impeccable swing fundamentals were the envy of golfers at the time.
(BOB THOMAS/ GETTY IMAGES)

In the third round, Weiskopf reacts after making a birdie on the 18th hole to take the 54-hole lead by one over Nicklaus.
(AP PHOTO)

Beginning the final round with an out-of-sync swing, Nicklaus quickly corrected it.
(BOB THOMAS/ GETTY IMAGES)

Miller watches as his birdie attempt on the 6th hole just misses on Sunday.
(BETTMANN/CORBIS/ AP IMAGES)

Weiskopf and gallery react as he sinks a birdie putt on the 3rd hole in the final round.
(AP PHOTO/ BOB DAUGHERTY)

On the 16th hole, Jack Nicklaus and caddie Willie Peterson watch as his 40-foot birdie putt nears the hole...
(AP PHOTO)

...and then improbably drops in to tie him for the lead with Weiskopf and Miller standing on the tee.
(AP PHOTO)

After the conclusion, contrasting expressions show on the combatants' faces during the trophy presentation.

(BETTMANN/CORBIS/AP IMAGES)

The previous year's champion Gary Player presents Nicklaus with a green jacket for his unprecedented fifth Masters victory.

(AP PHOTO)

And there was the success. Not only was Miller making golf look easy and receiving a lot of glory, but he was raking in the dough. In those days, $100,000 was a benchmark for off-the-course income. By now, Miller was making around $500,000 a year—only Nicklaus and Palmer earned significantly more. His first big endorsement came in the fall of 1973 when he signed a contract with Sears for the start of 1974. By 1975, he had other deals with *Golf Magazine*, MacGregor, Beautyrest, Ford Motor Company, Palmetto Dunes on Hilton Head Island, Mizuno (when playing in Japan), and Slazenger (when playing in the United Kingdom and Europe). As for purchasing power, he bought a house for his father in Napa, California, for $20,000.

"There was definitely jealousy," says Miller. "They would call me the Plastic Arm because I would compliment myself. They would make fun of me. They didn't like that I was getting a lot of write ups…. It was a little disconcerting."

Miller went out in the morning with Charles Coody, the 1971 champion, and shot a 71, a four-shot improvement from Thursday's opening round. Once again he had hit it well. He didn't feel like he was putting that poorly, but wondered as he sat at two over, "A lot of guys are hitting it like me and are one and two under."

Miller had done exactly what he didn't want to: he had fallen out of touch with the leaders. He badly wanted to win the tournament, to prove he could win multiple majors, but to do that, he needed to stay in contention. Presently, it looked like he'd blown up. His feast or famine style of golf was famished.

"It was about putting at Augusta," says Miller, who noticed his stroke was a little jabby, something that wasn't happening earlier in the year. "I was already hitting my putts and pulling my putter back. If you were off with your putting you've got no chance. Look at the guys who've won there."

By the time Miller finished, two-thirds of the field was still to come home. He told the press early that afternoon, "I am just not going to be around tomorrow." Miller left the course to catch some solitude by a fishing hole, the one place he could find solace. "That was the time I wanted to be by myself," he says. "It got me away from all the hullabaloo."

Of course following his round, Nicklaus was asked about Johnny Miller. "Golf's a bigger game than any individual. Really, if you win 20 percent of the time, you're on top. Of course, you like to have the best record. That's only human nature," said Nicklaus. Then, as a little dig at Miller, Nicklaus added, "It's easier to play when you're not in contention, but it's not as much fun."

After being on edge mentally all week, Miller wound up making the cut by three shots. "I was out of it," he admits.

He trailed Nicklaus by eleven shots, a seemingly insurmountable deficit considering no one in the history of golf's four major championships had ever come back from that many strokes after 36 holes to win.

LEADERBOARD AFTER 36 HOLES

1.	Jack Nicklaus	−9	68–67
2.	Billy Casper	−4	70–70
	Arnold Palmer	−4	69–71
	Tom Watson	−4	70–70
5.	Homero Blancas	−3	72–69
	Pat Fitzsimons	−3	73–68
	Bobby Nichols	−3	67–74
	J.C. Snead	−3	69–72
	Lee Trevino	−3	71–70
	Tom Weiskopf	−3	69–72
27.	Johnny Miller	+2	75–71
mc	Lee Elder	+8	74–78

| 8 |

MILLER

Johnny Miller had blown his best opportunity to win the Masters, and his critics reveled in the failure. To them, all the West Coast wins, low rounds, endorsements, and fame would never make up for the lack of a Masters title. By Saturday morning, they hammered away. Kenneth Denlinger in the *Washington Post* was one of the harshest: "Johnny. Hey, Johnny Miller. Let me tell you something. All those 61s at Tu-nix, or whatever, and all that money don't mean much unless you win some tournaments the big guys want, too. Get yourself some more majors, kid, then maybe I'll get excited."

Miller had no shot at a rebuttal. Going back to Hilton Head, the Golden Bear had now bettered him by thirty-three shots in the last four rounds when they were both in the field. In order to make up an eleven shot deficit on Nicklaus the next two days, he would have to pick up a shot on him every three holes the rest of the way. In the minds of the press and sports fans everywhere, that just wasn't going to happen. Not to Jack Nicklaus. Not at Augusta National.

This, however, was the Plastic Arm. Two days of marginal golf did nothing to dilute the unwavering self-confidence inside of Johnny Miller. By April 1975, he wasn't afraid of poor starts to tournaments.

He wasn't afraid of Jack Nicklaus. He wasn't afraid of going low. And he wasn't afraid of large deficits. Before the third round began, he could recall the midway point of the Masters four years earlier, when in Miller's mind, a green jacket should already have been in his closet.

IN 1971, Miller was in only his second full season on the PGA Tour. Although winless, he was starting to contend on Sundays. Three weeks before that year's Masters, he held his first 54-hole lead on Tour at the Greater Jacksonville Open. Playing in a field that included Nicklaus and Palmer, Miller battled thirty-mile-per-hour winds to shoot a 69 in the third round—the only sub-70 score of the day. Leading much of the final round, he walked up to the last green with a twenty-foot birdie putt to win the tournament. Instead of giving it a firm run, he left his putt two feet short. Then, unimaginably, he missed the par putt. His three-putt bogey left him one shot out of a playoff, which was eventually captured by Gary Player. The Associated Press reported, "(Miller was) in tears as he signed his card."

The heartbreaking conclusion was offset by a benefit—the high finish assured Miller of his first Masters appearance as a professional. In a category employed only once, Augusta National officials had instituted a points system based on finishes from the week after the 1970 Masters to the week before the 1971 tournament. Miller, who entered a whopping thirty-six events in that time span, was one of eight players not otherwise eligible who qualified off this list.

When Miller arrived at Augusta, he played all of his practice rounds with his friend and mentor Billy Casper. A fellow Mormon, Casper was also the defending champion, having defeated Gene Littler in a playoff the previous year. Miller felt like his game measured up to Casper's in those practice rounds, but his good play didn't translate to low scores the first two days. He opened the tournament with a double bogey on the very first hole, and, following rounds of

72–73, he trailed by seven shots at the midway point—seemingly out of contention.

In the third round, Miller began two hours and ten minutes ahead of the final group. After holing a twenty-foot par putt on the 4th hole to ignite his round, Miller made five birdies. Even a bogey at the 18th didn't prevent him from firing the low round of the day, a 68 (later matched by Jack Nicklaus). He had climbed to within four shots of Nicklaus and Charles Coody going into the final round.

On Sunday, Miller went off in the third to last pairing with Hale Irwin and picked up where he left off the day before. He birdied the 3rd, 4th, and 8th holes to go out in 33. Then at the 11th, he poured in a nine-foot birdie putt to reach four under on the day. "This (charge) drove the hordes mad," wrote Dan Jenkins in *Sports Illustrated*. "Suddenly, they personally had discovered the new Nelson, or Hogan or Nicklaus."

If Arnie had his army, Miller was quickly forming his own militia. "That was the most excitement that I had ever caused on a golf course," he says. "They were really pulling for me." With a willowy physique and blond mop-top, Miller already stood out, aided by what he admits were some pretty wild clothes. The Men's Fashion Association of America had voted him the flashiest dresser on Tour. On this day, his ensemble consisted of a pale lime-green shirt with wide collar, extra-wide white belt, and Technicolor pants with the seamless colors of army green, aqua blue, grey, black, and white vertical stripes.

This flamboyant figure right out of the *Mod Squad* was a striking juxtaposition against the backdrop of Amen Corner where Miller's young career was about to take off. On the par-three 12th, Miller played his tee shot at the middle of the front bunker, trying to fade a 7-iron to the far-right hole location. After hitting it, Miller thought the shot would end up stiff. But a gust of wind caught the ball, and it came up short in the bunker, buried deep under its front lip. Miller's run up the leaderboard appeared over. "It looks like I'm going to make bogey or double bogey," Miller says. "I hit it as hard as I could, and that thing popped out of that dang bunker, ran down the hill, and went right in the hole."

After a par on the next hole, he launched a long iron to within six feet on the 14th for another birdie. Suddenly, Miller was six under for the round, seven under for the tournament. The fledgling professional, just eighteen days shy of his twenty-fourth birthday, now led the Masters by two shots over Coody with four holes to play.

During this stretch, Miller had been completely in the moment. He didn't realize his position until walking to the 15th tee, when a patron told him that he was leading by a pair of shots. "I didn't know whether to believe him or not," says Miller. "But on the 15th tee, I'm thinking, my dad's watching this thing at home. I'm going to win the Masters, and he's going to be so excited."

Until then, Miller had just been trying to make birdies, like he would in a practice round. Suddenly, with the thought of actually winning the Masters for his first professional title—something only Claude Harmon had done in 1948—he had committed one of golf's deadliest sins. He had thought ahead to the end result.

With a rush of adrenaline, Miller did hit a good drive on the par five and, following some debate, went for the green in two with a 4-wood, his ball kicking into the right greenside bunker. To the gallery's delight, he nearly holed another bunker shot, but the ball ran six feet past the hole. It was not a tough putt, and a birdie would give him complete control of the tournament. Instead, the ball lipped out violently.

On the 16th tee, Miller—"like a dumbbell," he says—made an unwise decision to play at the flagstick. His 5-iron went directly at the hole, but the ball jumped into the back right bunker. After blasting out to eight feet, his par putt caught the right side of the hole, horseshoeing out for another crucial miss. Shortly thereafter, Coody, who two years before had led by one with three to play before bogeying each hole coming in to lose by two, made birdie at 15 and then another at 16.

Now Miller was one back. He parred the 17th, but then made another bogey at 18, failing to get up and down for par after a poor chip from short right of the green. Unlike in 1969, Coody didn't blink, even making a miraculous par on 17 after hooking his drive into the greenside bunker on the 7th. From there, he managed to hit to the front of the green with what he called "the greatest shot I ever hit in my life" and sink a seven-foot putt. On the last hole, Coody manufactured another par after a wild hook off the tee to win his first, and only, major championship by two shots.

Even with bogeys on two of the final three holes, Johnny Miller had again shot the day's low round with a 68 and elicited the most vocal cheers. He became only the fourth player in Masters history to shoot the low round each of the last two days. There were no tears this time around. "It was all a bit of a blur to me," says Miller. "I just got ahead of myself. I stayed awfully aggressive and hit good shots coming in. The putts just spun out."

Miller sat next to Nicklaus during the awards ceremony on the practice putting green, awaiting their silver medals as joint runners up. Nicklaus nudged Miller, leaned over and said, "Big deal, huh, second place." Miller, the youngest competitor to finish 2nd in Masters history, responded in kind, but recalls, "I wanted to say, 'You know, Jack, it is kind of a big deal'." Miller had recorded his best finish ever as a professional, more than doubled the largest paycheck of his life ($17,500), and upstaged the big four of the time (Nicklaus, Palmer, Player, and Casper). But looking back, he realized what Nicklaus meant: winning matters most.

For a short time, Miller became haunted by the ending of the 1971 Masters. He thought Coody got lucky and he got hosed. "I should've won that thing," he declares.

The one characteristic Johnny Miller did not lack was self-belief. The loss bothered him, but it didn't become him. He truly thought that he would win the Masters one day. In fact, he was destined to win it. Johnny Miller had always been—and would always be—a "champ." After all, Larry Miller had made sure of that.

JOHNNY MILLER'S FATHER served as the poster-dad for childhood affirmation. Laurence Otto Miller always spoke positive and encouraging words to his children. Johnny never remembers his father uttering a negative or derogatory comment toward him or any of his siblings. To him, anyone who tried hard was a "champ"—a term he called Johnny more often than his actual name. That praise and pronouncement would have a lasting effect on his son.

Genetically, Larry Miller also handed down quite a creative spark. He came from a family of artists—his grandfather was a noted sculptor, creating many pieces for the California State Capital in Sacramento. Johnny's father was highly intelligent—an outside-the-box thinker—with his ideas straddling the line between genius and quack. The wheels were constantly turning in his head. He came up with countless inventions, wrote poetry, and composed songs. But he was also fiery, driven, and harvested a temper he tried to hide as much as possible from his children. Once during the 1966 NCAA Championship at Stanford, he broke his hand after slamming it into a steel post when Johnny three-putted a par-five green he'd reached in two. "He would've been a Tommy Bolt if he'd played the Tour," his son reckons.

Miller's day job was at the RCA Corporation in San Francisco, where he missed only a handful of days in thirty-eight years of work. His expertise was in Morse code, and he could type a warp-speed 120 words a minute (forty is the average). During World War II, RCA sent him to the Philippines, where he served as a communications specialist to aid the United States's military effort.

At RCA, Miller met Ida Meldrum. A quite, introspective woman, Meldrum descended from Mormon pioneers. With jobs scarce during the Depression, she left Utah and ventured on her own to San

Francisco, where she found work in RCA's operations department. There, Meldrum relayed messages from one wireless telegraph operator to another while zooming around on roller skates.

Johnny Miller may have received his father's wiring—inquisitive mind, creative veins, energetic soul—but off the course, he took after his mother, who was reserved and tranquil and never raised her voice. Religion was the bedrock of her life. With children in tow every Sunday morning, she hopped on the K Car to Sloan Boulevard, caught an L bus to 19th Avenue, and then walked a third of a mile to church (she didn't learn how to drive until in her fifties).

Larry and Ida were a perfect match for each other. "It was quite a yin and yang with my dad—so much passion and energy—and my mom who was very calm," Miller says. But the vastly different styles and personalities they passed on to Johnny created a walking paradox: someone committed to his family, deeply religious, loyal, caring, yet antsy, competitive, egocentric, and overly confident. Johnny Miller would tussle with these contradictions throughout his life, especially when it came to golf.

John Laurence Miller was born on April 29, 1947, the couples' third of four children—all spaced two years apart. He would become the first Baby Boomer golf star. To his dad, he was "John" or "Champ." To his mother, he was "Johnny." Later, to local golf writers, he was "Little Johnny Miller."

In the fall of 1952, Larry Miller decided to introduce golf to the entire family. He had not taken up the game seriously until after marriage in 1942, but he now played regular Saturday games and had fallen in love with it. Soon, he began shooting rounds in the 70s and wished that he had started playing sooner. He wanted to pass the game on to his children at an early age.

The Millers had recently moved into a new house on Keystone Way near the southern city limits, not far from Lake Merced. The home featured a full basement that Larry Miller turned into an indoor golf practice facility. He purchased a half dozen canvas tarps from an Army Surplus store and layered them in a corner. He placed down a mat and hung up an oversized mirror. On a table, he laid out the top instruction books from the game's greats: *How To Play Golf* by Sam Snead, *Power Golf* by Ben Hogan, *Winning Golf* by Byron Nelson, and *Hit 'em a Mile* by Jimmy Thompson. With a set of cut-down clubs, he began to teach his children golf's basic fundamentals.

The oldest child Ronnie liked swinging the clubs at first, and their two daughters showed some proficiency. But Ronnie enjoyed tinkering more with carpentry and mechanics, and his sisters' artistic talents were more advanced. Their brother, however, was different.

Little Johnny appeared as if he was put on Earth for the sole purpose of hitting a golf ball. Right from the beginning, he had a knack for it, and his father noticed immediately. He approached his bosses at RCA and asked to take the night shift from 12:00 a.m. to 8:00 a.m. so he could sleep while his children were at school and then work with Johnny when he came home in the afternoon. They would start at 4:00 p.m. and hit balls until dinner. The fundamentals came first. They would practice grip, set up, and posture. Although naturally left-handed, Miller swung right-handed. He used the mirror to mimic the swing positions of Nelson, Hogan, and Snead. He learned ball flight—deciphering exactly where each club should hit on the canvas—and could detect a solid strike of the ball versus a poor one solely by feel and the sound of the clubface colliding with the ball. "I could never hit enough balls for him—in a nice way," he says.

The Larry Miller teaching method, though, went well beyond the game's basics. Long before sports psychologists tutored the top professionals, Larry Miller was preparing his son mentally. He instilled self-esteem. Everything was a positive. After his son hit each ball, his immediate response was either "good shot" or "good swing." He instilled attitude. He taught his son how to look and act like a pro. He taught Johnny how to put on a glove and how to squint his eyes. He instilled work ethic. Prepping for any eventuality, he instructed his son to hit balls left-handed, from up against lips of bunkers, from behind trees. Shots were practiced from every place imaginable, even from ice plant—the thick, tangly ground cover West Coast golfers dreaded most. Johnny didn't see anyone else doing those things. As he got older, his father created a checklist of exercises to do: push-ups, pull-ups, squeeze grips, and running. Miller ran to school most days and, by the fourth grade, was running five miles a day.

"He would give me ten things to try," Miller says. "One out of ten was fantastic. The other nine, I had to figure out why it was a stupid idea. I had to get my brain in all these strange rooms that you normally wouldn't get into of thinking why something would work or wouldn't work. Now whether he knew to do that, I don't know. But he had some strange, weird things he would try."

The thought process stayed with him. "That guy, I couldn't believe what runs through his mind," says Jack Nicklaus.

On a daily basis, Miller was making multiple deposits into the Johnny Miller Golf Account. Of his father's teaching, he explains, "His theory was if you're willing to do things no one else is doing, you're going to be better than the rest of the kids. If you want to be the best, you got to be willing to do what no one else is willing to do. I was just doing things no one else was doing."

When Miller began entering junior contests, the outcomes were never in doubt. "I knew when I went into tournaments, because of this deep training, I was going to win," Miller says. Of the thousands of ideas and inventions that Larry Miller came up with during his life, this was his greatest—the shroud of confidence that he cloaked over his son. The tour players should have known that it wasn't a plastic arm patting Johnny's back, it was Larry Miller's arm.

As Johnny's game progressed, his father knew that a more knowledgeable golf mind was needed to handle the game's technical intricacies. He heard that the head professional at San Francisco Golf Club was a Mormon, and that was good enough for him. So in the fall of 1954, he put Johnny in the family's 1951 Chevrolet and drove two miles to the private club whose A.W. Tillinghast designed course was considered one of the country's best. They parked in the gravel lot, and Johnny waited in the car while his father stepped inside the tiny pro shop. After a few minutes, he returned with a middle-aged man. Whatever his father had said worked. John Geertsen instructed his young assistant pro, Tony Lema, to tend the shop. He was going to take a look at this boy.

The unassuming Miller picked the clubs out of the trunk, and he and Geertsen walked to the practice area. This time, it was dad who stayed in the car. Geertsen, forty-five, must have thought that this was a practical joke. Even at age seven, Miller was small. He had the body of a four- or five-year-old. He had suffered sickly spells as a youngster—his father thought he might be anemic—and was a regular at the doctor's office. Even in ninth grade, he was barely over five feet and 100 pounds—the smallest person in his class. Miller didn't experience a significant growth spurt until age seventeen—sprouting from five feet, two inches to five feet, eleven inches in one year. And it didn't stop until age twenty-five, when he fully topped out at nearly six-feet-three.

There, on the practice range, it was Little Johnny Miller, hitting balls for half an hour. He went through virtually every club in his bag, and Geertsen did not utter a word. After he had seen enough, they walked back to the car. Geertsen told Miller that the boy had potential. He would like to work with him. Their relationship lasted nearly forty years.

In addition to sound principles, Geertsen taught Miller to do something most others didn't at the time—an early hinge of the wrists on the backswing. Not only did this promote a solid position at the top, but it resulted in a downswing that was led by a ninety-degree wrist-cock to the right hip and a solid impact position with the shaft perpendicular to the ground. This action became the foundation for Miller's precise iron play, which was imperative growing up since, being undersized, he didn't hit the ball very far. Geertsen was also an expert at trouble shots and showed Miller how to work the ball any way he wanted. Another plus was hanging out in the pro shop at San Francisco Golf Club, where Miller learned how to fix clubs and regaled in hearing Geertsen's stories of playing with the authors of his father's instruction books: Snead, Hogan, and Nelson.

"It was a heck of a one-two punch," Miller says of his father and Geertsen. "If there was a way of rating the opportunity to be a champion because of a teacher and a father, I know I'd be in the top-three. I think it might be number one, and it has nothing to do with me."

Miller dabbled in other sports at school such as baseball and track. No one was faster in grammar school, but any aspirations of track stardom were squashed when he ran up against a kid named O.J. Simpson in junior high. His father also arranged lessons in a variety of vocations: swimming, piano, ice skating, singing, and guitar. Larry Miller wanted his children to have all the things he didn't. But with Johnny, eventually it always came back to golf. "My dad said when you're in school, you're in school," Miller says, "but when that bell rings, you're a golfer."

When Miller was eight years old, a voice from within spoke to him. It would be one of many times this spirit would visit. According to Miller, it told him: "Don't worry, your destiny is chosen. You're going to be a champion golfer, just like your dad says. Continue working hard." From then on, Miller never questioned his future. It was such a clear voice, such a strong confirmation, that Miller had no doubt where it came from: "It was really the Holy Ghost if you want to know the real truth."

His older brother Ronnie hadn't needed a voice to tell him that golf wouldn't be a good career move. When the children ventured out to play the nine-hole Fleming Course at Harding Park for the first time in the spring of 1955, Johnny soundly beat Ronnie. "That didn't go over too good," Miller says. It was no fun having a brother four years younger that much better at something. Ronnie stuck to his passion. "He was a fishing nut, and I was, too," says Miller, who started fishing with his father and brother even before he began playing golf. "Give me the choice if my dad wasn't around, I'd probably go fishing." Rods in hand and lines in the water—that's how he and his older brother connected. Ronnie even made their own lures and weights. They fished a lot at Lake Merced. They went to the beaches to fish for striped bass when they were running. Surfperch under the Golden Gate Bridge were another favorite target.

On October 11, 1958, fifteen-year-old Ronnie and two of his best friends took their gear down to a favorite spot on the Pacific near the famous Cliff House restaurant. It was a dangerous area. No swimming signs warned of the severe undertow ever present in the water. Standing on the rocks, Ronnie never saw the rogue wave that arose suddenly out of the ocean and pulled him under. The Coast Guard and police spent days searching for him. Even when they gave up, his father never did. Every day, Larry Miller walked the shore from sun up to sun down. Finally, after seventeen days, he found his oldest son's badly decomposed body.

For eleven-year-old Johnny, it took months for the loss to soak in. "As a kid, I just couldn't believe he really died," Miller says. "Every night I went to bed thinking, okay, he's going to come home." The one comfort for the family was their faith. Three years earlier, the Millers had been sealed together in the Los Angeles Temple of the Church of Jesus Christ of Latter-Day Saints. It was an ordinance they believe unites children and their parents for eternity. Eventually, the family knew they would reunite with Ronnie in Heaven. Still, it hurt, and Miller never stopped thinking about him. The tragedy made everyone prioritize the most important things in their lives— an understanding that would take an even greater hold of Johnny years down the road.

JOHNNY CONTINUED with his golf, pouring himself into the game increasingly more. Harding Park was his first playground.

Considered one of the nation's premiere public facilities, Miller would get dropped off there at 7:00 a.m. in summer, play the back nine, and then practice his short game for four to five hours. In between, he hustled grown-ups in putting games for a nickel until he had pocketed thirty-five cents, which was all he needed for lunch. Adults fared no better against Miller on the course. During one match in the San Francisco City Amateur at Harding, twelve-year-old Miller faced off against a strapping six-foot-five man accompanied by several of his friends who were confident of an easy win for their buddy. As the match progressed, the friends vanished. After nine holes, Miller was 5 up. On the way to the 10th tee, his opponent veered toward the parking lot and said, "Be right back." Miller watched as the man opened the trunk of his car, put his golf clubs in, and drove off. "What's he doing?" Miller asked his dad, who answered, "I believe he's had enough."

From San Francisco Golf Club members to friends from his church, people could clearly see Miller's talent and determination, and many extended helping hands to him and his middle-class family. Leon Gregoire was one of those people. A member at famed Olympic Club, Gregoire became acquainted with Miller through his son Steve, who played with him in junior tournaments. Along with Jack Flanagan, whose son John was also a junior golfer, the Gregoires invited Miller to play as their guest on occasion, and Miller later began caddying at the club. In 1961, Gregoire helped Miller become the first merit member of Olympic Club—a junior membership for someone whose parents weren't club members. A private club was like another world to Miller, but he earned his stripes quickly, both off and on the golf course.

"Those were crazy kids," says Miller. "There were about twelve to fifteen junior golfers at Olympic Club, and to survive, I had to blossom verbally to handle myself. That group, man, you said what you thought. You had to stand up for yourself." The bunch not only forced Miller to sharpen his linguistic jabs, but they stoked Miller's competitiveness. They constantly played games, whether it was a putting contest or a race from the tennis courts to the junior locker room. The boys also tested Miller's discipline and faith. To no avail, his club friends introduced him to alcohol (he was always the designated driver) and smoking (which Miller tried for all of two days). But above all, Miller took full advantage of the first-class practice facilities and honed his game on the sloping, tree-lined fairways and small greens that had tested the game's best during the 1955 U.S. Open. It all helped Miller become invincible among his Olympic peers.

"They were good players—San Francisco City Junior champions, Northern California Junior champions. They never beat me one day in ten years," Miller says of his junior cohorts. "I was competitive in a funny way. I would not allow anybody to beat me."

The Olympic Club crew was just another part of Johnny's circle of friends—from church, from school, and from the golf course. "I had different groups I was interacting with," Miller says. "It's interesting I didn't go the wrong way." In another contradiction, here he was growing up, a teenager in San Francisco in the early- and mid-1960s, just the time when it was becoming, in Miller's words, "the craziest spot in the whole world." Knocking right on his doorstep were the drugs, the hippies, the flower children, the riots, the racial tensions, the Vietnam War. For Johnny, they were thousands of miles away.

But Miller was influenced by San Francisco on the links. It was the fourth corner of his golfing foundation: great father, great coach, playing at great courses, and the influence of other great players. The region's golfing talent in the 1950s and 1960s was astounding. At Harding Park, he sometimes watched Ken Venturi, whose father was the professional there, strike brand-new balls down the 1st fairway out of his Uniroyal shag bag. Miller knew Bob Rosburg, the 1959 PGA champion. He would go out at the Olympic Club with future Masters champion George Archer. He would compete in games of sixsomes at San Francisco Golf Club with Tony Lema, who had made it as a top echelon Tour pro, and Harvie Ward, a two-time U.S. Amateur champion. He would compete against future PGA Tour players Ron Cerrudo, Jim Wiechers, and brothers Dick and John Lotz. Bob Lunn, the 1963 U.S. Amateur Public Links champion, was even his high school teammate and would go on to win six times on the Tour himself. "I was riding this tidal wave of great players coming out of the Bay Area," Miller says. "It made me work harder and made a difference having those kinds of players to set those standards to meet."

Just to keep up with the expectations from friends, press, and fellow golfers, Miller had to paddle faster and faster, but soon, he grew into a local legend himself. He won the San Francisco Junior Championship, the Northern California Golf Association Junior, and even the Northern California Golf Association Stroke Play. He always played well and rarely hit a poor shot. At age seventeen, however, Miller remained a golfing unknown outside a ninety-mile radius of San Francisco. Of course, it's hard to get discovered outside northern California when the farthest you've been from home is Fresno.

That changed in July 1964, when Bill Powers, a Northern California Junior Golf Association official, persuaded Miller and several other locals to try qualifying for the U.S. Junior Amateur, which was being contested in Eugene, Oregon. His father sent in the entry form, and Miller made it through sectional qualifying with a 71 and medalist honors at the Olympic Club. Powers drove Miller and a handful of other kids 500 miles north to Eugene. On television, Miller had already seen Ken Venturi win the U.S. Open the previous month, and Tony Lema win the British Open two weeks earlier at St. Andrews. He couldn't let San Francisco golf down.

At Eugene Country Club, Miller set a stroke-play qualifying record of 71–68=139—a mark that stood for thirty-two years. As the number one seed in match play, he was out first every day at 7:00 a.m. with his average match lasting just a little over two hours. His only tough contest was a quarterfinal tussle with Floridian Bob Barbarossa, considered one of the nation's best juniors, but he prevailed, 1 up. In the final, he faced Enrique Sterling from Mexico. On the 17ᵗʰ hole, Miller laced a 1-iron from 210 yards to fifteen feet to seal the championship with a 2 and 1 victory. "The thing I remember most is his dad yelling at him," Miller recalls, "how he'd let the country of Mexico down and how could he lose. It was pretty mean." He had never seen anything like it. Mr. Sterling was the antithesis of Larry Miller.

The next level had been reached. Bye, bye "Little Johnny Miller." Hello "John Miller." After the U.S. Junior, people looked at Miller differently. His victory was chronicled nationally, including a mention in the "Faces in the Crowd" section of *Sports Illustrated*, whose forty-seven-word blurb called John Miller, "a San Francisco high school senior who tries to play 'as boldly as Arnold Palmer'."

Johnny Miller may have been better prepared than any player in the game's history for the road that lied ahead. He had mixed the ultimate cocktail for golfing success: father, teacher, golf courses, and influences. Even Miller knew it: "There was no doubt in my mind that when I turned professional I was going to be successful."

FOLLOWING THREE and a half years at Brigham Young University, Miller dropped out and mailed in his entry form for the PGA Tour Qualifying Tournament in April 1969. A group of members at San Francisco Golf Club put up $15,000 to sponsor Miller, who used the money for his entry fee and a one-year lease on a new Buick Riviera. He picked up the car and first drove to Provo to visit his fiancée Linda Strouse, to whom he proposed on Valentine's Day. From there, it was on to Palm Beach Gardens, Florida. About midway through the solo, five-day, 3,000-mile journey, a shot of doubt entered his mind for the first time in his life.

"I will never forget getting to Mississippi, all by myself," Miller admits, "and it finally occurred to me, 'What the heck am I going to do if I don't make this qualifying?' It never occurred to me that I might miss it." Miller would be playing on a course he'd never seen and on coarse Bermuda grass greens that gave him fits during his first Masters. He had grown up playing bentgrass and *poa annua* putting surfaces. "I didn't know what Bermuda was, that grain could make a ball go sideways," says Miller. Plus, there were 120 players competing for a scarce 17 cards. Miller played just well enough. He earned his playing privileges by one shot on his birthday.

From southeastern Florida, he drove straight to San Antonio for his first professional event, the Texas Open. Future PGA Tour commissioner Deane Beman wound up winning, but Miller made the cut and finished tied for 23rd. His initial paycheck was $810. "It never occurred to me that I could make money," he says. "Money, really, money? I guess it was for the purest reasons that I turned pro." For Johnny Miller, getting paid was just the start of it. For the next year, he was more Arthur Frommer than Arnold Palmer. Miller may have missed it when the world came to San Francisco in the 1960s, but now this twenty-two-year-old Bay Area kid, who had hardly traveled anywhere, was going to see the nation himself. Some kids backpack through Europe. Miller drove through America playing professional golf: Houston, Charlotte, Cleveland, Detroit, Minneapolis, New York City, Milwaukee, Boston, Hartford. In one year, he drove more than 63,000 miles by himself in that Buick.

Everything was absorbed, including the golf courses he was seeing for the first time. Although he failed to record a top-ten finish during his first season, he felt no pressure and imposed no timetable on himself to succeed. "I knew I could compete," Miller says, harking back on his successes as an amateur. "I had a lot of confidence on Tour. I wasn't shell-shocked to be out there." Larry Miller's shroud was still in tack.

The following season, Miller notched seven top-tens. He fired a 61 at the Phoenix Open to record his first top-ten as a professional, which got the attention of a lot of folks. It wound up as the lowest round of the year on Tour. Late that season, he hooked up with a young caddie named Andy Martinez, who previously looped for Miller's friend Grier Jones. Like Miller, Martinez had lost an older brother, who died in a surfing accident at age twenty. But it was Martinez's work ethic that attracted Miller. They connected immediately and remained a tandem on Tour for most of the decade.

By 1971, Miller was playing practice rounds with the likes of veterans such as Trevino, Snead, and Casper, who influenced Miller with their tips, wisdom, and humor. Off the course, Jerry Heard was the player with whom he bonded most closely. A top junior player from central California, Heard was a bit more mature and worldly than Miller but just as confident. Heard liked to tell people he could fall out of a car on the 1st tee before every round and still earn $100,000 a season. "He was like the Fonz," Miller says of Heard. "He made life look easy." Once Heard won the American Golf Classic in August of 1971, however, Miller's laissez-faire outlook changed completely. Heard provided Miller with his very own stimulus package. "Hey, maybe I should be winning," recalls Miller, who believed he was just as good as Heard, if not better. "He sort of broke the ice. I wasn't upset I wasn't winning at all until Jerry started winning."

Just five weeks after Heard's maiden victory, and five months after finishing runner-up in his first Masters as a pro, Miller snagged his initial PGA Tour win in, of all places, Georgia. Originally, Miller had planned a fly-fishing trip in Montana with Heard for the second week in September, but tournament director, and Nicklaus friend, John Montgomery talked him into coming to Columbus instead. Green Island Country Club was the site of the Southern Open—a course designed by George Cobb, the man who built the par-three course at Augusta National and had helped make revisions to several holes on the regulation course. To Miller's consternation, that dreaded common Bermuda grass covered the greens in western Georgia, and according to Miller, the ones at Green Island were "the grainiest greens ever." Players joked that it was the only course on

Tour where the ball whistled as it rolled on the greens. "Of all the courses you'd pick I'd win at," Miller says, "I'd figured that'd be the last place I'd win."

Miller, though, modified his pop stroke on the greens. He decided to put his hands behind the ball in what he called a reverse-back-lock grip, which got the ball rolling quicker on top of the Bermuda. It worked. Miller blitzed the layout—he was the only player with all four rounds in the 60s—and won in wire-to-wire fashion by five shots over Beman. "A young golfer who doesn't smoke, drink, or three putt," *The Atlanta Constitution's* Charlie Roberts wrote of Miller. The victory earned him $20,000—a check that he turned over at the trophy presentation to his wife Linda five days before their second wedding anniversary.

Miller won his second title the next year at Hilton Head (again in the South and on Bermuda). Soon thereafter, Ford Motor Company picked him to be one of the faces in its Five Young Thunderbirds campaign. It was Miller's first major endorsement. Jerry Heard, Lanny Wadkins, Grier Jones, and Jim Simons rounded out the fivesome that Ford tabbed as the players to challenge the game's established stars. They were each given a car a year and $10,000 for a few outings.

In a little more than three-and-a-half years on Tour, Miller had two wins and was pegged for stardom, but he'd let plenty of tournaments slip out of his grasp on Sunday afternoons. His confidence on the greens had declined. And he'd yet to win a top-tier tournament against the game's biggest names. In 1973, everything changed with three seismic events that would catapult Miller to superstardom.

The first happened on February 3 at the Hawaiian Open. Miller's putting, which had been so good as a teenager, was a source of mounting frustration as a pro. Languishing in a tie for 54th entering the third round that Saturday morning, Miller vividly recalls the idea that popped into his head on the practice putting green: "I was probably the best player on Tour tee-to-green at the time. I still wasn't putting well, so I thought maybe I'll copy Nicklaus, with that hunched over posture, 90-degree right-arm bend that he locked in and used as a piston."

He took his new stroke out on the Waialae Country Club layout and shot a 65 with it that day. A 69 followed on Sunday to vault Miller into a tie for 6th. The confidence he felt on the greens as a youngster returned. The weakest part of his game had been rectified, for now.

With his newfound putting technique, Miller recorded eight top-tens in his next thirteen starts, including two runner-up finishes. In spite of his stellar run, he entered the 1973 U.S. Open at Oakmont Country Club in June without a victory. It didn't deter a woman sitting behind the 9th green—someone Miller had never met—from telling him every day that he was going to win that week.

In the first two rounds, USGA officials paired Miller and Lou Graham with Arnold Palmer and his army on his home turf of western Pennsylvania. "It was crazy, more crazy than Tiger's galleries, and sort of rough," says Miller, who maintained his focus to shoot rounds of 71–69, two shots better than Palmer and just three off the lead. "When I look back, the real thing I'm proud of is somehow I was able to play with the great Arnold Palmer in Pittsburgh and still win. Seriously, it was totally cool."

On Saturday, however, Miller's concentration faded. He had left his trusted yardage book in the pants he'd worn the previous day. By the time his wife Linda brought it to him on the course, he was already on the way to a 76. Miller dropped into a tie for 13th, six shots behind the leaders. For the first time all week, the lady who told him after every round that he was going to win the U.S. Open was gone. So, it seemed, were Miller's chances of winning.

The next day, Linda didn't even go to the course, staying behind to pack and meet her husband immediately after the round to catch a flight. Once on the practice range, a funny thing happened. Miller says the voice revisited him. The same one that told him at age eight he would be a champion golfer. Now, that voice spoke clearly again:

"Open up your stance, way up." Miller thought this was crazy, but the voice had never let him down. He did it and began hitting balls as well as he ever had. Miller, teeing off an hour before the leaders, birdied the first four holes and went out in 32. By the time ABC Sports came on the air at 3:30 p.m., he had caught the leaders. Linda rushed to the course in time to see his finish. Staying aggressive with four more birdies on the inward nine, he shot a 63—the lowest round in the history of major championship golf. Johnny Miller was his sport's national champion.

So long Heard, Wadkins, Jones, and Simons. Johnny Miller's fame and talent had outpaced the Five Young Thunderbirds. Just three days later at the next Tour stop in Akron, Ohio, Miller fully comprehended his new standing in the world of golf. Hitting balls on the practice range, veteran Bert Yancey strode up to him and said, "You're the U.S. Open champion now, make sure you act like it," turned, and walked away. The comment floored Miller, who tried his hardest to lengthen his stride. But winning the national championship with the greatest final round ever didn't boost his confidence like many believed it had. That came later in the year.

As U.S. Open champion, Miller was selected to represent the United States in the World Cup of Golf. The other American to complete the two-man team would be the year's PGA champion— Jack Nicklaus. The two had become friends since the 1966 U.S. Open, but they had never displayed their games in front of one another for an entire week. "To play with Jack that many days.... I always thought Jack was up here (as Miller lifts his hand above his head), and I was somewhere closing in on him (his hand lowers to his neck line), maybe," Miller says.

Thanksgiving week, they traveled to Las Brisas in Marbella, Spain, where, despite five weeks off, Miller was laser-like with his irons, hitting shots so close that the soft, spiked-up greens didn't matter. In the second round, he fired a course-record 65 in which every approach shot landed inside fifteen feet. The U.S. team went on to win by six shots, and Miller captured the individual title by three over Gary Player. Nicklaus finished four back. "I thought, Nicklaus hits his driver a little longer and his 1-iron a little better," Miller says, "but starting with the 5-iron on down, I was better than him." That 3-wood Nicklaus hit seven-and-a-half years earlier at San Francisco Golf Club had been erased from Miller's mind. In its place was Las Brisas. "I thought, 'I'm ready to beat this guy. I *can* beat this guy'," states Miller. "The 1973 World Cup was really the turning point for me. That's what '74 was all about—a springboard off that World Cup."

Indeed, the boost of confidence that Miller acquired that week, added with his new Nicklausesque putting stroke and U.S. Open victory earlier in the season, changed the game of golf for the next year and a half. In the sixteen months to come, Johnny Miller would shoot eight rounds of 65 or lower, notch sixteen top-ten finishes, win eleven times, and confirm Larry Miller's premonition twenty years earlier.

AMAZINGLY AFTER the World Cup, Miller didn't pick up a club until the first week of January 1974, when he drove down from Napa to the season opener at Pebble Beach. There was no rust on his game as he won the rain-shortened Bing Crosby National Pro-Am by four strokes. The next week in Phoenix, Miller shot all four rounds in the 60s and birdied the final three holes to win by one over Lanny Wadkins. Then the week after that, two hours down the road in Tucson, Miller opened with a course-record 62 and led wire-to-wire for a three-shot victory. Three events played, three wins, and another mark in the record book: the first player in PGA Tour history to win the first three events of a season. Inexplicably, he took off the next week at San Diego.

In late March, he led wire-to-wire again at Hilton Head. In April, he stormed back from nine down after the first round to win the Tournament of Champions. Four more sub-70 rounds at

Westchester in August set a tournament record of 19 under par. A course-record 63 at famed Pinehurst No. 2 in September led to a playoff victory over Nicklaus, Bob Murphy, and Frank Beard. A resounding eight-shot win on his home course at Silverado at the end of the month rounded out the year. In the end, the tally was eight PGA Tour victories (not counting a late season win at the Dunlop Phoenix in Japan as well)—the most in one year since Arnold Palmer captured the same number in 1962.

Miller led the money list with a then-record $346,302 and was named PGA Player of the Year. There were more cover photos on *Sports Illustrated*, *Sport*, and *The Sporting News*, along with stories in general news publications such as *Time* and *People*. All celebrated one of the greatest seasons in golf.

"I was at the top of my game physically, finally really strong and in great shape," says Miller, who used working on his ranch and duck hunting as exercise routines. Now twenty-seven, Miller hit the ball as far as nearly every pro and had a clubhead speed of 117 miles per hour with what were heavier clubs at the time, a far cry from his teenage years. He says, "When I was winning, I would feel a sense of weightlessness. I remember being over the ball and feeling as light as a feather. I could do anything I wanted with the ball."

He had reached the pinnacle of his profession, but little did anyone know Johnny Miller's interest in golf was waning. "By '74, I was starting to realize, hey, I'm playing really good—one of the top players in the world—but I don't want to do this every week," Miller says. His third child, Casi, had been born in July, and his priorities resided at home where he was more interested in being a good dad and a good husband. He often cited two church sayings: "No amount of success can compensate for failure in the home" and "The most important work you'll ever do is within the walls of your own home."

"The golf tour was in total conflict with trying to do that," asserts Miller. "On the one side I loved it; on the other, I resented it keeping me from my kids." His priorities were family, church, teaching, Boy Scouts, and ranching. What's really important in life? Remember Ronnie? He decided to cut down his schedule to mimic Nicklaus's. After playing thirty events in 1972, he played just twenty-two in 1974. Only the West Coast events and the year's first three majors intrigued him. And golf didn't even come close to Miller's love of fishing. In fact, he began picking certain tournaments to play not because the course suited his game, but because they had excellent fishing on site. "It's amazing I won as much as I did," Miller says, "because I was just doing it in my spare time."

The other problem was that he was playing too well. "I was a little cocky," Miller admits, "a little too cocky." Why practice when you're hitting it so good? While at home, Miller rarely touched a club, sometimes going weeks between hitting balls. Before going to a major, he would hit a few dozen balls or play nine holes. That was it. Miller had fallen out of love with the process that had driven him to the top of his sport. "It was boring to tell you the truth," he confesses.

"I should've had somebody there to kick me in the butt," Miller says. "My dad could have done it and said, 'You know you are on track to really be a great player—a fifty-win player—but you've got to practice and work on your game'." Not a single friend or family member confronted him. He was doing too well.

It's hard to believe during the greatest year of his career, Miller was no longer doing any of the things that brought him to this point. Remember Larry Miller's axioms: "If you're willing to do things no one else is doing, you're going to be better than the rest" or "If you want to be the best, you've got to be willing to do what no one else is willing to do." "I definitely had screwed all that up," Miller says. "Instead of depositing money into the bank account, I was now just withdrawing off all those years of putting in." The principal in the Johnny Miller Golf Account was being eaten away. "I was going bankrupt," he says, "but I was going broke slowly."

Miller didn't even practice the parts of his game that needed work: chipping and putting. He was a poor chipper, using an improper technique with too much acceleration on shots around the greens. When Miller missed greens, he didn't have a short game to fall back on. That shortfall was magnified in the majors, and his putter felt the brunt of the pressure. The bigger the event, the more important it was, the more jittery Miller got on the greens. "I was still just a little too dang nervous in the majors putting," confesses Miller. "That was my Achilles' heel."

He may have been everyone's Player of the Year in 1974, but his performances in the four majors that season were in sharp contrast to his other tournaments. He finished 15th at the Masters, tied for 35th in defense of his U.S. Open title, 10th at the British Open, and tied for 39th at the PGA Championship. In sixteen rounds, he broke 70 just once. His scoring average in the majors was a pedestrian 73.3; in his other eighteen PGA Tour events that year, it was a sizzling 69.5. Gary Player won two of those majors in that season, finished top-ten in the other two, and would gladly tell anyone that he bettered the Player of the Year by thirty-nine shots in those four championships. And Jack Nicklaus chimed in: "Eight victories is certainly good for the bank balance, but what I bet is on his mind as he looks back—and forward—is his major championship record."

Miller realized the lack of a big title in 1974 left a void in his otherwise stellar season. He knew he should have won a major. In 1975, he was determined not to let it happen again.

AT THIS POINT, Johnny Miller was the ultimate golfing enigma. No one knew it, but the world's best player at the time put virtually no work into his game. Still, he was winning. And when he wasn't, he was shooting a 64 or 65. He didn't know when—sometimes, it was in a pro-am or practice round—but he posted a low score at least once a week whenever he played. "I was never sure what I was going to do," says Miller, who admits it made him a bit skittish. "But I could get hot quicker than anyone else.

"In those days, one round a week was going to be low. That's all there was to it. It might be in the pro-am; it might be in practice. There was going to be one day I was going to turn the lights on. It was going to happen."

And that's why on Saturday, April 12, he didn't think he was out of it.

In fact, Miller had already shot rounds of 63 or lower seven times on the PGA Tour—the same number as Nicklaus, Palmer, and Weiskopf in their entire careers combined. Of course, a 63 at Augusta National was a bit far-fetched. But a 63 at Oakmont had been as well. At least a 64 or 65 was necessary to get back in contention at this Masters. He was eleven back after all.

"In my mind, any day could be a good round, and one round could win an event," states Miller. "It was like having a big club in my bag that nobody else had."

The paradoxes abounded. Miller was shaky on the greens, yet he could shoot a 63 at any time. He rarely practiced, yet he had been the game's hottest player the previous year and a half. Golf was the lowest of his priorities, yet he really, really wanted to win the Masters, to validate his career, stick it to Nicklaus, Player, and the likes of Kenneth Denlinger, and leave no doubt as to who was the game's best player.

There was one certainty. On this day, Miller desperately needed that fifteenth club to show up in his bag. There was still a little principal left in his account. But time was running out.

| 9 |

SATURDAY, APRIL 12

To golf fans, Willie Peterson had the best job in the world. For one week every year, the forty-five-year-old was the caddie for Jack Nicklaus at the Masters, his portly figure and raspy voice exalting balls toward the hole. He carried a big, white bath towel draped over his arm that he'd wave in the air every time Nicklaus made a putt. He could have been a cheerleader on the sidelines in Athens, Knoxville, or Tuscaloosa. It looked like such fun.

Nicklaus's regular caddic on Tour was Angelo Argea, a curly-haired Greek from Las Vegas who first caddied for Nicklaus at the 1963 Palm Springs Classic, which they won. Argea became his regular Tour looper in 1968, but he couldn't caddie in the Masters. Neither could Miller's caddie Andy Martinez or others. Outside caddies were not allowed to work the tournament. The same held true at the time for all three major American championships. Only local caddies were allowed inside the ropes, no professional tour caddies. Because of this rule, many players became dependent on themselves.

In 1975, all of the caddies who worked at Augusta National Golf Club were black. They strode the grounds in their club-issued long-sleeved white jumpsuits, green caps, and Converse Chuck

Taylor white canvas shoes. They shagged balls on the practice range for their players, and, on the course, they picked the ball out of the hole for them. Multiple forecaddies sat by each green to assist with play. Before players arrived at the green, they would fix pitch marks in the greens. After they left, they would rake bunkers as necessary. The caddies would jump for joy and run around to celebrate good shots; they would throw their hands up and stomp around to commiserate bad ones. They added excitement, flare, and energy to the tournament. "They loved it," says Bob Kletcke. "A month before they'd get all fired up, and they'd stay fired up until a month afterward."

Even with Nicklaus's talent, the caddies initially avoided him like the plague. Pappy Stokes was the dean of Augusta National caddies, winning five Masters with four different players—the most of anyone—and got assigned to Nicklaus in 1959. "Jack was paying good money, but he'd go out there at 7:00 in the morning and come back at night," said Stokes, who gave him up. The line to pick him up wasn't long. He hit too many balls on the range. He practiced too much on the course the week before. He took too long. But Peterson, who'd caddied at Augusta National since he was a teen, didn't mind. He was given Nicklaus's bag in 1960. "I knew I had a winner," said Peterson. "I figured he'd win ten Masters before he was through."

Like Argea, Willie Peterson was more a bag toter than a caddie. "As long as he's there on time to carry the bag, that's all I'm asking," said Nicklaus. The only trepidation he had about Peterson was that one day he would be so overcome with excitement that he would hit a ball while swinging his towel. He rarely gave Nicklaus—or Mr. Jack as he called him—direction or advice. Nicklaus did his own thinking, pulled his own clubs, and figured his own calculations. He even created his own rudimentary yardage book—a club scorecard with notes on it. (A professionally measured and charted yardage book of Augusta National wasn't produced until 1983.) Beside each hole, Nicklaus had jotted down approach shot distances—measurements to the front and back of each green in yards. It was a concept noted amateur Gene Andrews utilized in the 1950s, and Nicklaus picked up the idea from Deane Beman in 1961. "Last ridge 222–250," he wrote beside the 2nd hole. "Last tree on right 190–235," he wrote beside the 13th. The only hole at Augusta without a note was the 12th—the yardage there was always 155 yards from the ball washer. Nicklaus didn't feel the need to chart the greens. He had them memorized. "This man doesn't miss a trick," said Peterson.

"I saw the world's greatest player get his own yardage, choose his own clubs, read his own putts, and never ask a caddie anything about how to play golf, how to play a shot, how to play the course," says Tom Weiskopf. He, Johnny Miller, and others followed suit.

With Elder gone and Nicklaus leading by five, a majority of the writers, commentators, and players believed this Masters was effectively over. Willie Peterson was going to cash in again and pad his annual "annuity" as he called it.

"Nobody can catch Nicklaus with a lead like that," said Bruce Devlin.

"Jack will be almost impossible to catch," said Tom Watson.

"I would like to see anybody else than Nicklaus at 10 under," said Bobby Nichols.

"If someone gets behind him, he'll just make more birdies," said Bud Allin.

Nicklaus wasn't having any of it. If leading by a large margin, he never got too high. If trailing by a large margin, he never got too low. Always, he kept an even-keel. "I've been coming to Augusta for many years," he said. "I've blown five-stroke leads before, and I've come from five behind before. I've seen many strange things happen."

ONE ABNORMAL occurrence had already happened on this Saturday that didn't please Nicklaus. He had been placed with Arnold Palmer in the final tee time.

The pairing was a renewal of golf's most famous rivalry and heightened the anticipation for the third round, so much so that it felt like a Sunday. For the previous twenty years, they had been the faces of golf—the two most popular players and the two most successful players. They were one-two in career earnings. They were one-two in endorsements. And they were one-one in Masters victories—the only two four-time champions.

"I don't know why they paired us together. Usually, they pair one with three, but they do things differently," said Nicklaus. By the order of finish on Friday and scoring, Nicklaus would usually have been paired with Tom Watson, with Palmer in the next-to-last group alongside Billy Casper. "They thought that would be exciting for television people," says Nicklaus. "They looked at it and said, 'Let's put Arnold and Jack together'."

The two first met on September 25, 1958. It was "Dow Finsterwald Day" in Athens, Ohio, and eighteen-year-old Nicklaus had been asked to come down to fill out the foursome in an exhibition match to celebrate Finsterwald's recent PGA Championship triumph. Finsterwald's good buddy Palmer, already twenty-nine years old, shot a course-record 62 that day. But when Nicklaus outdrove Palmer in a driving contest, the rivalry started. It wouldn't be one between peers so to speak, but one of the established King trying to hold off the upstart kid. Their first duel famously occurred at the 1962 U.S. Open at Oakmont just a short drive from Palmer's hometown of Latrobe, Pennsylvania. Nicklaus had put on a little weight in college, and shouts of "Fat Jack," "Ohio Fats," "O'Blobo," and "Whale Man" were omnipresent. So angered was Nicklaus's father that, of all people, Woody Hayes had to calm the moment and hold him back from confronting those fans. The crowds never bothered Nicklaus outwardly, but gave him even more resolve to beat Palmer.

It could be just as worse at Augusta. "In the old days, when the fans were so much for Arnold and against Jack, Jack and I just sort of let it go in one ear and out the other," said Barbara Nicklaus. "Depending on your viewpoint, Jack came along at either the right time or the wrong time. Arnold was a hero when golf needed one so badly. How could we blame Arnold's fans for feeling the way they did about him?"

"That was Arnold's territory," says Kaye Kessler. Augusta, Georgia, was where posting bogeys by Nicklaus on the scoreboards once sent the galleries into gleeful approval. "Anything Jack did bad they would cheer," he says.

Nicklaus was rarely affected by goings on outside or inside the ropes. Although he admitted, "No, I don't have any problems playing with Arnold," there was still something about his rivalry with the man ten-and-a-half years his senior. They continued to duel in the 1960s when Palmer was in the prime of his career and the young-gun Nicklaus was just starting his. Now, their positions had changed. It was Nicklaus, thirty-five, at his peak, and Palmer, forty-five, past his.

They each had their legion of fans now. Nicklaus had Jack's Pack. Palmer had Arnie's Army, which on this day included actor Jackie Gleason, who was attending his first Masters. In fact, it was at Gleason's tournament in Fort Lauderdale six weeks earlier where they had last played together, as part of a threesome with Bob Murphy in the final grouping on Sunday. Murphy saw firsthand the self-destructive dynamic a Nicklaus-Palmer pairing could bring out.

"As we played, it became apparent to me that Arnold and Jack weren't talking to each other that much," says Murphy. "I thought they would sort of stick together, but they didn't. One or the other would come over to me. So I ended up having little conversations. It turned out to be even more relaxing for me."

He continues, "One of the most incredible incidents happened in that tournament that I've ever experienced in all of golf." The 7th hole at Inverrary Golf & Country Club's East Course was a dogleg right par four around a lake. Nicklaus hit his drive to the left. Arnold was in the middle. Murphy was closer to the water, but with a shorter shot well in front of the other two on the angle.

With a strong breeze in their faces, Nicklaus went first. "I hear Jack hit this shot, and he hit it absolutely fat," says Murphy, who watched the ball fall well short of the green. "Arnold, with his lack of hearing, could not hear the fact that Jack hit it fat."

Nicklaus handed the club to his caddie Argea, and said with a load of sarcasm, "I hit that 4 pretty good." Palmer, farther up the fairway, then took a 5-iron, and after a solid strike, watched it sail clear over the gallery behind the green.

"We're walking across the bridge," says Murphy, "and I hear Creamy (Palmer's regular Tour caddie Ernest Carolan) say to Arnold, 'Why did you hit 5-iron? I was trying to tell you that was too much club.' And Arnold said, 'Jack said he hit his 4 pretty good, and it was short of the green'."

Palmer and Nicklaus each made bogey while Murphy made birdie. While watching the pair play each other, Murphy went on to win. Palmer shot 74, Nicklaus 73, and Murphy 68. "There was some gamesmanship with them all the time," Murphy says.

"Maybe he was a little distracted by beating Arnold," adds Murphy. "They did find themselves occasionally, when they were paired together, concentrating on only beating each other and forgetting about what the event was doing—and maybe playing some shots that weren't called for at the time."

Now they were preparing to rekindle their battle. On the putting green just before their 2:10 p.m. starting time, Nicklaus glanced over to see what scores were being shot. He noticed Johnny Miller's name, which wasn't on the board at the start of the day, had been added. Up-to-date scoring was another Masters innovation. Underground cable was first installed on the course in 1941, and by 1955 a phone network was stationed at each green, where each player's score for that hole was called in. Now, there was 327,904 feet of telephone wire throughout the property—nearly sixty-two miles—and recent changes in the tournament scoring office, located on the second floor of the tournament headquarters, meant scores were being relayed quicker and more accurately than ever to the twenty-five scoreboards operated throughout the grounds.

It was the main leaderboard on the 18th hole at which Nicklaus was peering. Nicklaus is partially red-green color blind, though, and couldn't tell whether the "4" beside Miller's name was red (for under par) or green (for over par). He figured they wouldn't have put it up if he was going backward.

Palmer, dressed in a red v-neck sweater and white visor, noticed Nicklaus checking out the board and motioned toward it: "He must be four under for the day."

Nicklaus corrected him, "No, Arnie, you're wrong. He's four under for the tournament."

"Pretty good nine for Johnny," added Nicklaus.

"It wasn't bad, was it?" said Palmer.

Nicklaus responded, "No. Nobody's ever done it before."

A POSTULATE OFTEN referenced in tournament golf states that the third round is moving day. It's the day to get into position to win in the final round. Moving day is a bit of a myth, though. Prior to 1975, each year's Masters champion had actually shot his lowest score most often on Thursday, followed by Friday—a trend similar to that in the U.S. Open. But this Saturday at Augusta would do nothing to dispel the "moving day" myth.

Johnny Miller had woken up Saturday morning fighting a headache. He and his wife Linda had been staying in a rental house set up by their friends Dudley and Marie Posey, who owned Posey Funeral Home across the river in North Augusta, South Carolina. They met the Poseys through Billy and Shirley Casper and became like family to the Millers. Together, they would go out to dinner several times during the week, a favorite stop being T's Drive-In and Restaurant just south of town for catfish and hushpuppies. "It was a real social week for me," says Miller, who normally didn't venture out much while on the road.

Miller's tee-to-green game had been stellar the first two days, as it had been ever since the beginning of 1973. That's when he assembled a bag of golf clubs that changed his career. "I had a real personal interest in this set," says Miller, "I put this set together with my hands."

First came a collection of Tommy Armour 915-T stainless steel irons made around the time of the Second World War. His father, who was a club collector himself, picked up the heads at a second-hand store. They were stainless steel because at the time chrome was needed for the war effort. Miller, who could never get that shank he hit at Pebble Beach out of his mind, liked them because the heads were a little larger than the Tourney Customs MacGregor manufactured in the early-1970s. "I was so freaked out about these little, tiny headed irons being made then that I thought it'd be really helpful if I had a little bigger head," says Miller, who also lamented the fact the sweet spot on the Tourney Customs was right next to the hosel.

Miller took the vintage heads to the Orlimar club factory in Oakland and had Lou Ortiz cut down the long hosels on them. Miller then reground the top-line and bottom sole, re-shafted them, and added lead tape on the back to make up for the weight lost by taking down the hosels.

"I thought those irons were sort of magical," says Miller. "They just were the best feeling irons I'd ever used."

Miller cared for his woods just as much. He refinished them himself, shellacking the wood with two parts linseed oil, one part orange shellac, re-wrapping the hosels, and re-gripping the shafts. And they were just as old as his irons. His 4-wood was an ivory-inserted Tommy Armour pre–World War II model. His 3-wood was a 1948 Tommy Armour shallow faced. And his driver was a 1955 Tommy Armour Velocitized with 10.5 degrees of loft.

"The minute I started using that driver, I started hitting it longer than I had ever hit it in my life and straighter," says Miller. "I wasn't as long as Weiskopf, but I was probably closing in on being as long as Nicklaus then."

"I thought I had put together this magical set," says Miller. "When I started using them, everything just clicked."

Although one wouldn't have thought so from that week, that included his putter. It was a Bullseye, one of the original ones manufactured in 1952 by John Reuter. With little money, Reuter went around to factories in San Francisco with a bucket to sweep brass tailings off the floors. That's why Miller's putter had a kaleidoscope of different gold colors in it. When Miller obtained this putter head, he attached a thirty-six-inch shaft to it.

"This set was probably the oldest anybody had ever used in history to win tournaments," says Miller.

Saturday morning, he bypassed the range once again and proceeded to the practice putting green with an extra putter in tow. "I had a Tommy Armour putter that I was always threatening my Bullseye with when it wasn't working," says Miller. The recent struggles on the greens represented his longest putting slump in more than two years. He thought the club cost him a shot to win at both Doral and Greensboro. Putter in his hands, Miller bent over—nose perpendicular to the ball, shoulders parallel to the ground, arms tucked in so close that his hands were virtually touching his thighs—and stroked a few putts. He decided he would give the old Bullseye one more go.

Subconsciously, some extra motivation would be provided by his playing competitor this Saturday. Miller was paired with the thorn in his side from 1974, Gary Player, for a tee time an hour and forty-five minutes before the last twosome. One year earlier, Player had shot a 66 in the third round with a record tying five birdies in a row from holes 12 to 16 to put himself in position to win. Player told everyone that his two majors in 1974 made for a better year than

Miller's eight wins. Miller understood the comment, but it still irked him somewhat. Miller always recalled playing with him several years earlier at Doral. Coming down the stretch, Player told him, "I cannot remember hitting it better than this." By his estimation, Miller had hit it inside him fifteen times and shot a 65 to Player's 70. "I figured I must be a pretty good player," he said.

"I'm here at Augusta, and I'm a little teed-off that I've gotten off to this crappy start," says Miller. "I know I'm due for a good round."

It was not long before Miller discovered that "15th club" was with him on this day. The momentum he was looking for came early and quickly. After playing the 1st hole well, just missing an eighteen-foot birdie putt, Miller put on a birdie display never before seen at Augusta National:

Hole number 2: driver, 5-wood (into front bunker), sand wedge to a foot.

Hole number 3: 3-wood, pitching wedge to fourteen feet.

Hole number 4: 2-iron to ten feet.

Hole number 5: driver, 4-iron to fourteen feet.

Hole number 6: 5-iron to one foot (with applause even from Player).

Hole number 7: 3-wood, pitching wedge to thirty-five feet just off the left edge of green.

Six consecutive birdies was a new Masters record, besting the previous mark of five by Player and Hale Irwin in 1974. "Shoot, I might shoot nothing today," Miller thought at that point. When he put his second shot right in front of the green on the par-five 8th, a seventh in a row looked nearly certain until he saw that the ball had rested in a divot. His pitch shot with a pitching wedge came out thin and carried thirty feet past the hole. He was unable to convert the putt.

When he handed in his scorecard to the rules official behind the green after parring the 9th, the numbers read: 443 232 354. He was out in 30—another Masters record. Officially, he took only ten putts in nine holes, but most importantly, he was back in the tournament at four under par with a course-record 64 in sight.

It caught everyone's attention. "I could hear the hollering in back," says Heard, who was playing in the group directly in front of Miller and Player. Amateurs Gary Koch and Craig Stadler, who had stayed on Saturday to hang out and watch golf on the second nine, scurried back up to the 9th after seeing Miller's score and followed him for a few holes. "I thought, 'Oh my gosh, he's come out of the pack'," says Vin Scully, who was still waiting to go on the air at 4:30.

Mark Eubanks had been waiting four years to witness one of these runs. He had been on Miller's bag at the Masters since 1972 for just this reason. Miller used Eubanks to read some of the greens. But like Nicklaus, Miller calculated his own yardages, picked his own clubs, and made his own decisions—quickly. On this day, Eubanks's excitable nature would even cause Miller to pull clubs out of the bag himself. "He would get so nervous, his hands were like Niagara Falls," says Miller. "Water would just pour out of his hands. My clubs would be so watery by the time he gave them to me." Miller found himself calming his caddie instead of the other way around.

Miller already had enough water to deal with as he made the turn. There isn't a visible water hazard on the first nine holes at Augusta, but there are five on the back: holes 11, 12, 13, 15, and 16. "I don't think I ever got comfortable with water hazards," says Miller, who saw very few growing up playing on Northern California courses. "I learned how to treat them and had enough shots. I always respected water maybe too much."

Whether it was the water on the bag or on the course, Miller's putter cooled on the second nine. He made birdie at the 13th, fortunate that his 5-wood second shot stuck in the creek bank. He pitched up to six feet and made it to go seven under on the round at that point. But he would get no lower. He failed to convert birdie putts of ten feet at the 10th, fifteen feet at the 12th, and six feet at the 17th. On the 18th, forty-five feet above the hole, he eased a putt down the slope that slid inches by the hole. Miller came home in 35 and shot a bogey-free 65—one off the course record. It was eight shots lower than Gary Player's 73.

"If it wasn't the Masters and I wasn't so nervous…Normally when I'd shoot 30 on the front nine, we weren't talking about 65. But that was the sign of a major. If that had been anywhere else that would have been a 62 or 63, even if it was the same course," believes Miller.

When asked afterward if his round was his best ever, he responded: "No way it was as good as Oakmont. The round at Tucson was the best in my life. Eleven under par on that course is super. I should have had a blood test after that round."

With just twenty-eight putts, Miller's Bullseye putter was back in good graces. "Maybe my old one just needed to be threatened a little," he said. Miraculously, he was back in contention, excited and relieved at the same time. "I just wanted to come in the top-twenty-five. I thought if I shoot 63, he still might run off and leave me. I wanted to play a good tournament so you guys wouldn't say I was a dog this week. I also wanted to let those guys (the other players) know I'm here," he said.

When Miller finished more than two hours in front of the last group, he had already jumped into 3rd place by himself.

"All the players know I'm an explosive player. I don't know if that bothers them, but they know it. Deep down inside them, they know that I might go berserk again," said Miller. "But Nicklaus isn't worrying about me. He's worrying about Jack Nicklaus."

OR ARNOLD PALMER. All along, Nicklaus knew the second half of a golf tournament could be the longer half. He said as much in the media center the previous evening: "This is a hard course to hold the lead on. It's not so bad on the front nine, but on the back there is so much water. The par five holes have the potential to be '3' or '7' holes." It had happened before. In 1972, he built a five-shot lead during the third round only to have it completely erased.

"Being ahead won't affect my play," he admitted, "except maybe at the danger points."

Having seen Miller's low number brought some concern, and not just because it was a hot Johnny Miller who had found his mojo. He also saw the course conditions changing as mid-afternoon approached. Augusta was getting its teeth back. "Back in those days," says Weiskopf, "the weekend is when it brought out the best of Augusta. They didn't quite get it there early in the week." After the overcast skies and occasional rain shower the first two days of tournament play, the course was beginning to dry out. "The greens are getting so slick your ball marker will slide off of them," joked Hubert Green following his round. Some greens with full exposure to the sun, such as the 9th, would speed up quicker than the 13th, which stays in the shade much longer. The sky would remain sunny all day with highs reaching the upper 60s. The ten to fifteen mph winds from the east and northeast would turn to the west by the end of the afternoon, making the swirling gusts through the pine trees at ground level even more confusing to judge. Birdies could be made, but Nicklaus knew he would have to proceed cautiously.

Nicklaus had enough to think about. Now the distraction of playing with Palmer factored in as well. Hoots and hollers of "Go Arnie!" and "Get 'em, Arnie baby" rang out when they arrived on the first tee. Then, ever the club aficionado, Arnold had to have a look at Jack's new driver before they began.

"It seemed like everybody was with that group," says Koch, still a Palmer guy, who walked a few holes with the twosome after watching Miller. With the large gallery, he eventually gave up and drove back to Florida Sunday morning.

The afternoon got off to a bad start right away for Nicklaus. His approach shot found a greenside bunker on the 1st, and he missed a six footer for par. When Nicklaus made the bogey, someone in the gallery yelled, "That's one, Arnie, now get the rest."

At the 2nd, he picked the shot back up. Leaving his second in the greenside bunker, he used his new sand wedge to blast to four feet for birdie. But Nicklaus couldn't get anything going. He lipped out a birdie putt at the 8th. On the next hole, with the wind having turned from the north and whipping the red flag marked with a large white "9", he ran his birdie putt twelve feet by. Before it had a chance to roll off the front of the green, he hustled to mark it, using one of the three pennies he always carried in his pocket when playing. He failed to make the par putt. The greens were getting faster, and the wind was picking up as well. On the 11th, it was against him on the tee and with him on the approach shot, causing him to leave it on the right front edge of the green. The fifty-foot putt came up three feet short, and he couldn't hole the tricky curler he left himself. It was a three-putt green and another dropped shot.

After no bogeys in his first thirty-five holes, Nicklaus now had made four in his last twelve. His five-shot lead at the day's start was no more. "On this course, you have to get it over the hump to get the scoring going," he said. "If you get it going you can keep it going. If you can't, it gets harder and harder to get it going."

With the flagstick cut on the left side of the 12th green, which meant the hole played its shortest distance, Nicklaus hit a towering iron shot ten feet left of it just as the wind died down. He holed the birdie putt to retake the outright lead briefly at eight under—his left hand flicked his putter toward the hole as the ball went in. On the 13th, he hit the green in two shots but left a sixty-foot eagle putt from the back of the green some ten feet short on the shaded, and therefore slowish, putting surface. He missed the birdie effort—his third of three, three-putt greens on the day.

Nicklaus's success on the par fives had been startling. To this exact point in his career, he had played the par fives at Augusta National in a combined 99 under par, while being 11 over on the par threes and 48 over on the par fours. He was six under on them this week. But Nicklaus knew the dangers of their give-and-take nature. "All the par fives are designed as four and a halves," said Nicklaus "If you miss-hit the ball, you'll find out what they are. They become sixes right quick."

After over-shooting the green at the 14th and making par, Nicklaus strode to the tee of the par-five 15th. Curtis Strange thinks what many do about Nicklaus on this hole: "Ever remember him not hitting the fairway at 15 or not hitting the ball on the green in two there." In reality, the hole was not kind to him as an amateur. He played it eight times before making his first birdie. In the last three Masters, it had cost him one title and nearly another. On Friday in 1972, one day after making eagle, Nicklaus hit a fairway wood long and into the pond behind the green, resulting in a double bogey. On Saturday in 1973, with his ball lying on the upslope of a mound, he gambled and hit a 3-wood thin and into the front pond. After taking his penalty drop, he lost his patience and compounded the error by hitting his wedge fat and into the water as well. The triple-bogey eight matched his highest score in the Masters and, in the end, was the difference between winning back-to-back titles and finishing tied for 3rd two shots behind champion Tommy Aaron.

With the wind now coming from the west and against him, Nicklaus gave his tee shot an extra lash, but the ball tailed off to the right and missed the fairway. He then hit his lay-up shot too hard, running it through the other side of the fairway. From there, he struck a wedge to seven feet but couldn't make the putt. Walking off with tightened lips and a shake of the head, he glanced at the leaderboard and knew he had given up a lot on the holes that had given him so much in the past. He had birdied only one of the four par fives on this day.

Arnold Palmer fared no better. He hit only six of eighteen greens in regulation. He salvaged what he could of the round by one-putting nine greens. "If I had not scrambled extremely well," he said, "I would have shot an 80. Every ball I hit went left." Palmer's only birdie all day came on a scrambling effort on the par-five 2nd that epitomized his round: drive left into the trees, punch-out with a 3-wood, 7-iron from 150 yards to four feet, and conversion of the birdie putt.

The headliners had played more like the undercard. Dan Foster of the *Greenville (S.C.) News* wrote, "It had the nightmarish effect on their galleries of two guys staging a fistfight while their boat was sinking."

Walking up the 18th fairway, they turned to each other and said, "We did it to ourselves again, huh?" A raucous ovation didn't mask that once more they hadn't played well when paired together. Palmer shot a 75. Nicklaus stumbled around the course with a 73. They combined for a grand total of three birdies.

Nicklaus, who usually excelled at blocking out emotions and distractions, thought he had an answer to their struggles: "Arnie's gallery is hoping for him to beat me, and mine is pulling for me to beat him. This makes us want to beat each other, and we forget about the field. It's detrimental to both of our games. We would probably play all right if everybody else stayed at home."

"We were kicking ourselves, but we laughed it off, too," recalls Nicklaus. "I laughed it off a lot more than he did because he was gone."

Palmer was disheartened to fall further behind and to have his chance for an elusive fifth green jacket become more remote. The day marked the end of an era for the two foes. It would be the last time that they would be paired together in the final group on the weekend of a major championship. Palmer would turn fifty years old in just a little over four-and-a-half years. The oldest person to win a major had been Julius Boros, age forty-eight, at the 1968 PGA Championship.

Meanwhile, his archrival was still in position to win that fifth Masters. After starting the day with a five-shot lead, he now trailed by one. So much for a runaway Nicklaus victory. Playing the best golf of his life, he had frittered away some of his edge and wasn't happy.

"I felt like I had a good chance to extend the lead," he said. "The third round is important. I had a chance to make a runaway, but you often probably can make up more in the fourth round. Why?" Nicklaus asked as he turned the question to himself. "It's because some just can't quite finish the tournament."

NICKLAUS'S STRUGGLES had left the door open for others, but few took advantage. Miller's 65 was an anomaly. The course average was the highest of the week at just over 73.8. Only nine of forty-six players broke par with just three rounds in the 60s, the first of the day being Ralph Johnston's 69. Frustrations were particularly high in the two pairings next to last.

Billy Casper bogeyed the first two holes and struggled to get anything going. He holed a few long putts just to stay in contention with a 73. There was no extra practice for Casper as he left with his family after the round.

Tom Watson scrambled around the golf course as well until arriving at Amen Corner. He hit his approach shot into the pond at the 11th and made bogey, and then he made another bogey on the 12th after hitting his tee shot in the front bunker. The resilient Watson, however, came back with birdies on the 15th (for the third consecutive day) and the 17th. He made a solid par four at the 18th for a four-birdie, four-bogey round of 72.

The soft conditions that had helped faders and lower-ball hitters like Bob Murphy, who shot 80 on Saturday, and Lee Trevino were gone. Frustrated as he watched Nicklaus stonewalled on the leaderboard, Trevino struggled with both the quicker pace of the greens and his attitude, which he could never put on the back burner. Over their second shots on the par-five 8th, J.C. Snead goaded him into hitting since he couldn't get there. Trevino couldn't resist:

"Oh no, I'm not breaking any rules out here. I'm not going to give them anything to say about me this year. I'm even afraid to take a divot out here." After striking his 3-wood, he retorted, "See, I didn't even bend the grass." Trevino's hook wasn't cooperating either on this day. He failed to make a single birdie in his round of 74, and his playing competitor J.C. Snead didn't make one either in his round of 75.

In the fifth pairing from the end, Bobby Nichols didn't look like a contender on the opening hole. Up against a tree after a wayward drive, he hit his next shot left-handed with a putter. Able to gather himself, Nichols went out in 35 before finding pay dirt on the back.

On the 12th, Nichols used the advice that Dr. Cary Middlecoff gave him years before during a practice round. "No matter where that pin is, don't ever look at the left or the right. You look right over the top of that trap. You try to hit it there every day," says Nichols, who doesn't remember ever hitting it in the water there. So Nichols fired a towering short iron right at the middle of the green. It cleared the bunker by mere inches and plugged. After a drop right next to the bunker, he didn't have a stance to take, so he played another left-handed shot, nearly holing it for a birdie.

On the 13th, he hit a 4-wood to fifteen feet and holed the putt for an eagle—the only eagle of the day on any hole. On the 14th, after his drive hit a tree, the first-round leader rolled in another fifteen footer—this one for birdie—that moved him within a stroke of the lead at six under.

Then, the glow of his orange golf glove faded. In perfect position from the middle of the fairway, he three-putted the par-five 15th for bogey, missed an eight-foot birdie putt at the 16th, missed a par putt just inside three feet at the 17th after leaving his approach in the front bunker, and left a ten footer short on the 18th for par after hitting a really poor second in the right bunker. In less than an hour, three bogeys in the last four holes dropped Nichols from one back to six back. "I had myself in the hunt, but I kinda blew myself out of it," said Nichols. "If I were Johnny Miller and I thought I could shoot a 65, I would feel great about tomorrow."

UNLIKE OTHERS, Nichols's playing competitor Tom Weiskopf hadn't conceded anything to Nicklaus, even though he had been six back at the start of the day. Weiskopf had to think back only two weeks earlier to the South Carolina Lowcountry. There in the Heritage Classic, Nicklaus also held a six-shot lead after 36 holes over Weiskopf. But Nicklaus shot 74 in the third round while Weiskopf recorded a 68 to get right back in it. With nine holes to play, Weiskopf was even in front of a struggling Nicklaus, whose swing had gotten flat and loose by letting his hands drop too much. After losing his shots to the right, he made an adjustment. Nicklaus would win by three, but Weiskopf's confidence had returned. It flourished further with victory the following week at Greensboro.

Like Miller, Weiskopf felt he had played really well the first two days but putting woes gnawed at him. And also like Miller, Weiskopf was doing the damage tee-to-green with clubs that were meticulously put together and cared for. When Weiskopf turned professional in 1964, MacGregor sent him four sets of Tommy Armour Silver Scot irons (1-iron through pitching wedge, all with four degrees difference in loft). Every iron, though, was two degrees weak and upright to match his swing. "That helped get elevation," he says. Out of the four sets, he picked the two best irons out of each to create the two best sets. The first-choice team stayed in his bag for eleven years. "I started with them in 1965 and gave them to the R&A in the fall of 1975," he says.

"I'd change my (leather) grips sometimes after every round," states Weiskopf, who kept his backup set in a box at home, ready to be shipped at a moment's notice. "I checked the lies and lofts all the time because the steel was so soft, and they had pretty long hosels. If you played on hard turf your loft would change. I was fanatical."

Weiskopf originally had a MacGregor Tommy Armour driver as well until it broke on a practice range in 1969. When it happened, a few of Weiskopf's expletives caught the ears of Bobby Nichols, who offered him two extra H&B PowerBilt drivers he had with him. Weiskopf hit three balls with the first one and each took off like a rocket. He didn't even hit the other. Weiskopf says, "After the round, I gave it back to him and he said, 'How'd you like it?' I said, 'It's terrific.' He said, 'It's yours'."

Weiskopf, Nichols, and Nichols's old driver teed off thirty minutes before Nicklaus and Palmer, and Weiskopf felt particularly good today. He was dressed in his favorite color—yellow—with a golden mustard-colored argyle cashmere sweater and chocolate-colored slacks.

After playing the first five holes in even par, Weiskopf, in his words, "got it going" at the 190-yard, par-three 6th where he hit a 4-iron into the wind to eighteen feet and made birdie. He added a tap-in birdie at number 8 and at the 9th nearly chipped in for another as it kissed the flagstick dead-on but failed to drop. Following a 4-iron approach on the 10th, he rolled in a thirty footer for another birdie. On the 12th tee, he reached into his back left pocket and pulled out a piece of legal pad paper and his scorecard. Weiskopf checked his notes, yardages, and arrows on greens, then walked twenty steps off the green to judge the wind. He hit a lovely short iron to eight feet, but missed the birdie putt low.

Weiskopf chose his 3-wood again on the 13th tee. After he hit it, caddie LeRoy Schultz implored the ball to "stay there." Weiskopf immediately assured him, "That's tremendous LeRoy," as they watched it turn around the corner. It was the longest of the day on the hole.

If there was an advantage for Weiskopf at the Masters, unlike Miller and Nicklaus, Schultz was his regular Tour caddie. An Augusta native, Schultz had caddied for Weiskopf's friend Bert Yancey in previous Masters and quickly saw the potential in Weiskopf. In 1969, he approached Weiskopf and, with a mumbling, southern accent, said he sure would like to caddie for him at some point. Weiskopf offered him a tryout on Tour, but Schultz declined and waited for twelve months. He began caddying for Weiskopf at the 1970 Masters and held the job for twelve years.

"He knew my game really well, and he could read the greens pretty dog-gone good, I can tell you that," says Weiskopf. "He rarely made a mistake."

Otherwise, just like Peterson and Eubanks, Schultz was a hands-off caddie. "I got all my own yardages and usually chose my clubs," says Weiskopf, who asked Schultz for advice on a green read or a club selection maybe three or four times a round. "He was more of a cheerleader, too."

"I wasn't a difficult guy to caddie for. I always blamed myself" says Weiskopf. "I needed a head psychologist, not a great caddie."

Schultz moved slowly and stayed quiet most of the time, but his excitement level began to pique this afternoon. After a 3-iron to the middle of the green on 13, Weiskopf two-putted from thirty feet for birdie. When he parred the 14th, he was tied for the lead with Nicklaus at seven under.

The 15th could have been a turning point. With the hole playing into the wind, Weiskopf decided against going for it and laid up to the far left side of the fairway just in front of the water. From there he hit a delightful half-wedge shot three feet above the hole. After making birdie on the first three par fives, Weiskopf hit the putt firmly but it failed to touch the hole and missed on the low side. He made the comebacker from a similar length on the other side (just after Bobby Nichols had missed the same putt). He rued the missed opportunity as he walked to the next tee.

"It doesn't matter where you are, what course, what tournament, the holes are not the same for all of the cast of characters involved. There are always holes that you feel so comfortable with, regardless of where the pin is, regardless of how the wind's blowing. And then there's always holes that, geez, you just have a hard time playing them. Sometimes they can be what others think are the easy holes," says Weiskopf.

For him, more than any hole at Augusta National, that was the 16th. The par three had originally been built as a 145-yard hole with the green set against a hill on the left and a stream that wrapped around it from right of the green to the front. Bobby Jones felt the hole lacked drama, so in 1947, he had architect Robert Trent Jones (no relation) design a new hole. He created a two-tiered, kidney-shaped green to the right of the creek, which was dammed and turned into a pond. Three bunkers surrounded the putting surface that sloped severely from back right down to the water. "It was the damndest green I'd ever seen in my life," says Curtis Strange.

"I never felt comfortable on the 16th tee for some reason," Weiskopf admits. "I didn't like the pin front right and didn't like it top right. I was a versatile player. It's not that I couldn't cut the ball to those pins. It's not that I couldn't draw a shot to a certain pin, hit it low and skip it up, or hit it high and hold it."

On this day, the hole location was back left, in the same spot when Weiskopf hit it in the water in 1974's final round. Weiskopf's tee shot was never in danger this time. "Be the right distance honey," commanded Schultz as the ball flew right over the flagstick, landing fifteen feet behind the hole. Weiskopf trickled the putt down the hill, and when it fell in the hole he clinched his fist and punched a soft upper cut into the air. Schultz retrieved the ball from the hole. A little revenge on the par three pulled him back into a tie for the lead with Nicklaus.

Weiskopf couldn't convert a fifteen-foot birdie putt on the 17th before he headed to the difficult 18th. As usual, he left the driver in the bag. "18 was only difficult because I had to lay up," he says. "I didn't like where the bunkers were located. I didn't mind laying up, but I liked to drive the ball."

He pulled out a 3-wood, then put it back and took the 1-iron. Weiskopf found the middle of the fairway and then hit a towering

7-iron hole high just twelve feet away. He hit every green in regulation on the second nine. There had been only two birdies on the final hole, but he smoothly rolled his in. Weiskopf bent his knees and held his putter firmly with both hands to the sky, as if not wanting to let go of the moment. He smiled from ear to ear. He made seven birdies and one bogey for a 66, including a career-best 32 on the second nine, a stretch of holes on which he'd struggled compared to the first nine throughout his career.

"When you are in the position that I was, a great round puts you back in it," he said. "It's the saving round. It's the single most important round of the tournament. Five or six shots is nothing with the caliber of players we have today. I didn't say, 'Gee Whiz, Jack's won the golf tournament.'

"I knew I had to play a super round of golf today if I was to get back into the golf tournament. I played more aggressively today. I had my concentration and desire going." Under toughening conditions, Weiskopf's six-under 66 was the only score in the last eleven pairings under par. "Tom played a helluva round," said Nicklaus.

Weiskopf's 66 wasn't the lowest round of the day—that was Miller's 65. In one day, Weiskopf had picked up seven shots on Nicklaus; Miller eight. Miller vaulted up the leaderboard from a tie for 27th to 3rd; Weiskopf from a tie for 5th to outright possession of the lead.

"At the start of the week, it was between Nicklaus and Weiskopf," said Miller. "I was just a remote third. I think I'll play well tomorrow. He (Nicklaus) had better not make a mistake. I'm certainly not going to choke. I could blow him right out of the box."

Asked about Miller's round, Nicklaus said, "No, there's one other guy (Weiskopf) who's four shots ahead of that boy."

Weiskopf was a leader in the Masters for the first time after any round. It was his second 54-hole lead in a major—he won the 1973 British Open wire-to-wire—but he was just eight of twenty in converting final round leads on Tour (and just one of the last six).

"There's two pretty good golfers behind me," said Weiskopf.

For once, the pre-tournament chatter might live up to its hype after all. All one had to do was look at the leaderboard.

LEADERBOARD AFTER 54 HOLES

1.	Tom Weiskopf	−9	69–72–66
2.	Jack Nicklaus	−8	68–67–73
3.	Johnny Miller	−5	75–71–65
4.	Tom Watson	−4	70–70–72
5.	Billy Casper	−3	70–70–73
	Bobby Nichols	−3	67–74–72

| 10 |

WEISKOPF

Of all the great rounds and low scores Tom Weiskopf shot in his career, the digits he can't shake from his memory have nothing to do with golf.

ER15767567. His rank, file, and serial number.

In October 1968, just six months after playing in his first Masters, Tom Weiskopf entered basic training at Fort Polk in Louisiana with dog tags around his neck. He had passed his physical with the U.S. Army in May. He was classified 1-A and cleared for active duty. But in early July, he was able to enlist in the Army Reserve in Columbus. He wouldn't be going to Vietnam—at least not yet—but the Reserve was a six-year commitment.

He wasn't the first golfer or athlete to be drafted into the United States military. Tour pros Bud Allin (Johnny Miller's college teammate), John Jacobs, and Walter Morgan experienced combat in Vietnam. More than 3.4 million men were deployed to southeast Asia, and 90,000 never came home. There were some serving like a young Larry Nelson, who hadn't picked up a golf club, but would later win three professional majors. Of all these young men, Tom Weiskopf was the first player leading the money list to be summoned to active duty.

He won again in July at the Buick Open and topped the money list into mid-August. After his final event on September 22, he was second, just behind Billy Casper. "As good as I was playing and with the confidence that I had, if I could have continued to play the fall swing I would have won the money title," he says. Instead, he finished third with $152,946.

Golf had already been good to Weiskopf. He had earned more than $225,000 in his career. He had traveled outside the country, even shooting a *Shell's Wonderful World of Golf* television episode in Morocco in 1967. It was in contrast to what he experienced at Fort Polk. "I met some guys who had never been farther than twenty or twenty-five miles from their house in their life," says Weiskopf. "Eighteen-, nineteen-year-old guys who broke down crying when they were given the first pair of boots they'd ever had for themselves that weren't a hand-me-down. Guys who wouldn't shower in front of other guys, they were so shy. I heard guys crying that first week at night in bed. The stuff—unbelievable." It placed golf in a different light.

Weiskopf was placed in the Army Reserve. "It was all legal," says Weiskopf, who insists he asked for no special treatment. At any time he could still be called for active duty. "I volunteered. That Reserve Unit was open. It was a very controversial thing at the time in regard to people getting in that program."

"If I wasn't in that unit, I might not be here today," he admits.

For five-and-a-half years, Weiskopf reported to the Ohio Headquarters of the Army Reserve in Columbus for four hours of desk duty every Monday night—even on holidays—as an Army clerk typist. "I did absolutely nothing," says Weiskopf. While other pros were practicing or with their families, he spent each week traveling to central Ohio either Sunday night or Monday morning, then going to his tournament Tuesday or reconnecting with his family. His two-week summer camp of active duty was held in December.

"I never missed a meeting in five-and-a-half years or my summer camp obligation," Weiskopf says with pride, knowing the reputation of other athletes and sons of prominent citizens who never fulfilled their obligations in the Reserve. "I feel like a very, very fortunate person that I had that opportunity to avoid the Vietnam situation," he says. Still, the arrangement took a toll on him.

"It affected me," says Weiskopf. "Even though I felt fortunate, it affected me." For starters, there was the interruption to his schedule, the days he could have been practicing, his toddler Heidi asking why daddy's leaving, the missed time with his family and friends, the logistical headaches of going back-and-forth, and even the inability to write-off the associated travel costs. When you added up all the days, nearly one-and-a-half years of his life was taken up by his military obligation.

Still, he interjects: "It wasn't so much that. It was, 'Why me?'"

That's a question he would ask himself often over the course of his career.

WEISKOPF'S BASIC training ended just a little over a month before the 1969 Masters. While in Louisiana, he had played one round of golf in six months, a casual outing with the Commanding General of Fort Polk. Yet soon he would have his best chance to win a Masters.

"I want to tell you when I came out of that six months of basic training, I was really fit," says Weiskopf. "I think that's what helped me." He went to Doral for his first tournament in almost a half a year, hit tons of balls, and finished tied for 19th. The next week, he shared the first-round lead in Orlando. The week before the Masters, he lost in a four-way playoff at Greensboro to Gene Littler.

In Augusta for his second Masters appearance, Weiskopf opened with rounds of 71–71–69. On Sunday, he played in the next to last group with George Archer, a six-foot, six-inch professional born in San Francisco, who grew up playing Harding Park. When you added Weiskopf's six-foot, four-inch frame, it was possibly the tallest twosome ever in contention on a Sunday at Augusta National. "Tall guys usually don't do real well at Augusta," says Johnny Miller, who was six feet, three inches himself. "It's tough for tall guys to hit a ball off hilly, downhill, sidehill lies. You've got to be real good at striking it solid." Weiskopf concurred with that assessment. Archer, who actually picked Weiskopf to win at the beginning of the week, was one who never appeared comfortable playing golf. Gangly looking, he squatted down, like the clubs didn't fit him, and swung off-balance. Most of his ball-striking deficiencies, however, were off-set by his ability to putt. "He was so good around the greens," says Weiskopf.

A key sequence that day happened on the 15th. Weiskopf hit driver, 4-iron into the green, while Archer hit driver, 3-wood in the water. After playing a bump and run shot into the bank, Archer was lying four, still outside Weiskopf's eagle attempt. Then, he knocked in his par putt, and Weiskopf missed his eagle try. The moment added to Weiskopf's bafflement on the greens.

"That's when we had continuous putting," says Weiskopf of the rule, in effect from 1966 to 1969, where you could only mark your ball on the green once. "I three-putted eight times for the week. He three-putted once and beat me by a shot. There was a stupid rule. There is one where I let the rule overtake me because I hated that. I didn't like to have to putt out. Nobody did."

After bogeying the 71st hole, Weiskopf's last chance to tie him came on a birdie putt from forty feet. When it missed on the low side, he walked off the 72nd hole with his head down. "When I lost to Archer, I should have beat him there," says Weiskopf, who could become frustrated when players of lesser ability defeated him. Weiskopf's game was tailor made for Augusta, and he was picking up its complexities. As it was for Miller in 1971, the loss didn't bother him initially. "Impetuous youth," he says. There would be plenty more Masters, plenty more chances to win.

Weiskopf's solid play at Augusta National continued, finishing tied for 23rd and tied for 6th the next two years. Then, on the final day in 1972, he played in the last group with Jack Nicklaus, who was the third-round leader. In blustery conditions, both players shot 74 on one of the most difficult Sundays for scoring in Masters history. Weiskopf finished tied for 2nd, three behind him.

In 1974, Weiskopf was in contention once again. After playing with Nicklaus on Saturday and shooting a 70 to his 72, he was poised to strike on Sunday in the second to last group with Bobby Nichols. He made a birdie at the par-five 8th to go nine under par and tie Gary Player and Dave Stockton for the lead. Weiskopf then dropped back with a bogey on the 10th and then another on the 11th after his ball had settled in an old divot in the fairway. Others were having trouble as well, so when he got up-and-down from the back fringe for birdie at the 15th, Weiskopf moved back into a tie for the lead at nine under with Player.

Then at the 16th, with the hole location back left, he aimed just right of the flagstick with a 5-iron. Weiskopf hit the ball fat, and it splashed in water just short of the green. He salvaged a great bogey, getting up-and-down from the forward tee, and had a final opportunity on the 72nd hole. His sidehill, downhill birdie attempt from twenty feet looked perfect, but it hit the right edge and spun out. He dropped his putter, slumped his shoulders, and shook his head—his reaction a carbon copy of 1969.

"I'm very disappointed," he said after taking 136 putts for the tournament (35-34-33-32). "I only made one putt over ten feet all week. Frankly, I am a very good putter, but I've never putted well here. Why, I don't know."

Weiskopf had played the second nine in a pedestrian even par. In contention on the final nine holes three times, he had let opportunities to win slip away, finishing second in 1969, 1972, and 1974.

"Everybody thought if anybody ought to win at Augusta, it ought be Weiskopf as long and high as he hit it with that," says Jerry Heard. "I'm surprised he didn't win probably four of those Masters," says

Nichols. "If you saw him play golf, you'd say, of all places, the Masters ought to be perfect for him."

Tom Weiskopf should have been Jack Nicklaus. That was the consensus among the game's pundits. It was Weiskopf who should have had multiple green jackets in his closet instead of three runner-up finishes. It was Weiskopf who had the most talent and the best swing. In many observers' view, the only person standing in the way of Tom Weiskopf was, well, Tom Weiskopf.

Shoot, Tom Weiskopf hadn't even wanted to be a golfer, even though it was in his blood.

ON NOVEMBER 9, 1942, Thomas Daniel Weiskopf was born in Massillon, Ohio, to Tom and Eva Weiskopf. A few years later they moved forty miles north to the southeast Cleveland suburbs where Weiskopf would grow up. He had a sister, JoAnne, who was five years younger, but his brother Dan didn't come along until sixteen years later. His parents were excellent golfers and loved the sport. They were public links players and not a part of the country club set.

Weiskopf's mother was a champion golfer herself. "I was very close to my mother," he says. "She was a very gracious, quiet, hard-working woman like any mother that had to raise kids." Before children, Eva Shorb had played competitively. Her first venture with fame came in the first round of the 1936 U.S. Women's Amateur at age eighteen. The Associated Press wrote, "She has the game and the courage to make a name for herself," in describing her play against the previous year's runner-up (and future Hall of Famer) Patty Berg, who won their match, 1 up. Two years later, she again faced Berg in the championship, this time in the third round, and sprinted out to a 4-up lead after nine holes. Suddenly, Berg started crying. "My mother, knowing her personality, she felt sorry for her," says Weiskopf. Berg came back to win the match, 1 up, and later the championship. "It's too bad she didn't have an opportunity because she would really have been something special out there," her son says.

Weiskopf's father was equally skilled at the game. Both he and his wife were plus-handicaps as amateurs with fundamentally sound golf swings. They were a powerhouse in Scotch mixed foursomes, once even shooting a remarkable 66 in the format. Not surprisingly, they actually first met on a golf course.

"My parents never forced it on me," he says in regard to playing golf. "It was a long time until I could beat my dad, to tell you the truth. It took me until the summer of my freshman year in college until I could beat him."

Weiskopf was blessed with a tall, athletic build and outstanding hand-eye coordination. He dabbled in a variety of sports growing up, including basketball and baseball. "I had two very close friends, Marty Malatin and Ernie Kellerman. We were all a year apart, and I was the middle guy. We played all these sports together and spent a lot of time inventing little things that occupied our time," he says. "The three of us were inseparable."

Golf was one sport they didn't play until the summer following their freshman year in high school. Their parents decided the boys should have jobs. "That's how I got into golf," he says. "The three of us took it up caddying."

To help indoctrinate his son into the world of golf, Weiskopf's father took his fourteen-year-old to the final day of the 1957 U.S. Open on Saturday, June 15. Early that morning, they climbed in the family's maroon Dodge Dart—a car that would be handed down to Tom seven years later when he turned pro—and drove two hours west to the Inverness Club in Toledo. "That was unbelievable," says Weiskopf. "That had a lot to do with wanting to play the game." But it wasn't just the golf. The trip was a significant step in their relationship. Unlike the Nicklauses, they were not best buddies. Unlike the Millers, they were not mentor and protégé.

"My dad was a tough guy," explains Weiskopf. There was discipline and strictness and routines that were to be adhered to. Dinner was eaten at 5:45 p.m. every day. There was a flat-top haircut every fourteen days. Mass was attended every Sunday. "He was hard to get to know, to tell you the truth," says Weiskopf. "A neat guy, but he just wouldn't open up." In addition to golf, his father actually loved fishing, hunting, and dogs—activities his son would later take keen interests in. Weiskopf didn't think poorly of his quiet father, but he yearned to be closer. "I was kind of frightened of him I guess," he says.

The reserved nature of his father could be traced to the job he held. "He was a train master," says Weiskopf. "He hired and fired people and crews on the railroad all his life." It was a stressful occupation experienced by the younger Weiskopf himself.

Upon answering the telephone at home, Weiskopf occasionally took a call that began with the voice on the other line asking, "Is this Tom?"

"Yes, this is him," Weiskopf would say.

"Well, I'm going to come over there and beat the hell out of you, you laid me off."

"What are you talking about?"

"Is this Tom Weiskopf?"

"Yeah," replied Weiskopf, realizing by now that the threatening call was for his father, who also went by Tom.

The elder Weiskopf was a man of conviction, but doing the right thing by the book took its toll on him. The decisions he made were black and white, but the grey areas tore at his soul. "It drove him to drink," Weiskopf says. "That affected him if he had to lay people off."

Young Tom didn't find out about the most heartbreaking story until his father was on his death bed. There had been a train wreck in which someone was killed, and Weiskopf's father was in charge of gathering evidence for the railroad. He discovered the person responsible for making the ill-judged decisions in routing the trains that led to the accident. He testified what he found out, and that man was eventually fired.

The dilemma was that man was the same person who hired Weiskopf's father out of college and became his mentor. That man was the one who saw to it he was promoted. That man took him fishing and hunting and spent time with his family. That man was six months away from full retirement and benefits.

The whole incident shook the resolve of Weiskopf's father. Instead of the occasional drink, he stayed drunk for three years. "That's the only way he could go to sleep it bothered him so much," says Weiskopf of the depression his father went through.

But on this day in Toledo, they were a father and his boy at the U.S. Open.

"My dad said, 'We're going to watch the greatest swing in golf'," Weiskopf says. They walked over to the range, and there was Sam Snead. "What a specimen he was back then," he says. They watched Snead a lot that day and others. One player they didn't see was seventeen-year-old Jack Nicklaus, who had missed the cut in his first U.S. Open the day before with two rounds of 80. "I'll never forget Cary Middlecoff on the 18th tee. He had to birdie the last hole to tie Dick Mayer," says Weiskopf, who observed him regripping more than a dozen times. "He was unbelievably slow." Middlecoff made his birdie, but lost in an eighteen-hole playoff the following day.

"The next year, I was obsessed with it," says Weiskopf. He and his friends would ride their bicycles to a nearby par-three course. While his buddies played for fun—Malatin would become a football and wrestling standout at Kent State and Kellerman would become an NFL All-Pro as a safety for the Cleveland Browns—Weiskopf played for keeps. "There wasn't enough daylight," he says. "I hit balls, and balls, and balls, and balls." His parents gave him some pointers but otherwise left him alone. Once he began playing the local public tracks, he was soon firing rounds in the 70s.

Despite not having the early start and advantages Nicklaus and Miller had been afforded, Weiskopf became a scratch handicap in short order. The Weiskopfs didn't have much spare change and weren't wealthy but made sacrifices for their son. "They gave up a lot," he says. "They put me in tournaments. They gave me good clubs to play with and were very supportive." Witnessing the fruits of their sacrifices was the difficult part. "My dad couldn't watch me," says Weiskopf. "He'd always have to be under a tree somewhere and get a report from somebody."

Weiskopf began playing in some area tournaments and won a few of them, but he didn't play in many big state tournaments or compete against upper echelon juniors around the country. Winning at a young age against many of the same peers they would see on Tour gave Nicklaus and Miller added confidence down the stretch of professional events. Weiskopf didn't achieve that.

In fact, it wasn't until he went off to college that he truly blossomed.

WEISKOPF PLAYED well enough in junior events to catch the eye of Bob Kepler, the golf coach at Ohio State University since 1938. He knew Weiskopf's mother from golfing circles growing up and offered him a grant-in-aid that was formally a baseball scholarship. Unusual for a college coach at the time, Kepler was a very good player himself, having won regionally and competed in four U.S. Opens, shooting a 69 during the 1947 championship to tie for 31st.

"He was the guy who really taught me the game and my fundamentals," says Weiskopf. Other than generic tips from his parents, Weiskopf was a self-taught golfer. His grip was, in his words, "a caddie grip"—so strong that he could see three knuckles on his left hand. Kepler saw Weiskopf's raw ability and knew changing his grip was the key to developing it. He turned his hands to the left on the club, placing them on top in a more neutral position. "I remember starting to hit balls and shanking them. Everything went straight right," says Weiskopf, who thought he already hit the ball pretty well and initially questioned his coach about the change.

"You can't cut the ball, can you?" replied Kepler. "It gives you more versatility in playing shots." Weiskopf slowly understood his coach and stuck with the new method through the fall and then into the following spring.

"It was a hard, hard first year," says Weiskopf of that freshman season. "Then, about the middle of the following summer, I gained distance. I gained height. I could cut the ball a lot easier. I didn't have to worry about hitting some real bad hooks. I went from a very inconsistent player to a guy who just mailed-in a 68 to a 70 every day at the Scarlet Course. I was always under par. The game just totally changed for me."

Weiskopf was also undergoing a physical transformation. Just five feet, ten inches tall at high school graduation, he sprouted nearly six inches during that first year in Columbus. "Guys who are tall like I am don't quite have the balance that the shorter guys have," he says, believing the ideal golfer's height to be six feet tall (ironically closer to Nicklaus's height which was five feet, ten inches). Any imbalance could adversely affect the swing's tempo among other elements (like George Archer).

Weiskopf had the physical ability to make a big shoulder turn with his backswing. "My trouble was I got a little quick, and I wouldn't complete my turn," he says. "I'd start my downswing and go over the top of the ball and hook it." Kepler worked with him on completing that full shoulder turn, keeping his lower body relatively quiet, and maintaining tempo. In time, what was once considered a disadvantage would be a distinct advantage.

Kepler's influence extended off the course, too. "Since I was never really close to my father, he was more of a father figure," says Weiskopf. "I had a great respect for him." Out of his regimented household back home, Weiskopf flourished in college, finally seeing what it was like to challenge authority, experience his first taste of alcohol, chase girls, and cause general mischief. Kepler was there to reel him back in. "He threw me off the team one time, rightfully so," he says after one such incident. "I didn't think he'd do it, but he did."

Weiskopf improved enough to win the Ohio Public Links Championship in 1961 and 1962 and to be selected second team All-America as a sophomore in 1962. But after two-and-a-half years, he left Ohio State. "School was not for me," he says, echoing Johnny Miller's sentiments. "I knew what I wanted to do." For now, golf consumed his life.

Weiskopf spent all his time playing and practicing. He won the prestigious Western Amateur in the summer of 1963 by upsetting Walker Cupper and two-time U.S. Public Links champion Dan Sikes in the semifinals and then reigning U.S. Amateur champion Labron Harris Jr. in the final. Weiskopf didn't turn professional because he had no money. Proof of $5,000 in the bank was a requirement for PGA membership at the time. He sold everything he won and saved the cash.

In June 1964, Weiskopf flew with Jim DeLeone, a friend and lawyer who would be his first business advisor, to watch the final day of the U.S. Open at Congressional Country Club outside Washington, D.C. When they walked through the gates, they stopped to watch a group tee off the 18th. First was Terry Dill, a big Texan, who drove off on the far left side of the tee—with his feet outside the markers—and played a towering hook that eventually landed in the fairway. Then Bob Rosburg, whom Weiskopf knew was the 1959 PGA champion, placed his ball down on the right side, took a baseball grip, and squeezed a big slice down the other side of the fairway. He turned to DeLeone. "Who's this guy here?" asked Weiskopf of Dill, who would finish tied for 14th. "Does he ever make any money out here on the Tour?" DeLeone told him he makes $500 or $600 a week. "That was like $50,000 a week to me," says Weiskopf. "I said, 'How do I turn pro? I can beat either one of these two guys.' We wrote a letter the next day to the USGA announcing I was turning pro."

TWENTY-ONE-YEAR-OLD Gary Koch was one of the nation's best amateurs when he arrived for his first Masters in 1974. On his first day at the club the Saturday before the tournament, he walked out the back of the clubhouse to the practice putting green, and noticed a lone figure hitting practice balls in the spacious clearing between the 18th, 8th, and 9th holes. He strolled over beside the 1st tee to get a better look. "Sure enough, I recognize it is Weiskopf's swing," he says. Koch, who'd never met him, eased his way down the hill to within twenty yards of him. "Whether he knew I was there or not, I have no idea, but he never acknowledged that I was," recalls Koch. "He's hitting what appears to me to be 3-irons to his caddie. He has this effortless swing and the ball's going way up in the air. The caddie's taking two steps to his right, catching it on the hop, and he takes a step in and catches one, couple steps to the left and catches it on the first hop.

"I'm sitting there watching this for about 15 minutes," continues Koch, "and I'm thinking to myself, 'I've never hit one 3-iron that looks like this, not one in my whole life. How could I ever beat this guy? How could anybody ever beat this guy?'"

Those were questions that people had about the man with the swing everyone envied.

Weiskopf stepped into the ball with an erect posture befitting someone who had gone through basic training. There was both an arrogance and an elegance to it. His height and full shoulder turn allowed him to produce a huge arc that, in turn, created tremendous clubhead speed. All of it was accomplished with a vertical motion on plane that sent balls straight up in the air. "That upright swing that I had and staying behind the ball helped me elevate it," explains Weiskopf.

But it was the tempo and rhythm that others swooned over. There was a grace and smoothness rare for a tall man who always finished perfectly on balance.

"Impeccable golf swing. Impeccable fundamentals. His strength. His power," says Roger Maltbie. "He could hit some of the most majestic long irons, and that's back when we were playing with things that looked like scalpels. Rarely did Tom miss-hit a shot."

As time passed, Weiskopf learned to control and harness his swing. "He could work the ball. He could play shots," says his friend Ed Sneed. "He could take something off the ball when he needed to. Obviously, Jack could do that and Johnny could do that, but I don't think they did it quite as well as Tom when he was in his heyday."

Weiskopf credits one man with influencing his swing.

"We are victims of an example," says Weiskopf. "Nicklaus was the example. Look at the way he swung the golf club. Well, that must be the right way to do it. You got to stay back behind that ball. Got to stay underneath it. When you do that it's easy to produce elevation on the shot. And a right-to-left swing."

Eventually he was able to produce with consistency a shot only a select few could even attempt: a high, soft draw. "That was what I knew I had to do if I was going to be effective in major championship golf," he says. It not only produced shots that could make him competitive in U.S. Open or PGA set ups, but it helped him shoot rounds that people still remember.

"I saw him play some of the most incredible golf," says Bob Murphy, who more than four decades later still remembers a 65 in the second round at Harbour Town the first year there in 1969 when the average score was around 75. "I could have putted one-handed, left-handed and made seven putts that he missed. That's how well he played."

Weiskopf's professional debut came in August 1964 at the Western Open, where he made the cut to earn $487.50. Soon thereafter, Tony Lema told him, "I wish I had all the money you are going to win on the Tour."

Once on the road, Weiskopf became influenced by hanging around veterans like Sam Snead and Tommy Bolt, the 1958 U.S. Open champion. Bolt was a snazzy dresser with an immaculate swing and legendary temper. They shared those three similarities. Bolt deepened Weiskopf's belief that style was nearly as important as substance.

"I'm a traditionalist. I used to get more satisfaction out of playing a great round of golf from tee to green aside from the score," Weiskopf says. "If I shot 70 or 69 and missed two fairways and maybe one green, I executed. I played the holes correctly under those conditions. That meant a lot to me. I got a little bit too caught up into being that perfectionist. It wasn't always the score."

"He very much believed in style points," says Maltbie. "You had to look good. You had to hit the proper shots. You had to execute them. Those were all very important to Tom in his own game, and as he viewed others. You better be able to do some of that stuff or he didn't hold you in very high regard."

It took three-and-a-half years before Weiskopf won, shooting a score to match his style at the 1968 San Diego Open.

"I approached the game as a living with no great expectations," he says. "Then I married, and it definitely was work. I had responsibilities. I took a lot of time for myself and did things with my friends that I liked to do.... It's a sport but it's still hard work."

Weiskopf was constantly on the go, and even with his Army Reserve duty, he still played more than most. "In retrospect, I think he played too much golf," says Murphy. "Had he played fewer times I think he would have been more ready to go when the time came, rather than finishing someplace on Sunday and making your way to the next stop."

With all of this talent, it begged the question: why wasn't Weiskopf winning more? In his first ten full seasons on Tour, he won a respectable eleven times and finished top-thirty on the money list nine consecutive years. It provided a nice living, but others saw a guy with the potential to be an immortal in the game.

WHY? WHY wasn't Tom Weiskopf more successful?

In short, the answer was Tom Weiskopf. His personality traits were in constant conflict with being the type of golfer so many thought he should.

"I used to worry about anything and everything," says Weiskopf. "I am a perfectionist. I can't stand mediocrity. Everything has to be done right." An example was his penmanship, which was exquisite. Autographing golf balls bothered him because the signature on a dimpled sphere could never be written to his satisfaction.

"I wasn't happy if I wasn't doing what I knew I could do," he confesses. "You can't do that."

When things didn't go as Weiskopf thought they should, he could get easily agitated. The results would be mood swings up and down that could change his personality in a flash.

"He was the kind of guy who could be very charming and engaging and fun," says Maltbie. "He might walk by you on the way to the practice tee and say, 'Hi Roger,' and then he might pass you a half-hour later and you didn't exist. He was a hard guy to get a read on."

Having a positive outlook could yield great results for Weiskopf, but when things weren't to his liking, the going could be rough.

"I had to be self-motivated, for whatever reason," he says. "I had to like where I was to feel like I could play good. I had to like the situation. If I didn't, I didn't care about it." If Weiskopf was playing well and in contention, there was complete resolve. If he was playing poorly, he could totally disengage.

"Nothing disturbed Nicklaus," says Kaye Kessler. "Weiskopf was so different from that." He didn't let things go. Things didn't stick in Nicklaus's craw, but they did in Weiskopf's. Temperament and concentration were Nicklaus's strengths. He could turn a 75 into a 70. Weiskopf would turn a 75 into an 80. Or higher.

"I was very spontaneous with my emotions," he says. "I showed my temper. I was never fined for throwing clubs. Never broke any clubs. Did I bury some in the ground? Of course I did."

Weiskopf was fined for other indiscretions. In the second round of the 1974 PGA, he played hockey with his ball on a green, then walked over to a rules official to withdraw due to an injury. When asked to describe his injury, he responded, "I'm 25 over par." For that, Commissioner Deane Beman fined him $1,000. After double bogeying the last two holes during the third round of the 1974 World Open, Weiskopf left the scoring tent without signing his card and was disqualified. That fine cost him $1,500. Then in January 1975, the tournament director of the Tucson Open accused Weiskopf of scraping in putts and conduct unbecoming during a score of 41 on the back nine in round two. Weiskopf countered that every putt was hit with his feet on the ground and two hands on the club. He even birdied holes 14 and 15 in an attempt to make the cut.

In any case, his reputation as a hothead and underachiever had seeped into the psyche of those in the golf universe. Terrible Tom. Tempestuous Tom. The Towering Inferno. Those nicknames bothered Weiskopf. To him, it seemed like the press would blow up any innocent occurrence to make him fit the part.

One year in Texas, Kessler remembers Weiskopf storming off the golf course after a round. Kessler followed him. There had been a photograph in the local newspaper showing Weiskopf throwing a golf club. The cutline said, "Weiskopf throws club in a fit of anger." Weiskopf claimed he had just tossed the club routinely to his caddie while walking out of a bunker. He was livid. Yet, Weiskopf couldn't get away from his public persona.

"My wife read something one time and said, 'Who's this guy I'm reading about here'," recalls Weiskopf, who met Jeanne Ruth, Miss Minnesota 1965, at the 1966 Minnesota Golf Classic. They were married just over three months later.

"Golf was never the most important thing in my life," he says. "It was at first when I learned how to hit golf balls. By 1975, I had another life, a good family, great friendships, terrific hobbies. I wasn't obsessed with being the world's greatest player, I just wasn't. Those other people wanted me to be that, I think. That's fine. I wasn't who they thought I was."

But Weiskopf still read the clippings and heard the talk. "He said one time, 'I'm getting sick and tired of reading about how much potential I have'," says Maltbie. Maybe he didn't need to be the greatest, but maybe all the expectations kept itching the perfectionist in him. "He expected so much of himself. I think for a big part of his career, Tom was a disappointment to himself," adds Maltbie.

One evening, he and Ed Sneed walked into a Jacksonville Beach, Florida, bar before dinner, when an older, white-haired gentleman approached. "Hey, isn't you Weiskopf," he asked. "Come up here, I want to buy you boys a beer. I'm Smitty." He shook their hands, turned to Weiskopf, and pronounced: "I want to ask you something, Weiskopf. I watch you on TV a lot. I want to know how come you fuck up so much." Weiskopf chuckled.

"People pretty much universally liked Tom," says Sneed. "He was a good guy. He was fun to be with. I think the pressure of the spotlight changed him. If he was in the locker room just sitting there, without the external pressure of the press, Tom was as fun to be around, to laugh, to tell a story. Tom's a pretty interesting guy, too. A lot of people don't give Tom the credit for being intellectually as strong as he is. He's a smart guy, a very smart guy."

It was even possible that Tom Weiskopf wasn't mean enough. Tommy Bolt once told him, "You've got the greatest swing in the world and all the potential. But you got to be mean. You've got to grind 'em down to win."

"Tom has a very, very soft and compassionate side to him when it comes to other people," says Sneed. "It's a side of Tom a lot of people would never see."

Weiskopf never saw a psychologist or sought help to address any characteristics that were impeding his golf game. "I should have," he says. "At that period of time in my life, you're an egomaniac playing the tour. I should have. I'd be the first to admit."

Instead, Weiskopf put it all back on himself. His guilty conscience worked in overdrive. "I didn't make any excuses," he says. "I blamed myself and took it out on myself."

Like his father found out, life is not black and white. Young Tom found out the pressures of navigating those grey areas were tricky. To combat them, he would fall into the same trap as his father.

WHY? WHY did Tom Weiskopf's father have to be an alcoholic?

Alcohol was a much bigger presence on the Tour in the 1970s. Before trainers, psychologists, nutritionists, and most importantly big money entered the game, the Tour was more like a traveling carnival. "There was a lot more unity," says John Mahaffey of that period. "You tried to beat the other guys like crazy, but you were buddies afterward."

Go in any locker room, and not only would beer be available, but a significant number of pros would be lingering and drinking it. There were players such as Johnny Miller who didn't drink or socialize, and there were those who drank socially and never let it consume them. And there were some who let alcohol ruin them.

"There are years I don't remember," says Mahaffey, a PGA and Players champion who admits drinking was detrimental to his career. "Anytime it affects your personal life, it's going to affect your golf game, too. I've been married four times, and alcohol was a factor."

Weiskopf started drinking in college, but by his late twenties his alcohol consumption increased. Beer, red wine, vodka—whatever he was in the mood for. He rarely mixed drinks at night, but once he started on something he could drink it dry.

"I wasn't a good drunk," confesses Weiskopf. "I wasn't a fighter, wasn't confrontational. But I could drink with the best of them. I didn't drink every day. I didn't drink because I was happy or sad. I had a problem."

Few people knew of Weiskopf's problem at a time when drinking too much either wasn't noticed or it was ignored.

"I didn't know it when I played with him all those years," says Murphy. "Had no idea that that struggle was going on." "It's not like he was coming in all red-eyed and you could smell it on his breath," says Heard.

Each stop on Tour featured its popular hangouts and old friends to mingle with. Ed Sneed was a frequent companion of Weiskopf and admits his game suffered as well from those evenings. "We probably drank more beer than we should have," says Sneed. "I'm not sure I realized it at the time because there were times when he might have kind of a binge."

When Weiskopf asks why he drank, he responds: "Was it because you play the game and all the things that are a part of that game that get to you? I don't know. People drink for different reasons."

"He was his own worst enemy," says Ben Wright, who had his own struggles with alcohol. "I remember one year at Hilton Head he never got upstairs to his bedroom. He would get so drunk he couldn't negotiate the stairs so he slept on the couch in the living room. He would be incoherent in no time."

"He used to say to me that if only Nicklaus hadn't been around, I'd have had a hell of a career," recalls Wright, "and I said, 'I doubt it. You're too damn stupid after dark.' He couldn't deny it."

Weiskopf admits that alcohol played a large role in why he wasn't as successful on Tour as many thought he should be. "It was a problem," says Weiskopf. "That alone would have been a whole new book about Tom Weiskopf had that not been a problem then or had it been confronted.

"Drinking affects your attitude. It affects your emotional side. It's a downer. The only reason I was probably able to mask it or get through it, or exist, or continue, or win… was the fact that I was so talented and in such great shape."

It's said the apple doesn't fall far from the tree, and unfortunately for so many, neither does the bottle. Weiskopf frequently made the connection between his drinking and his father's, but he couldn't sever it.

The frustrations with trying to make everything perfect, trying to be in control, trying to live up to his expectations and to those of others, boiled to the surface later in his career while drinking at a bar one evening. Sitting with Roger Maltbie and others, Weiskopf turned to them and stated: "I'm so sick of this. When I play golf, I'm trying to paint a beautiful portrait, and all these other guys are scribbling."

It spawned another nickname that night: Rembrandt.

ON CHRISTMAS DAY 1972, Weiskopf presented his father with a gift, a trip with him to the Crosby Pro-Am in late-January. His father had always wanted to see Pebble Beach in person. But once on the Monterey Peninsula, Weiskopf's father began feeling ill. At a local hospital, he was diagnosed with a brain tumor. After a couple of weeks, he was transported back to Ohio and admitted to the Cleveland Clinic. In between tournaments and the Army Reserve, Weiskopf carved out at least two days every week to visit his dad.

"That's probably the closest time I'd ever been to my father, those three months," he says. "We talked about all kinds of things we'd never talked about." Among the topics of conversation was his new grandson Eric, born two weeks before their trip to Pebble Beach.

His father passed away on March 14, 1973.

"That was the toughest thing I had ever gone through in my life," says Weiskopf. "I had finally understood this guy, I felt. And he understood me. We talked about a lot of my short comings. And he said, 'Tom, you've got all the talent in the world. If you just apply yourself a little more. And don't be so hard on yourself'."

In the end, Weiskopf came away with remorse and the feeling he had let his father down.

After three weeks off the Tour, he returned in April with mediocre showings at Greensboro (tied for 29th) and Augusta (tied for 34th—his worst Masters finish). After working through the mourning process, he began putting more work into his game. He finished tied for 8th at the Byron Nelson Classic in his next start. Only some substandard putting with his trusty Bullseye putter was holding him back until he ran into Johnny Miller at the Colonial National Invitation Tournament in Fort Worth, Texas, in mid-May.

"I made two Tommy Armour putters, cut the shaft way down, the hosel way down," says Miller. "I'm on the putting green trying them— one of them is laying on the ground—and he (Weiskopf) grabs this putter and says, 'I want to try this.' And he didn't say two words to me. He basically took my putter without even asking. Never said thank you after he was Player of the Year that year. And made every putt he looked at from that time on. To this day he's never said, 'John, that was nice of you to let me have that putter'." Miller never saw the putter again.

In full confession years later, Weiskopf believes that the putter came from Arnold Palmer via David Graham, who was the chief club pusher at the time. But what happened later wasn't in dispute. "He went nuts the rest of the year because of that dang putter," says Miller. "He just made everything."

Also that afternoon, Weiskopf's good friend Bert Yancey pulled him aside. Yancey was infatuated with trying to win the Masters himself, going so far as to construct scale models of the holes at his house. He had noticed that Weiskopf seemed to be out of his normal putting rhythm and wanted him to try a metronome he'd acquired. "So he set it up to that sequence. I counted 'one-two,' and as soon as my eyes came back to the ball I said, 'three,' and took the club back. It just freed me up," says Weiskopf.

New putter in hand, he went right out and won that week, his first of five wins in eight starts over the next two-and-a-half months. He didn't shoot a round over par in his next three events, finishing 2nd in Atlanta and winning in Charlotte and Philadelphia.

After coming in 3rd in the U.S. Open at Oakmont and tied for 5th at the American Golf Classic, he traveled to July's British Open at Troon in Scotland as the hottest player in the game. Every day there, he would see and hear the trains as they ran by the golf course, reminding him of his father. After opening with 68–67, Weiskopf was paired in the final two rounds with Johnny Miller, the U.S. Open champion from the month prior. All Miller saw was him making putt after putt with that Tommy Armour. By Miller's count, Weiskopf one-putted twenty-one of the last thirty-six holes. "His putting just wore me out," says Miller. Weiskopf won wire–to–wire for his first major championship title.

Two weeks later, he captured the Canadian Open and then the unofficial World Series of Golf against the year's other three major champions: Nicklaus, Miller, and Tommy Aaron. His year concluded overseas with a win in the South African PGA in December. His line on the PGA Tour: five wins, twelve top-three finishes, and third on the money list with $245,156. Moreover, in fifteen total starts around the world from mid-May until the end of the year, Weiskopf's worst finish was 6th at the PGA Championship.

"I dedicated that year in '73 to my father," says Weiskopf. "I talked to him all the time. When things got tough on the golf course, I told him I'm going to do it, watch this. I had this inner-conversation all the time. It's too bad he couldn't see me win my only major."

Even with a career year, Weiskopf still finished behind Nicklaus on the money list that season. He won seven times and earned PGA Player of the Year honors. Weiskopf was selected Player of the Year by the Golf Writers' Association of American and *Golf Magazine*. "I think Tom in '72–'73 was better than Jack tee-to-green," says Sneed.

"I think he had come into a groove in his swing. The shots that he hit were just marvelous."

With his Army Reserve duties up at the end of 1973, Weiskopf looked to be on his way to super stardom. But 1974 didn't lead down that path.

"I didn't like the exposure that went with the success that I had," he says. "I didn't like the lack of privacy." Having to put up with strangers coming up to him and telling him about seeing him play wasn't his cup of tea. "I admire Arnold Palmer and Jack Nicklaus and all the guys who could handle that. I did not like that at all," says Weiskopf.

Even his now rosy portrayal in the media rankled him. "I became Tom Terrific, and previous to that I was Terrible Tom," he says. "I was still the same guy.

"The press can label anybody and create their cast of characters and their storylines. Now everybody thinks I'm the greatest guy in the world. I haven't changed. Maybe I lived up to everybody's expectations. And finally maybe they're happier than I am. I didn't like that."

On top of the extra attention, Weiskopf started the year with an injury. Tendinitis in his left thumb hindered his play in the first three months of 1974. Other than some stomach problems that Weiskopf said were the result of "working himself up too much," this was the first golf injury he'd ever had. "It really, really hurt," says Weiskopf. "I should've taken off."

"It was very frustrating because '73 was such a great year," he says. He tried medications and anti-inflammatories, everything but a shot. His doctor told him to take a month off and he'd be fine, but Weiskopf says he couldn't put down the clubs, "Especially when you pick up the newspaper and see that guy did that, he won that. I need to get out there."

Because of the injury, he didn't practice as much and began compromising movements in his swing to ease the pain. He started playing golf with his right side only, a bad fault he had to fix once healthy. "He suffered a little bit when he had that thumb," says Sneed. "You can cut off any finger of my golf grip except for my left thumb. That's the most important digit on a (right-handed) golfer's hand. When you have pain there, it's hard to hit a shot with a lot of confidence and hit the ball hard."

With his thumb still bothering him, he held a five-shot lead going into the final round of the Western Open. Several uncharacteristically wayward shots down the stretch let Tom Watson capture his maiden PGA Tour win.

Weiskopf fell to thirteenth on the money list with three runner-up finishes in 1974. He failed to record a win. It wasn't a bad season by average Tour standards; however, by the standards the media and Weiskopf had set for himself, it was unacceptable.

AT THE START of 1975, Weiskopf stood at another crossroad in his career, made more challenging by the death of Bob Kepler early that year. The man who was like a second father to Weiskopf and his defacto swing coach had retired from Ohio State in 1965 and become head professional at Hound Ears Club in the mountains of North Carolina. "He knew my game so well. I could call him up on the telephone, and he'd always ask, 'What's the ball doing'," says Weiskopf. "I'd explain what I thought my problems were. 'Well why don't you try this, call me back tomorrow.' I'd go work on it, and 90 percent of the time he was right on the money."

Again as with the passing of his father two years earlier, it galvanized Weiskopf. "He believed in me so much," says Weiskopf. "He spent so much time with me. And he was such a positive guy."

Weiskopf did some soul searching, and by late-February he had rediscovered his game. He finished 4th in Los Angeles and tied for 7th at Inverrary, even though he bogeyed the final two holes. At Hilton Head, a 65 in the second round put him in contention, but his nemesis Nicklaus still defeated him. Then in Greensboro the very next week, he won for the first time on Tour in twenty months.

Now, Weiskopf was the 54-hole leader for the first time in the Masters. He was just eighteen holes from the greatest triumph in his life.

Saturday night, Weiskopf rested with the weight of all this on him.

Finally, maybe he could do it for his dad, do it for Kep. And if he could win, maybe he could finally see his own shadow—not just that of Nicklaus's.

| 11 |

SUNDAY, APRIL 13

Before Saturday ended in Augusta, Sunday had already begun in Welwyn Garden City, England, a small town just north of London. Five hours ahead and 4,000 miles away, anticipation ate away at a seventeen-year-old boy, just as it had the previous three second-Sundays in April. The final round of the Masters wouldn't be shown by the British Broadcasting Corporation until late that evening on a slight tape delay. He would just have to spend the day playing golf and waiting.

Nick Faldo loved sports. That suited his mother Joyce—anything as long as he wasn't sitting in front of the television. Her son had tried them all: swimming, track and field, tennis, skiing, soccer, rugby, cricket, etc. "A sportsman looking for a sport," he says. But in the first thirteen years of his life, golf hadn't been given a single thought until he watched television. Seeing the 1971 Masters on his parents' new color set changed his life. "It was the trees and these fairways … and the colorful golfers," says Faldo, who was one of many boys (and girls) in the United Kingdom whose interest in golf was ignited by watching the Masters since the first overseas broadcast of the tournament by the BBC in 1967. Faldo had already decided that he wanted an outdoor job and to be his own boss, which led to his two top career choices at the time: landscape gardening and the forestry commission. This beautiful place in Georgia was somewhere he'd love to work. "It was almost the surroundings of golf rather than the actual golf," he admits of his attraction. One didn't have to be a golfer or a fan of golf to be charmed by Augusta National. He wanted to try the game.

The very next day, his ever-supportive parents, who knew nothing about golf either, signed up their only child for a half-dozen lessons and later bought him a half-set of clubs. From there, his obsession with the game grew. In July 1973, just a week before his son's sixteenth birthday, George Faldo took him to see his very first professional tournament—the British Open at Troon. Father and son loaded up their camping gear and hopped in the family's white VW Beetle for the 400-mile drive north to Scotland. They would camp out at night and absorb the professional game during the day.

At the course each morning, George picked a spot and instructed his son to meet him back there at 5:00 p.m. Until that time, Faldo had complete run of the links. Kept warm in the chilly weather by wearing his pajamas under his clothes, Faldo scurried to take everything in. He would lie down beside the tee boxes to peak between legs, then hustle down the fairway to watch second shots before moving on to the green. Nicklaus, Palmer, Player, Trevino, the British idol Tony Jacklin—he saw them all at Troon. The practice range became his favorite stop, where he would let the rhythm of their swings and the big, colorful golf bags mesmerize him. But as much as anything or anyone, two players took hold of Faldo's fancy—Tom Weiskopf and Johnny Miller.

Faldo was already over six feet in height, and it was natural that he gravitated toward two of the taller players on Tour. But the attraction was deeper than that. "Weiskopf came down the range one evening talking with Jack and was hitting balls in his street shoes," he says. "I thought, 'wow.' That was showing off his tempo." Faldo followed him. "Weiskopf hit a 1-iron, and I'd never seen such a divot. It was as thin as your finger." Faldo was also enamored with the sound of his shots at impact. Even four decades later, he vividly remembers standing on the 7th tee, witnessing Weiskopf crack a 1-iron that kept pace with the driver of playing competitor Peter Oosterhuis.

The smoothness of Miller's swing and flight of his shots—hardly ever off-line—stuck with Faldo as well. "I remember seeing Johnny coming down those first few holes and watching the balls dance when they hit the greens," he says. "As a youngster, I haven't come close to getting backspin on a ball." Weiskopf and Miller were paired together in the final group for the final two rounds, and Faldo followed them as much as possible until he and his father had to make the journey back down south for work before the end of the last day.

At home, he returned to his local club and began playing imaginary games—his favorite a best-ball with two of the game's best taking on himself. The team of Weiskopf and Miller versus Faldo was a popular match. With Tom Weiskopf, Faldo would try to copy his meticulous address of the ball, his steady head, his tempo, his straight left arm, and his divots from those long irons. With Johnny Miller, he would mimic his walk into the ball, his milking of the grip, his leg action, and his high, ever-so-slight fade with the irons. As for his own game, Faldo would let all of the varying idiosyncrasies he saw at Troon seep into his swing—"accidental self-taught visualization" he would call it years later.

By April 1975, Faldo had quit school and crafted himself into one of England's leading amateurs. Golf was going to be his living. "I used to sit on the windowsill of my bedroom, look at the stars and dream this whole thing, just painting the pictures of the future," he said. On this night, the telly would frame the colors and hues of Augusta and reveal what lay ahead for those fortunate enough to realize their aspirations. And on this night, he would find out who tomorrow's competition would be. Weiskopf? Miller? Nicklaus?

"ALL RIGHT, let 'em go," hollered a security guard by Gate 3 after checking his watch one final time. It was 8:00 a.m. Time to open the gates. Cars had begun pulling into the club's main Number 1 parking lot at the corner of Washington Road and Berckmans Road long before sunrise at 7:01 a.m. This day would be the warmest of the competition, with afternoon highs nearing 70 degrees and less breezy, what wind there was now coming from the south. But as glorious early spring days can go in the South, the start was chilly with morning temperatures slow to warm off a near-freezing low.

A ticket to the Masters had never been hotter than on this day. Scalpers worked in the shadows right across Washington Road, out of sight but not out of mind. The club began producing a plastic ticket with a raised logo in 1966 to prevent counterfeiting. These season badges were numbered with a reminder on the back: "Seller reserves right at any time to take up this badge and cancel all privileges connected therewith." This year's ticket was red and mustard yellow, making the sporting event look more like a Washington Redskins home game. The four-day tickets, which the club sold for $30, had reportedly gone for as much as $1,000 a piece earlier in the week.

Even some without a ticket or the means to participate in the black market weren't dissuaded from trying their luck with the Pinkerton guards. They claimed to be press or PGA members. They lined up at Will Call spouting off names without any proof of identification. They approached with a bare safety pin attached to their clothing claiming their ticket had fallen off. Already this year a man who professed to be the Prime Minister of India had sauntered up to the gate. He wasn't. And the occasional bribe wasn't uncommon— both of the monetary and non-monetary variety.

Years later, holograms, bar codes, electronic scanning, and metal detectors would arrive. For now, the patrons only needed to show their badges and respect the rules, written and unwritten, inside. No periscopes. No running, even though the gaits on some patrons made speed walking champions jealous. Those through the gates first were in a slight hurry to stake their chairs at the most desirous locations on the course. Squatting was an unwritten custom and tradition at Augusta National going back many years, but chairs must be folding and canvas—lawn chairs and those with hard seats were outlawed in 1962 because patrons were standing on them.

On the way, patrons picked a pocket-sized *Spectator Suggestions for the Masters Tournament* written by Bobby Jones out of one green-painted box, and out of another a Starting Times and Pairings sheet with tee times on one side and a green, black, and red map on the other. There was a rush to the 12th tee, 13th green, 15th green, and the par-three 16th, where the most boisterous galleries tended to congregate on the weekend. But the prime spot for chairs was around the 18th green, where patrons would see a champion crowned. It would be ten hours before the final group walked onto the 72nd green. Looking down the pairing sheet, surely the winner would have to come out of the last four twosomes with thirty major championships among them at the time and all major winners except the youngster Watson:

1:36	Bobby Nichols, Arnold Palmer
1:44	Billy Casper, Lee Trevino
1:52	Jack Nicklaus, Tom Watson
2:00	Tom Weiskopf, Johnny Miller

The fact that Weiskopf and Miller—number one and number three on the leaderboard after 54 holes—were paired together for the final round was an oddity found only at the Masters. The other majors at the time paired players 1–2, 3–4, 5–6, etc. with any ties determined by the order of returned scores on Saturday (or Friday in the case of the British Open, which finished on Saturdays until 1980). Meanwhile, the Masters featured a hodge-podge of pairings over the years. For a while, the 54-hole leader was always paired with

Byron Nelson, and the leaders used to never go out last. Since 1969, tournament officials had paired one and three on the leaderboard in the final group with the second and fourth place players in the penultimate group (a practice that would stay in place until 1982). Instead of a Weiskopf–Nicklaus final twosome, that meant Nicklaus and Watson would be going off just ahead. It was Miller's first time in the final group at the Masters after being in the fourteenth-to-last on Saturday and barely making the cut, but it was his second in a major—the other being that 1973 British Open with Weiskopf. There wouldn't be a lot of conversation in that final group, but there would be a lot of watching and looking ahead to the man playing just in front of them.

"I'd rather be two strokes ahead going into the last day than two strokes behind," observed Nicklaus years later. "Having said that, it's probably easier to win coming from behind. There is no fear in chasing. There is fear in being chased."

WEISKOPF ARRIVED at the course Sunday, carrying his pair of burgundy slacks on a clothes hanger, size 34 waist and 34 ½ inseam. Weiskopf was one of the snappiest dressers in golf and borderline obsessive in his meticulousness. The crease on his pants had to be straight down, otherwise he wouldn't wear them. A pair with a double crease met the same fate. On this morning, he ironed them himself and carried them to the course so they wouldn't wrinkle while sitting in the car.

"I got that from my mother," says Weiskopf, who adds that she always dressed his father well. He also took cues from Tommy Bolt, whom Weiskopf considered the best dressed player he'd ever seen. "It's easy to coordinate two colors, but when you get three and four that look good together, now you've done something pretty special," he adds with a twinkle in his eyes.

There were few clothing deals at the time, so Weiskopf bought all of his clothes himself. His slacks were custom-made by Hamilton-Taylor in Cincinnati—the same company that manufactured Augusta National's green jackets—and his sweaters were designed by Pringle in Scotland. "My sweaters were one of a kind. I used to sit down with their guy and choose my colors. They would never make another one," says Weiskopf of the cashmeres that ran $300–$400 apiece. The jumpers, as they are called in Scotland, were shipped to Weiskopf in the off-season. "I'd start thinking about what outfits I'd wear at Augusta around Christmas time," he says. Going through a shipment of new arrivals in late 1974, a purple sweater with an argyle pattern on the front stood out. "I said, 'I'm going to wear that next year'," Weiskopf remembers.

"I always felt good if I wore certain colors," he said, yellow being one of his favorites which he wore on Saturday. For Sunday, he reasoned differently: "I'd worn green and finished second three times so I thought I would wear something that clashed."

Two players who did have clothing contracts were Miller and Nicklaus. Miller was another player who enjoyed wearing snazzy attire. At the end of 1973, Miller signed a deal with Sears, Roebuck and Company, the largest retailer in the United States Johnny Miller Menswear would become ubiquitous, but Miller felt his style, which once featured custom-made clothes and shoes, took a hit. "Their clothes fit well," he says, "but they were not that high quality." Today, he was dressed conservatively in a light blue golf shirt, white pants with light blue checked stripes. None of the three players wore a hat, a visor, or had a logo of any sort on their clothing this day.

For Saturday and Sunday rounds that would be televised, Nicklaus had his outfits picked out months in advance by the Hathaway Company. He came out of the locker room in white pants and a green-colored shirt with white horizontal stripes—as close to "Masters" green as you could get with the tag inside the collar stating: "The Hathaway Golf Classic shirt, 100% Cotton Lisle (L), Wash Warm, No Bleach." He felt ready as he walked onto his preferred practice spot on the west side of the range to meet Willie Peterson, who gave him a strange look. "Aren't you going to put your shoes on," he asked. Nicklaus looked down. His street shoes were still on his feet. "That's what you call real concentration, isn't it?" said Nicklaus.

Once Nicklaus changed into his white, tasseled golf shoes, he returned to the range and encountered a more pressing problem. His swing tempo was off.

SIGNING AUTOGRAPHS while walking from one side of the clubhouse to the other, Nicklaus made it to the 1st tee with Tom Watson. Unfortunately for him, the hiccup in his swing followed him as well. "My opening tee shot was always a tough tee shot," says Nicklaus. "You always had to hit it hard enough to get over the bunker, but you also didn't want to hit it into the trees on the left (a dozen of which had been added two years earlier to narrow the landing area)." With a swing out of sync, his opening drive of the final round went right, hit a tree, and bounced further right into the trees. Fortunate to have any play, he clipped a tree on his recovery shot and then left his third shot with a wedge short. He made bogey on the opening hole for the second day in a row. "I could've kicked myself," Nicklaus said. "The swing wasn't long enough. It was slow enough but too short." He was now two back.

Just as Grout and Jones had taught him, Nicklaus remedied a fix on the spot. He told himself to "complete the backswing." That would remain his primary swing thought for the rest of the day. "A lot of times I would get very quick at the top of my swing," says Nicklaus. This meant he would get his weight all the way back on his right foot and rotate too quickly, moving his shoulders and hips left of the target. The result was a block to the right, as on the 1st hole, or dropping the hands inside and flipping the club. "My thought was to make sure to finish the backswing and give me time to collect myself and move forward," he says of the remedy.

Historically, the tee shot on the 2nd hole was another that gave him problems. This time, Nicklaus hit the fairway and reached the greenside bunker in two shots. But it was the bunker farthest away, nearly thirty yards from the hole. For the second day in a row, he took out his new forty-year-old sand wedge and blasted out to three feet for a birdie. The rhythm returned in his swing and in his stride. On the 3rd hole, he spun his pitching wedge approach to within tap-in range to tie Weiskopf for the lead.

Weiskopf and Miller teed off eight minutes after Nicklaus, and Weiskopf had already made a key decision. He wouldn't use his driver today. Weiskopf's MacGregor 3-wood was strong—almost 12 degrees—and went nearly as far as most player's drivers but with greater accuracy. Miller noticed Weiskopf's strategy and how well he was playing. "He was playing very conservatively, hitting a 3-wood off almost every tee, which was a new game plan for him," says Miller. "He was pretty bulletproof then."

The back-and-forth battle commenced. After pars on the opening two holes, Weiskopf made his first birdie of the day at the 3rd to retake the outright lead. Nicklaus struck a 5-iron to four feet on the 5th for his third birdie in a four-hole stretch to tie Weiskopf at 10 under par. Fifteen minutes later Weiskopf rolled in a six footer from behind the hole at the 6th to go 11 under. With the golf and temperature heating up, Weiskopf shed his cashmere sweater. In the fairway on the 9th, Nicklaus knew from his scorecard that from the last ridge in the fairway, it was 130 yards to the front of the green, 160 to the back. He hit an 8-iron seven feet behind the hole and made the birdie putt.

Nicklaus was out in three-under 33. Weiskopf would make the turn right behind him with a bogey-free 34. Counting ties, the lead changed hands five times in the first nine holes.

"These guys just wouldn't throw me a bone," says Miller. "They were playing great golf."

Weiskopf recalls little of his own play early in that round but can still see Miller. "I don't remember hardly anything about the front side except for Johnny Miller was knocking the flag down," he says.

Miller was enjoying the freedom of a pursuer. He birdied the 2nd hole, but a bogey from over the green at the 3rd dropped him five shots behind Weiskopf at the time. Then, Miller got hot: a six-foot birdie at the 4th, a fourteen footer at the 6th, two putts for birdie from twenty-five feet on the 8th where he barely missed an eagle, and a fifteen footer from right up the fall line on the 9th. He shot 32 on the first nine with five birdies. That was 10 under on holes 1–9 on the weekend. He had made up half his deficit from the lead and was now just two back.

"I was in chase mode and totally aggressive," says Miller of the pressure-free feeling. "Enjoying the fact I was hitting every fairway and every green and not getting in any trouble whatsoever."

"He was really, really playing well. Nicklaus was playing well," says Weiskopf, who as the overnight leader felt he may have been a little too cautious. "I was playing okay. I was a little tentative."

With nine holes to play Nicklaus, Miller, and Weiskopf had separated themselves from the field, even though scoring was the best of the four days. The course average that Sunday was 71.3—two-and-a-half strokes lower than in the third round.

Earlier, the reigning U.S. Open champion Hale Irwin made the most of the improved conditions. After making just five birdies the first three days, Irwin birdied the first three holes and was off and running. "I didn't play all that well, really," he said. "I missed some shots, but when I missed, I missed in the right places." Irwin holed lots of putts, including three from more than twenty feet in length. After eight birdies (tying Art Wall's 1959 record for most in one round), he had the opportunity for one more on the 18th, just off the front-right of the green, thirty feet from the hole. It was a putt for 63, which would match Johnny Miller's at the 1973 U.S. Open for the lowest in a major championship.

"When it got about two feet from the hole, I said, 'I just set a record'," Irwin said. Instead, it slid just right. His 64 matched the course record held by Lloyd Mangrum in 1940, Jack Nicklaus in

1965, and Maurice Bembridge in 1974. It also jumped him from a tie for 19th into a tie for 4th at day's end.

Of the other challengers, Bobby Nichols got to six under with a twenty-five-foot birdie putt at the 12th. Normally, with all the danger and rewards ahead, he wouldn't have been out of it. But, he pulled his tee shot on the 13th into the woods, made par, and then missed a two-and-a-half footer at the 15th just as he had on Saturday. He scrambled around the rest of the way for a bogey-free 69, finishing at six under par with Irwin.

Nichols's playing competitor could not get back in the tournament either. Arnold Palmer's day could be summarized in one hole. With the hole location on the right side of the 12th green about four yards on, his tee shot nicked the bottom of the flagstick and struck just beside the hole. The ball finished twelve feet away, though, and he missed the putt—from a near hole-in-one to a routine par. Palmer finished with a 72 and wound up tied for 13th—his last top-twenty finish in the Masters.

In the second to last group, Billy Casper shot a 70 to finish tied for 6th. Lee Trevino shot 71 to finish tied for 10th. He would never finish better in the Masters.

Tom Watson was the only player within five shots of the lead after turning in 34 thanks to holing a shot from the back bunker at the 7th and another birdie at the 9th. Although he would never get closer, Watson's play would be a significant factor in the outcome.

The remaining nine holes for the game's top three golfers would determine not only the Masters champion, but their places in the game's history.

"It is definitely a game of misses," says Weiskopf. But the fewer the misses, the more accentuated those become. Any mistake could be disastrous. With these three playing so well, would there even be a miss?

"FIVE, FOUR, Three," Frank Chirkinian counted down, "Two, One … Sing, Vinny." That was the guidance Vin Scully received before

CBS came on the air. "It always seemed to lift me, make me rise to the occasion," says Scully of the Chirkinian command.

Before the days of the internet and mobile devices and all-sports cable stations, CBS television and radio was the nation's lone connection to up-to-date play at the Masters. The first time the nation saw Augusta that Sunday came just before 4:00 p.m., as CBS gave an update into the NBA playoff game that preceded the golf. "The Augusta National Golf Club has seen some marvelous finishing rounds, and this fourth and final round of the 1975 Masters might very well be a story that will live for many years to come," were the first words out of Scully's mouth. Chirkinian showed Nicklaus's second shot on the 9th on tape and then his seven-foot birdie putt from behind the hole to tie for the lead before sending it back to Brent Musburger.

Scully couldn't believe his fortune. The storyline at the beginning of the week remained the storyline late Sunday afternoon. "The three men that I was thinking about the most are all locked in on Sunday," says Scully. There were no cameras on holes 1–8, but he didn't need sight to figure out what was happening.

"I'll never forget the sounds of Augusta," says Scully who took in the scene from his tower at the top of the hill, just to the golfer's left of the 18th green. "You would sit at 18 with that large gallery around the green and all of a sudden, like cannon-fire, you'd hear a roar, sometimes a muffled kind of a sound, but always a roar. Immediately everyone would look over at the leaderboard, and then they would change a number.

"Well on Sunday, you started to hear the roars, and you started to see that this was going to be Nicklaus, Weiskopf, and Miller. I couldn't believe that the storyline held up all the way through, but it did. There they were: the big three. And it was amazing."

Indeed, the game's best three players—each at the top of his game going to the final nine holes—all with a chance on the closing holes was rare. In major championships, there had been plenty of two-

man duels. Jones–Hagen. Snead–Hogan. Nicklaus–Palmer. Nicklaus–Trevino. But never the top three.

In the 16th tower, Henry Longhurst had just taken the single red
rose out of the glass that cameraman George Drago left him before
every broadcast. Then, he made haste of the glass's remnants—gin.
About 150 yards away, Ben Wright was in his position just behind the
right corner of the 15th green. With nothing but the years of Masters
winners jotted down on a pairing sheet, he summoned the advice Longhurst gave him several years earlier: "We are nothing but caption writers in the picture business. If you can't improve the quality of the pictures
with your words, then keep you damned mouth shut." Like Scully,
they didn't want to screw this up—not only for fear of their boss—
but because they were the soundtrack to golf's greatest moments.

It's not known when or who coined the phrase, "the Masters
doesn't begin until the back nine on Sunday," and whether or not it
was widely acknowledged before or after 1975. Of course, that was
the case at most any tournament when the nerves were ratcheted
and pressure heightened on the closing holes. But that Masters myth
certainly gained traction following this day with an epic finish that
would earn the tournament much of its reputation.

In the heat of battle on the finishing holes was where Jack Nicklaus was most confident at this stage in his career. "I was a good
closer," he said years later. "In part, it was because I had a lot of opportunities; in part it was probably a function of my temperament.
I'm sure some players have a counterproductive personality or temperament for handling pressure and finishing off a tournament.
Good golf requires a lot of self-knowledge."

Nicklaus continued to think about completing his backswing. He
played the percentages and made pars on the first three holes of the
second nine. Meanwhile, the final twosome ran into difficulties on
the two downhill holes, 10 and 11.

As soon as he was just two shots back—the closest he'd been all
week—Miller's pesky putter reappeared. He missed an eight-foot

birdie putt at the 10th, leaving it a few inches short, right in the heart. At the 11th, his birdie attempt from thirty feet just missed on the high side and ran by two feet. When he hit the comebacker, the ball caught the right side of the hole and spun out to the left. "I didn't hit a bad putt, it just broke more than I thought," says Miller, who stared at the ball for five seconds. "That was a huge, huge putt for me, though, to stop a little momentum."

Weiskopf parred the 10th hole after a simple chip from the front of the green to tap-in range. He found himself at a perfect angle on the left side of the fairway at the 11th. "It was kind of a hairy lie," he says of the ball in the fairway, a lie you could get at Augusta National in spots where the overseed hadn't come in.

"When you are really good at what you do—and I was good at what I did—with every club I was within two steps one way or the other of that distance," says Weiskopf. "Now the wind comes into it, now the excitement, the nerves, the pressure of the shot, the choice of the shot, the lie—good or bad. That's what makes it difficult—it's not the yardage."

With a 5-iron, he aimed away from the left-rear hole location tucked along the edge of the pond. It wasn't far enough right. Weiskopf pulled the shot, and the ball hit on the bank and rolled back into the water. Because the ball had initially carried the hazard, he was able to drop on the other side between the hole and point of entry instead of a more difficult angle on the ball drop. He dropped the ball over his right shoulder—as was the rule then. Still, there was just ten feet of green between the water and the hole on the ninety-foot shot. "That shot's impossible," says Miller.

"I took a chance," Weiskopf says. "It's either going to be a good choice or a bad choice. I was comfortable with that shot because I had a really good lie… I felt like I could get it eight or ten feet past the hole." But Weiskopf didn't hit it hard enough. His heart was in his throat for a split second before the ball barely clearly the bank and rolled up three feet from the hole. He made the putt to salvage a bogey. It was an important up-and-in, but it was his first dropped shot in twenty-seven holes. For the first time all day, he trailed.

Jack Nicklaus now possessed the outright lead. At 11 under par, he led by one over Weiskopf and three over Miller. There were only seven holes to play.

Miller stayed aggressive and fired right at the flag on the 12th but was a club short. It barely carried into the bunker (the only one to find that bunker on Sunday)—the same one he holed out from in 1971. Only this time with the new sand, it didn't bury. He escaped to three feet and made par. Weiskopf hit a 7-iron to the left of the pin and two-putted from forty feet for his par.

Standing in the fairway at the 13th, Nicklaus had been striking the ball as well as at any point during the week. He hadn't missed a shot since the opening hole. On his second shot, however, he got too fast with his long-iron into the green. This time, it resulted in a pull to the left in between the first and second greenside bunkers. It settled just a few feet off the green but 100 feet away, Nicklaus chose to chip it to the back-right hole location. The ball barely got halfway to the hole, leaving him more than twenty-five feet for birdie. He couldn't make it and had thrown away the first of two par-five opportunities coming home.

Back on the tee, while Nicklaus and Miller remained in short-sleeved golf shirts, Weiskopf pulled his sweater out of the bag and put it on. His 3-wood off the tee didn't turn over and went straight behind the pine trees, forcing him to lay up. He hit his wedge shot strong and mis-read his birdie putt coming back down the slope.

The only one to take advantage of the easiest hole on the course was Miller. His drive around the corner of the dogleg left him a long iron to the middle of green. He two-putted for birdie to get back within two of Nicklaus.

The 14th hole marked the halfway point of the second nine. Sandwiched between the more famous par fives, the 13th and 15th, the uphill, dogleg left hole never got any respect. It was the only hole on the course without a bunker—or any hazard for that matter—since a large fairway bunker on the right side was removed after the 1952 tournament.

The hole, which awkwardly moved to the left while the terrain sloped to the right, had not been kind to Nicklaus since bogeying it in his very first practice round here sixteen years earlier. "I always had a hard time with 14," he admits. In his career, he had played it in eight over par. Of all the holes at Augusta National, only the 18th had been tougher on him at 10 over. One year earlier, he bogeyed it from over the green in the final round when just one off the lead.

In the fairway after a perfect drive, he had hit an 8-iron ten yards over the green on Saturday, and now thinking the wind was with him again, he chose a 9-iron. The green was the second largest on the course, but with a large rise from the front right to the back left. A third of the green was a false front, and the hole location was back right just over that incline. After he struck the 9-iron, the wind seemed to turn and the ball finished short and rolled back off the front. A frustrated Nicklaus tossed some leaves of grass into the air again after the shot. On his next shot, he used his putter but hit it too firm. It scooted just off the back of the green, sixteen feet past the hole. He left the comebacker a foot-and-a-half short. Nicklaus used his putter three times, but it was officially a one-putt green. Nicklaus felt like he'd let two shots slip away the last two holes. "I thought the tournament had gotten away from me on 13 and 14," he admitted.

The 14th hole had been tough on this day, yielding only two birdies when the final twosome came up. Miller exasperated its difficulty by pulling his drive into the pine trees on the left. He had hit every green in regulation to this point and showed his anger at the mistake by slamming his right fist into his left palm walking off the tee. Taking a long iron, he unsuccessfully gambled on his second shot when his ball hit more tree limbs and failed to get out of trouble. After all those birdies and stellar play, Miller looked to be throwing away his chances on this one hole. For his third shot, Miller stepped off his own yardage and decided to hit a rope-hook 7-iron around the trees. The ball bounded up the green, hit the bottom of the flagstick, and almost went in. The anything-but-routine par drew a wry smile from Weiskopf.

After a beautiful drawing 3-wood into the center of the fairway, Weiskopf hit an 8-iron that never left the flagstick to six feet in front of the hole. He rolled the putt right in and waved to the crowd as he regained the outright lead with four holes to play. To those watching, it looked like this would finally be Weiskopf's Masters. Only Weiskopf didn't yet think so.

"I never thought I was going to win," he says. "I knew that guy in front of me wasn't done. I knew that guy playing beside me wasn't done. I had a lot of shots to play.

"Maybe that's where I fell short."

TO HAVE ANY shot at winning, Nicklaus knew he needed, at worse, a birdie on the 15th. It was a hole MacKenzie originally sketched as a long par four with the green fronted by a tributary of Rae's Creek. Changed to a par five before construction began, it was now a player's last good chance at birdie.

Off the tee, Nicklaus didn't hit the most solid of drives, but it went down the right-center of the fairway and fortunately stopped just short of one of the mounds on that side. When Nicklaus and his caddie Willie Peterson arrived at the ball, Nicklaus took out his notes from his back pocket and calculated that he was 245 yards to the hole, 235 to carry the pond that fronted the green twenty-five feet below him. The lie was virtually flat, slightly on the upslope if anything. He first grabbed a 3-wood, then had Peterson put it back in his bag. He bent down to pick up some grass and stepped a few yards in front on the top of the mound, tossing it in the air. He watched the clippings come back toward him. Then he took the 3-wood out again.

And Peterson put it back again. Nicklaus placed his hands on his hips with a slight shake of the head and bite of the lower lip because he just didn't want to hit that club. He checked the wind again. This time the grass fell nearly straight down. He pulled the 1-iron.

Lee Trevino once advised that if in a lightning storm you should hold up a 1-iron into the air, because even God can't hit a 1-iron. But for professionals like Nicklaus and Tom Weiskopf—those with tall, wide arcs who could make balls soar instead of scoot—the 1-iron could produce magic. "Jack Nicklaus could hit a 1-iron higher than I could hit a pitching wedge," says Gary Koch. His MacGregor VIP 1-iron had been in the bag for nine years. With the head only 3 ½ inches wide and the club 40 ½ inches long, it had already produced two of the greatest shots in the history of golf. The same 1-iron from 238 yards on the 72nd hole at Baltusrol wrapped up the 1967 U.S. Open for him after a poor drive and chunked recovery shot. He sank the twenty-foot birdie putt to shoot 275—one better than the lowest score ever in that championship by Ben Hogan in 1948. On the treacherous par-three 17th at Pebble Beach in 1972, he chose the 1-iron again, this time into a stiff ocean breeze from 218 yards. Feeling his clubface shut at the top of his backswing, he adjusted on the downswing, delaying the release just enough to hit the ball square. The ball bore through the air toward the tiny hour-glass green. It rattled the flagstick and dropped next to the hole for a birdie and a third U.S. Open title.

With the 1-iron in hand, Nicklaus quickly got over the ball and began his pre-shot routine. He didn't hit the club as far as he used to—this distance was now at the maximum of his range—but the adrenaline was pumping and he knew it. He picked out an aiming spot just in front of his ball—a trick he developed playing St. Andrews during the 1970 British Open. His eyes moved along three points. Ball. Spot. Target. Spot. Ball. Spot. Target. Ball. Spot. Target. Spot. Ball. Nicklaus cocked his head to the right, took the club straight back, completed his backswing, and took a mighty lash, sending the ball straight up in the air at the flagstick. He immediately walked after it, admittedly thinking the ball might hop in for a double eagle as it did for Gene Sarazen forty years earlier. It landed eight feet in front of the hole, took a big bounce six feet in the air, landed again just a foot of so from the back-right hole location, and rolled twelve feet by.

Nicklaus smiled and raised both his hands, dropping the club in the process. He rubbed Peterson's head, and a grinning Peterson patted Nicklaus's back. "I couldn't have hit it any better," said Nicklaus, "That might have been the best full swing I ever took." The shot had everyone in awe, from Scully to the patrons surrounding the 15th green, who gave Nicklaus a standing ovation as he strode down the hill and onto the green. He didn't hit the eagle putt hard enough, missing the uphill twelve footer to the right, but a tap-in birdie tied the Golden Bear for the lead again. He was back in it.

NICKLAUS WALKED to the final par three, the 16th. Even though players hit over a pond that cut around the left side of the green, unlike Weiskopf, Nicklaus never felt like it was a dangerous hole. He had made a two there on his way to winning his first Masters in 1963, holing a crucial twelve footer to win by one. But in 1974, one off the lead in the final round, he made a critical mistake by hooking his tee shot into the left bunker and making bogey. On this day, the hole location sat in its most difficult spot, back right on a small plateau. It was nearly impossible to end up close to the hole, which was just a few feet over a ridge and sat on a crown. There had been only three birdies in forty-two tries in the final round, and if you were long or right, a bogey-four was a near certainty.

Meanwhile, even hitting to the generously wide 15th fairway, Weiskopf stuck to his game plan by taking a 3-wood off the tee. It left him several yards behind Miller's drive. "That wasn't normal for Weiskopf to be hitting first every hole," says Miller. Weiskopf could still go for the green and went for it with his 1-iron. Instead of a high fade, Weiskopf's ball drew slightly toward the left center of the green and bounced eighteen feet over. Miller, who nearly came out of his shoes on the tee, had already hit each of the par fives in two shots and then taken two putts for birdie. He selected his 4-wood this time and hit his second to the front right of the green.

On the 16th tee, Nicklaus chose to hit a 5-iron, but he didn't catch it cleanly. "Get up," Nicklaus barked as the ball approached the green. It hit just a few feet right of the water and stopped quickly and short. From there, he would face a treacherous, uphill putt of forty feet. The intended line traveled just left of a pronounced ridge. And going away from Rae's Creek, it would be extremely slow. It was a putt no one made.

Immediately after Nicklaus, Tom Watson, who by his own measure had been hitting the ball on the final nine as well as at any point all week, pulled his tee shot well left and into the water. Unsure of whether the ball crossed the margin of the hazard by the green, he walked all the way up to the green to determine it.

Weiskopf studied his third shot. "Those are tough shots over that green," he says. The ball sat on a tight lie, and he had little green between him and the hole seventy feet away. Weiskopf carried the ball too far, and it ran more than ten feet past the hole.

After finding out his ball never crossed land, Watson walked back to the forward teeing ground for his next shot on the 16th. This forced Miller, a fidgety and quick player, to wait on his eagle putt on the adjacent 15th green. Watson proceeded to hit his third shot in the exact same area of water. He quickly dropped another ball and hit his fifth shot in the middle of the green, the ball funneling back down the slope just outside of Nicklaus's.

After waiting more than two minutes, Miller resumed his pre-shot routine. For the first time in the tournament, he had a putt to tie for the lead. Miller missed his eagle from a little more than twenty-five feet—it just barely went by the right edge too firm. Putting into his shadow, he would make the nervy three footer for birdie.

To keep up with Nicklaus, Weiskopf faced a similar, but shorter, putt—downhill, slightly right-to-left, twelve feet. At that moment in time, it was the biggest putt of his career. After he struck it, there wasn't a doubt it was going to drop. Weiskopf displayed his most demonstrative reaction of the day, raising his right leg and giving an upper cut with his arm. "I'm feeling really good, really confident," says Weiskopf. "Just like everything came together." He retook the lead by one with three holes to play.

From his vantage point beside the water at the 16th green, Nicklaus had a lot to take in. Right hand on hip, leaning on his putter, he had watched Miller's eagle attempt and Weiskopf's birdie. Moments after Weiskopf's putt, he turned his attention to Watson's putt from nearly the same spot as his. He observed him strike his ball up the slope and saw exactly how it turned to the left at the top of the hill. Watson tapped in for his quadruple-bogey seven. Nicklaus put down his ball, walked behind, and knelt to study the putt. A three-putt bogey was more likely than him holing this putt. Even Peterson had to tend the flagstick. Just get it close and make par.

Once Miller was in for birdie at the 15th, Nicklaus stood up after his final look. For such a lengthy putt, the line had become very clear to him, about eighteen inches of break to the left. Under these circumstances, he would gladly take two putts and move onward. Suddenly, he had the silliest feeling come over him. "I think I can make this," he thought to himself. Due to Watson's travails on the hole, Miller and Weiskopf were now on the tee waiting.

More than eight minutes had elapsed since he'd hit his tee shot. Nicklaus now tugged on his glove and addressed his putt. His senses were heightened. Nicklaus crouched over the ball to take a single practice stroke, still seeing the line in his mind and sensing the necessary speed of the putt. Then he righted himself and looked at the line again. He told himself, "Make it." After four glances at the hole, Nicklaus took his George Low Sportsman Wizard 600 back and hammered the ball. He watched as it weaved its way up the slope. Peterson pulled the flagstick out of the cup. It had plenty of speed, enough to go several feet by. But within two feet of the hole,

Nicklaus raised his putter in the air with his right hand and Peterson bent his knees. With a last second turn to the left, the ball hit the back of the cup and fell in.

If making the putt had been unexpected, the celebration that followed was completely unforeseen. Peterson, clutching both the flagstick and a cigarette in his left hand, jumped up and down behind the hole. Nicklaus left all stoicism behind. Turning away from the hole, he leapt in the air as well, breaking into a trot around the front of the green, as if celebrating the winning touchdown at Ohio Stadium. "I don't often hole forty footers on the 70th hole," he explained. He ran right off the green and on to the 17th tee, leaving Peterson to pick the ball out of the hole. Nicklaus never looked back at the tee. There was no need. It was a cruel enough blow. The dagger had been delivered to Weiskopf again.

"It's an impossible putt—a putt you just don't make," says Miller.

The past can repeat itself in strange ways. Just as he had sixteen years earlier in his first round ever at Augusta National, Nicklaus played the 14th, 15th, and 16th holes bogey–birdie–birdie. This time, those scores of 5–4–2 might propel him to a fifth victory.

Johnny Miller actually didn't see the ball go in the hole. Upon being asked after the round if he saw the putt, Miller said, "See it? I had to walk through the bear prints."

WHY HIM? Why did Nicklaus make that momentous putt in front of Tom Weiskopf of all people? Why did he make it when the tournament was all but Weiskopf's to put away? And why, of all places, did he make it on the 16th—with Weiskopf left next to play the tee shot that gave him the most discomfort of any at Augusta National?

Tom Weiskopf tried not to ask himself those questions; however, after seeing Nicklaus's putt drop in the hole, he had one. "Good gracious, how do you make that putt?" he asks. "I can't believe he made that putt. You could stand there the rest of your life and never make that putt. But he did. That's why he's Jack."

Only ninety seconds after possibly the most important holed putt of his career, a shaken Weiskopf now had to steady himself. It was as if the 44 Long green jacket was over both arms, only to rip at the seams. As Nicklaus pranced up to the 17th tee, Weiskopf poked a broken tee into the left side of the tee box—he always used a broken tee on par threes—but the spot didn't feel right. He scoured the ground to re-tee, moving to the right. Weiskopf took some extra time tapping the ground down behind the ball with his foot.

"LeRoy, I'm thinking of a little five. I'm going to hit a high-cut 5-iron," he initially told his caddie Schultz. "But I had 6 in mind," he says. Pulling the 6-iron out of the bag, he addressed it behind the ball and waggled a practice swing. Then he handed it back to Schultz and picked the 5-iron. The same club he hit left into the water in the exact same position on this hole in the final round one year earlier. The same numbered club Nicklaus just hit slightly heavy.

"Whether I lost my concentration," says Weiskopf, his voice trailing off as if still searching years later to fully explain what happened next. "I wasn't afraid of the shot… But it's one of those holes I never played well." Whether because of pressure, nerves, emotions, or Nicklaus, he made his worst swing of the day, catching the ball high up on the clubface after coming down too steep on his angle of attack. He knew it immediately, staring down blankly at the divot as soon as he'd completed his follow through. It cleared the water by only a few feet and finished short of the green, some 100 feet from the hole. "It was the right club, just a bad swing," felt Weiskopf both then and now. "I made probably four or five bad swings the whole week," he says, "and that was one of them."

"That was basically Jack Nicklaus making him do that," says Miller. "That putt he made was a nasty thing for Weiskopf to see."

Now, Weiskopf was in an even tougher spot than Nicklaus had been moments earlier. Not only was he twice as far away, but between his ball and the hole was the ridgeline that ran through the entire green. He couldn't get around it. If the ball had been two feet left or two feet right, he could have. He never considered chipping it. Instead, he believed his best choice was to putt the ball to the right of the ridge and try to leave it eight feet away on the top level. After walking up to the hole twice to survey the terrain, he struck the putt on his intended line but didn't hit it hard enough. As the ball approached the hole, it lost speed and caught the wrong side of the slope, trickling down the hill toward the water before finishing eighteen feet away. The ensuing par putt was on-line as well, but he failed to hit that hard enough, too.

"I thought Tom might have trouble playing the hole, and he did," said Nicklaus. "I knew with Tom back on the tee watching me that he was going to have a time playing the hole after I'd made a two. It turned out I was right. It was a two-shot swing, and the tournament."

"It didn't deflate me," maintains Weiskopf. "I accepted the results. I have two more holes to play. Anything can happen." But the momentum had turned.

For the second straight year, the 70th hole of the tournament had impaired Weiskopf's chances with a bogey four. Leading by one moments earlier, he now trailed by one.

A ONE-SHOT lead with two holes to play meant the numbers game Nicklaus was so skilled at playing returned in his favor. "Play first to win," he thought, "which means figuring and playing the percentages." After getting his emotions back under control on the tee, he placed his drive in the right side of the fairway at the 17th, then hit his approach shot to the center of the green, giving him a twenty footer below the hole which he lagged to four inches. On the final hole, he continued his conservative play, hitting a 3-wood off the 18th tee that finished just in the fairway on the inside of the dogleg. The hole location was cut in its customary front-left Sunday position, just seven yards over the left-front bunker. In thirty-eight Masters, only eight champions had birdied the 72nd hole. Nicklaus aimed slightly to the right of the pin with a 6-iron, which finished hole-high eleven feet away. Watson hung back to let Nicklaus walk up by himself. "There is no more fun than coming down the last fairway neck-and-neck," he said.

As Nicklaus was receiving a standing ovation while striding up the incline to the 18th green, Weiskopf stepped in to a birdie putt at the 17th. He had striped his 3-wood—the first time he'd tried to hit a ball really hard all day. From there, it was an aggressive short iron to the back of the green, about fifteen feet from the hole. "It was tracking," says Weiskopf of the relatively simple uphill putt, but he left it half-a-foot short. "I hit it too easy, and it just came up short underneath the hole and broke away."

Incredulous to what was going on around him, Miller had made par on the 16th after hitting his tee shot twenty-five feet left of the hole. All day, he had tried to catch up—like a dog chasing a car, only for the car never to run out of gas. Two solid shots on the 17th had left him in the middle of the green in a similar spot to Nicklaus, only closer. From twelve feet away, he wasted no time in reading the line, stepping into the putt, and striking it. "It was in halfway there," says Miller, who raised his right hand up when the ball was still four feet from falling in. He was within one shot of the lead for the first time the entire week. "Now I got a shot of adrenaline after that putt went in like I've never had in my life," says Miller. "My hair was standing up on the back of my neck and my arms. It was like, oh my gosh, I might finally have a chance to catch these guys. Finally." One hole remained to complete the greatest weekend comeback in major championship history.

Ahead on the final hole, Watson, after being in one of the fairway bunkers, holed a birdie putt to shoot 73. His blunders at the 16th may have helped Nicklaus, but a par there would've put him in solo fourth instead of a tie for 8th. Still, he walked off the last hole feeling confident about his ability to play the course and compete against the likes of Nicklaus, Miller, and Weiskopf.

Nicklaus had a very makeable putt himself on the 18th. It would break off hard to the left at the hole and run out, but he was only eleven feet away. A three-putt from Nicklaus wasn't likely. "It's a putt he should make half the time," says Miller. But before he putted, Nicklaus heard a roar from the 17th. Immediately, he went into stall mode. "I was curious to know whether or not I was ahead," he said. "I might have been more aggressive if Tom had made birdie at 17. If John birdied, then I would go at it as a lag putt."

So Nicklaus walked around the hole again, glancing at the large hole-by-hole leaderboard facing the green. After a short pause, they posted the scores. Weiskopf stayed at 11 under. Miller went from 10 to 11. "He's that cagey this guy," says Miller. "I'm not sure why he waited. It shouldn't have made any difference. He should've just said, 'I'm knocking it in, take these guys out'." Somewhere inside him, Nicklaus didn't believe Weiskopf or Miller had it in them to birdie the 72nd hole at the Masters to tie him. So he chose the cautious route, easing the putt that broke more than a foot to the left right up to the hole. Nicklaus tapped in for par to finish with a 68 and a total of 12-under-par 276 for the tournament.

Miller and Weiskopf stood on the 18th tee, the only two players left on the course. Miller had the honors. He took a driver, mimicking Lee Trevino's swing to produce a baby cut that landed in the middle of the fairway. Weiskopf hadn't wavered from his game plan all day, taking 3-wood off nearly every par four and five. "LeRoy said, 'What do you think?'" says Weiskopf. "I said, 'driver'." Driver! Now he pulled the driver. "I said, 'I'm not laying up'," Weiskopf recalls. "The only chance I have is I've got to drive it. If I'm going to win this thing I've got to give myself a short second shot." Just as the CBS truck and Scully picked up on it, Weiskopf made the point moot. The ball took off over the right tree line and appeared as if it would never come down. "He hits the longest drive maybe we've ever seen on 18," says Miller. Weiskopf concurs: "I hit one of the best drives I've ever hit in my life."

Miller's ball was some fifty yards behind Weiskopf's. For his approach shot he picked a 6-iron out of the bag. After pushing the accelerator to the floor all weekend, a tinge of conservatism entered his thought process at the worst time. "Instead of aiming at the pin, something told me to aim twenty feet right of the pin (to protect again pulling the shot)," says Miller. "That's just a terrible thought. I should have just said, 'Hey, I'm going to knock the flag out'." As soon as he struck the ball, he and Eubanks began motioning for the ball to hook left. It stopped just past pin high but eighteen feet right of the hole. "I hit it within an inch of where I was aiming," says Miller. "That's the only regret I had about that whole tournament."

Weiskopf's ball actually sat on a slightly downhill lie, and with just over 100 yards to the hole, he debated between a really hard pitching wedge and a little 9-iron. He chose the 9-iron—the least amount of club hit into the 18th all week. Weiskopf aimed straight for the hole. The ball started right at the flagstick, landed three feet in front of the hole, bounced five feet in the air ten feet past the pin and came back slightly. He was unlucky the ball didn't wind up closer than eight feet. If the ball would have hit a foot or two higher up the slope, it would have gathered more momentum and finished even closer to the hole.

They walked up the fairway to the same thunderous applause that greeted Nicklaus. One final putt for Nicklaus's two biggest threats—of the day and the era—to tie him and force a playoff.

Nicklaus peered out from the scorer's tent just behind the green to watch. His presence was felt by everyone.

As Miller looked his putt over first, the roars of the day had turned to complete silence. Putting directly into the sun, he took two practice strokes and addressed the ball, looking at the hole four times before striking it. The ball missed by just a few inches on the low side of the hole. "I hit a good putt, just under read it," says Miller, who hit it right where he wanted. Miller grimaced to the sky. "I played a twenty-seven-inch break and the ball broke thirty inches," he says.

"Nicklaus," laughs Miller. "He was smiling after I missed because it was like, 'I don't want to play that guy tomorrow'."

Weiskopf looked at his putt from the side and then from behind. He lay eight feet from vanquishing the demons. He had seen Miller's putt break quickly to the left. "I said to myself make sure you hit it firm," says Weiskopf. Just like Miller, there were two practice strokes and then four looks at the hole after addressing the ball. As Weiskopf stroked the putt, his head moved with the ball with anticipation. "When I looked up," he says, "I thought I'd hit a good putt." He truly believed he had made it, but somehow at the very end, the ball stayed right, never touching the hole. It was a putt that had fooled many players over the years—one that looks like it's got to work slightly to the left towards the 11th green. This time, it didn't turn back until eighteen inches after the hole. When it finished, the hole was directly between the ball and Weiskopf. With a blank look on his face, Weiskopf hit the putter's face with his right fist and sighed. The heartbreak was evident.

"I just hit it too hard," says Weiskopf. "I hit it through the break. That reflected back to the 17th hole. We are all victims of what happened previously. I didn't want to miss it on the low side and thought there was a break.

"It was tough."

Before his two challengers tapped in for their pars, Jack Nicklaus exited the back of the scoring tent. He was the winner of the 1975 Masters Tournament.

NICKLAUS WAS whisked away to the basement in Butler Cabin first for the television presentation, somewhat surprised. "I just knew one of them was going to make it," said Nicklaus. "I figured that if Johnny makes his putt, Tom wouldn't and if Johnny misses, Tom would make his and we'd have a playoff. I never wish anybody any bad luck. I was happy he didn't make it, but I wasn't rooting against him."

The cabin was built in 1964 and the following year hosted the made-for-television green jacket ceremony for the first time. At the time, runners-up were also a part of the proceedings, so sitting shoulder-to-shoulder on a leather green sofa were Nicklaus, Miller, and Weiskopf.

It was the first time Cliff Roberts had seen Weiskopf's purple palette up close. He had earlier told Pat Summerall, "No wonder he didn't win, look at that outfit he's wearing." Weiskopf never wore that sweater again, placing it in storage for his son Eric. Ironically a dozen years later, Augusta native Larry Mize pitched in on the 11th hole in a playoff to win the Masters in a purple ensemble almost identical to Weiskopf's.

Gary Player, the defending champion, presented Nicklaus with his jacket, size 44 Regular. "I watched it on TV. I was choking more than you guys," he said, to which Nicklaus replied, "We didn't have time to choke. Everybody was making birdies." George Burns, who wrapped up low amateur honors at four over par, one shot better than Jerry Pate, was also there.

From Butler Cabin, the combatants walked thirty yards to the practice putting green for the actual trophy presentation where Roberts proclaimed, "What a threesome. What a golf tournament. What a champion."

Again, Weiskopf, Miller, and Nicklaus sat side-by-side-by-side. It was there that Nicklaus leaned over to Miller and said: "Thanks for making that the most fun golf I've ever played in my life."

"He says, 'Thanks for making it so much fun for me.' Not for us. But for me," says Miller. "That was the e-ticket ride. He wanted a couple of guys who would push him and he just barely beat us."

For winning, Nicklaus received a record $40,000—$5,000 more than Player got in 1974. Miller and Weiskopf earned $21,250 each. Nicklaus would also take home a gold medal, a bas-relief sterling silver replica of the Masters trophy, and a silver cigarette box engraved with the signature of every player in the field.

"This is the best I've played ever, including 1965 (when he set the Masters 72-hole record of 271)," said Nicklaus. "I never bogeyed a par five or a par three. I played the par fives in eight under and didn't make a mistake, and I played the par threes under par."

True to his formula, Nicklaus was the champion of limiting his mistakes. His six bogeys for the week were the fewest of anyone in the field. He didn't hit a single ball in a water hazard.

"I had the best feeling of control over the golf ball for a stretch of four days that I can remember," said Nicklaus. "A lot of it I'd say was due to my driver."

He had shot 141 on the weekend. "Normally, you would win by six or seven shots," said Nicklaus, "but there were a couple of talented boys who played extremely well. I'm just damned glad to win the tournament.

"This is the first time that I have played a major championship that none of them gave it away. All of us had a right to win. Tom played well enough to win. John certainly did. I was lucky to have won. They certainly played well enough. That to me is fun. I think it is wonderful that something like that can happen in America today—to be in that kind of a fight. It's fun to be involved. For three men to play to win and none of them fall on their faces. Obviously I enjoyed every minute of it."

"They'll win their Masters, and they'll win a couple of them," he continued. "These two guys have more talent than any young players today. They're going to dominate golf from now on."

The victory delighted Jack Nicklaus more than any other in his career. For the rest of the evening, he wore a giddy smile on his face. It was in sharp contrast to his adversaries. Miller was disappointed. Weiskopf was disconsolate.

"In all the time I have played golf, I thought this was the most exciting display I had ever seen," Nicklaus stated upon having the green jacket draped across his shoulders for a record fifth time. In one afternoon, and with one putt, he had changed the game.

AFTER HOLING OUT on the 72nd hole, Miller had playfully put his ball in his mouth and bit it. He then tossed it into the gallery.

His weekend scores of 65–66=131 added up to the lowest final 36-hole total in major championship history. It also set the Masters record for lowest final thirty-six-hole total and lowest consecutive 36-hole total, breaking Nicklaus's 64–69=133 in 1965. His final fifty-four-hole score of 204 broke the Masters record held by Ben Hogan (1953) and Nicklaus (1965). Eight birdies on that Sunday tied the tournament record for most birdies in one round. Ten total Masters records were broken or tied by Miller—an incredible feat for someone who didn't win. He actually beat Nicklaus by ten shots on the weekend in which he missed only two greens in regulation. "I didn't think anybody could play this course like he did the past two days," said Nicklaus.

It was pretty impressive for a guy who didn't hit a ball on the practice range all week.

Even in defeat, Miller looked at his performance as a victory in certain respects. "I think this proves to people that I can play in tournaments besides Phoenix and Tucson," said Miller.

He had responded with a pretty good answer to those critics who said he couldn't stop Jack from winning when he wanted, his U.S. Open was a fluke, and he can't play in majors. "A lot of people are saying I'm not really as good as my record indicates," he said. "Ask Gary Player and Tom Weiskopf. They will tell you that I'm not shooting all those low scores by chipping in or sinking forty-foot putts. They will tell you I can play a pretty good game of golf. I want to play well in major championships, and I think I can play well in them. I feel I have the game to win any tournament I play in. I've already won on almost every conceivable type of course."

"I was disappointed, but it was like, wow, that's cool," says Miller. "I didn't hold it against Nicklaus for that putt at 16.

"The difference between Weiskopf and me was like I was in a fun horse race trying to catch these fast horses, and I almost caught them, so it was sort of thrilling to make it that much of a run being that far behind. But for Weiskopf, he viewed it as his tournament and then Nicklaus makes that crazy putt at 16. He chunks it, makes bogey, two-shot swing, loses the tournament right there. It was really stinging, I think, to Tom."

"I REMEMBER sitting there and seeing a lot of faces. There were happy faces and a lot of sad ones too. And I was looking at them," says Weiskopf of the trophy presentation. "Mine was sad, I know that."

Arguably, Weiskopf had played better than Nicklaus and Miller for the entire tournament. He was the only player to play the par threes, par fours, and par fives each under par. He was also the only player in the field without a round over par—the fourth time he'd done that in the Masters.

"It usually gets down to a shot one way or the other," says Weiskopf. "And it's usually a putt, isn't it?"

"When you play that well for 72 holes, it makes it tougher," he says. "I finished it off at 17 and 18 playing those holes as perfectly as you possibly could play them, and it didn't happen. That's the tough thing about it. You had your chance. Not just one chance, I had two good chances."

Weiskopf's session in front of the press was a solemn affair. "It's very hard at times to put into words when you're very, very unhappy," he said that evening. "Someone once said you can't explain pain. There's no explanation. I just felt terrible. I'll win this tournament yet. And when I do the jacket will be tailor made.

"I'm not going to let it get the best of me. I'm disappointed as I possibly can be. There's only one winner in a golf tournament. Nobody remembers who finished second. And I'm going to try to forget it. I tried the best I could."

After speaking with the press and cleaning out his locker, Weiskopf left the course early that evening. "Oh brutal," says Weiskopf of that night. The consolations began right away. "It started walking in the locker room. It started with my caddie LeRoy. It started with my friends. It's a tough game. It takes no prisoners. There were a lot of people I didn't even know who were sad for me or John or both of us.

"I never cried, but I remember Jeanne just couldn't stop crying for the whole night. Sometimes it's tougher on people who are pulling for you."

The support continued once he returned home to Columbus. "There were some unbelievable letters that I still have, from former players and friends," says Weiskopf. He read every correspondence, even the ones from people he didn't know. And he responded to each of them. "Something my mother beat into me," says Weiskopf.

The silver medal he received for being runner-up would get locked away in a safe, along with the three others. Roberts even joked that a special second-place trophy should be made for him. With all the people who reached out to him, there was one person Weiskopf doesn't remember ever hearing from: Jack Nicklaus. What could he say?

FOLLOWING THE closing ceremony and press obligations, Nicklaus stayed at the club for a traditional dinner Roberts hosted for each winner the night of his triumph. For the intimate occasion, he, Barbara, and Jackie joined Roberts and a handful of members.

At 9:07 p.m., the club received a phone call from the White House. Nicklaus won majors during the terms of six different presidents, but only on two occasions did one call. The first was President Richard Nixon following the 1972 U.S. Open. The other was President Gerald Ford on the line this evening. President Ford talked with Nicklaus for five minutes, congratulating him on his victory. It's debatable how much of the tournament Ford had seen since he'd been playing a round of golf himself that afternoon at Burning Tree Country Club in Bethesda, Maryland—about a twenty-minute drive from the White House. Nicklaus liked Ford, whom he played with twice in the previous nine months, first at the World Golf Hall of Fame induction and then a month-and-a-half earlier during the pro-am for the Jackie Gleason Inverrary Classic when Nicklaus blocked out the distractions of playing a five-and-a-half hour round with Ford, Gleason, and Bob Hope in front of 40,000 people to shoot a 63. The Nicklaus's first golden retriever, Lady, was even a gift of the Ford's.

Upon leaving that evening, it was Roberts's turn to present Nicklaus with a surprise.

"That was the night that Cliff Roberts gave me a gift," he says. In his car, Roberts placed a case of 1952 Lafite Rothschild and two bottles of 1945 Lafite Rothschild. It was the Jack Nicklaus of wine. "He said one for each of your future Grand Slams with the 52 and a bottle each of the 45s for each Grand Slam. Needless to say I didn't drink any of the 45s. We did drink a couple of the 52s, but I didn't drink them necessarily to commemorate the majors, but that was his phraseology."

Once back at his rental house, Nicklaus went to bed.

With a smile. And a wink.

EPILOGUE

The next morning, nearly an inch of rain pelted down on Augusta. The conditions were not lost on Clifford Roberts. If Miller and/or Weiskopf had made their birdie putts on the 72nd hole, an 18-hole playoff would have been scheduled for Monday. Whether it would have been played was doubtful. Conducting another full round of golf was the playoff format in all four major championships at the time. Roberts wondered if an 18-hole playoff would have come close to matching the exciting climax on the 72nd hole Sunday afternoon. Was it worth the time and money of everyone involved—especially television—to come back for another day? Roberts pondered these questions, and the following February, he announced a change. There would be no more 18-hole playoffs. Instead, the Masters would be the first major to institute a sudden-death format, which would commence immediately following the conclusion of the final round. Even in triumph, officials looked for improvement.

Instead of a playoff, the tournament was basking in the glow of its magnificent finish. The best course, designed by the best architect, that hosted the best tournament had been won by the best golfer in the best finish. The superlatives flowed from every corner of the print world.

"Even a person who would not know a drive from a bunker could not fail to feel the suspense," wrote *The Economist*.

"The grand and glorious old Masters golf tournament, which has a way of producing dramatics so freely, has never seen a day like yesterday," wrote Ron Green in the *Charlotte News*.

"(It) will become the measuring stick for golfing drama," claimed Hubert Mizell in the *St. Petersburg Times*.

"There has never been a better finish than this in the history of golf," said the esteemed golf writer Herbert Warren Wind.

"It possibly could have been the greatest Masters, or any tournament, ever played," wrote Robert Eubanks on the front page of the *Augusta Chronicle*.

Back in the CBS offices in New York City, executives anxiously awaited the national household ratings from the Nielsen Company to be delivered four days later. The weather on Sunday had been good across most of the country, cool but sunny along the East Coast. Good weather meant more people enjoying outside activities, resulting sometimes in lower figures. That wasn't the case this time. The two-hour broadcast earned an 11.9 rating (35 share)—at the time, the highest in Masters history. Even by 2013, it remained the third-highest behind a 14.1 in 1997 and a 13.3 in 2001.

In the United States, an estimated 15 million people had witnessed the two hours of drama that Frank Chirkinian considered his masterpiece. Chirkinian, who died in 2011, felt it was the best broadcast moment in which he'd ever been involved.

The centerpiece of the show had been an exchange between Ben Wright at the 15th hole and Henry Longhurst at the 16th. There was irony that two men who were from the same county in England and members of the same club, Aspley Guise & Woburn Sands Golf Club in Milton Keynes, played such leading roles. Wright had always looked up to Longhurst, who mentored him and had suggested to BBC management in 1967 that he be promoted from radio to TV. Until that Sunday, the two had never played off one another in such a seamless way as if each was writing the other's lines.

The by-play ensued after Weiskopf ran in his birdie putt on the 15th. "Oh. What a tremendous putt by Tom Weiskopf," said Wright, feeling the hairs on the back of his neck stand up as Chirkinian went to an image of Nicklaus on the 16th. "And that is going to be evil music ringing in Nicklaus's ears."

Barely a minute later Nicklaus struck his putt at the 16th. "Now up the hill…," rumbled Longhurst with his gravelly voice. "Uh-oh, did you ever seen one like that? I think that's one of the greatest putts I've ever seen in my life."

As Nicklaus jogged off the green, Chirkinian cut to a camera showing the final twosome. "Back on the tee," Longhurst continued, "Weiskopf has to take it this time having dished it out on the hole before. I never saw such a putt in my life."

"I shall never forget that exchange with Longhurst," says Wright, who would work twenty more Masters. Longhurst passed away from cancer in 1978. "People ask me what was the most exciting thing you ever did," says Wright, "and I say, well, maybe '86 because of the circumstances. But for sheer, unadulterated excitement in that three of the best players ever to play the game came down the stretch with each one of them having a chance to win, '75 has to be it."

Vin Scully would be remembered for what he didn't say. After setting the scene for Miller and Weiskopf—with Chirkinian mixing in shots of Nicklaus staring out of the scoring tent, something he'd done throughout the day—Scully said, "So it is that simple, the roll of the putt." He then took the microphone attached to his headset and flipped it above his forehead to, as he says, "make sure I wouldn't step on the moment which I thought was absolutely supreme. Best thing I ever did was shut up," he says. "I don't have a trademark, but if I did, I think it would be laying out."

Scully would call seven more Masters, all the while still keeping his day job with the Dodgers, before moving networks to NBC in 1983. None of them resonate like his first. "Ask me about all the others, and I probably couldn't remember," he says. For Scully, the roars coming from the base of the bowl still echo, as well as the silence when the final pair stood on the 72nd green. Nicklaus's shots at the 15th and 16th holes are vividly etched in his memory. There's even a print of Nicklaus's putt at the 16th hanging in his home in southern California. "It seems like it was from forever," he says. "I will never forget that."

The images composed by Chirkinian, associate producer Chuck Will, and the rest of the crew had an effect even they couldn't have imagined. Their show proved golf could be fast-paced. Golf could be exciting. Golf could be cool. The broadcast was Emmy nominated for Outstanding Live Sports Special for that year (beaten out by Carlton Fisk's home run in Game 6 of the World Series), and Scully was nominated for Outstanding Sports Personality (he would earn the academy's Lifetime Achievement Award twenty years later).

Still, it wasn't an hour after the broadcast when Roberts entered the television compound, suggesting a new camera position for the 16th hole in 1976. Chirkinian's fascination with the place reached even higher plateaus. The following year, he moved to Augusta. But the actors and the scene would never be as compelling as that Sunday afternoon in 1975.

Over the years when Will and Chirkinian traveled together, Chirkinian would nap on planes. When he awoke Will, hoping he was in a good mood, would often ask: "I hope you were dreaming of the '75 Masters." Chirkinian would reply: "Dreaming you guys wouldn't mess it up."

IN CLIFF ROBERTS'S eyes, it had to have been the best Masters, but publicly no one would ever know. "The club's philosophy was every Masters was the greatest tournament," says Bob Kletcke.

"There was never any talk of this is the greatest Masters of them all or this was the worst. They were all on equal level."

Later, Roberts came close to revealing his opinion in his introduction to the official 1975 Masters film. "It's been forty-one years since the Masters Tournament was inaugurated," he spoke in a slow, deliberate delivery. "Many patrons of the game seem to think the 1975 Masters was the best ever. It's not for us, however, to make such a distinction.... I'll cheerfully admit, however, that having Nicklaus, Weiskopf, and Johnny Miller arriving at the 18th green separated by a single putt was something a bit special."

The winner of the 1975 Masters was, in fact, the Masters itself.

"The '75 Masters did a lot to enhance its importance," says Wright. "It was so exciting that it started to elevate golf to a major sport, rather than a minor one."

"It was the first tournament I ever watched," says Brandel Chamblee, who'd taken up the game just a month earlier. Afterward, the twelve-year-old ran out to the backyard and tore up his father's grass by copying the three players' swings until sundown. "It was maybe the greatest moment in the history of golf," he says.

Roberts passed away in September 1977, taking his own life below the par three course. After his death, future chairmen continued to balance the tournament's traditions with the need for refinement and progress. On the course, grasses on the greens were changed, holes were lengthened, more trees were planted, and even a cut of rough was added. Everything grew: televised hours, credentialed press, fan interest, sponsors, purses, etc. Even so, nothing diluted the stature of the tournament.

The Masters had become the biggest ship in the harbor of golf. The majors Jack Nicklaus coveted so much kept increasing in importance. And when the tide rose, the Masters ship remained floating above everything else. "The Masters is pretty magical, the stuff that people pull off there," says Miller. In 1976, the U.S. Open would finally be played in the Southeast, at Jones's home club, the Atlanta

Athletic Club. Five years after his death, Jones's dream would be realized. But the USGA was forty-two years too late. The other tournament in Georgia had already eclipsed it.

The club no longer had to address the question of when a black player would compete in the Masters, although the issues of race (and gender) at Augusta National and in golf continued to arise. Just days later, Lee Elder returned to Pensacola, the place where his Masters journey had begun twelve months earlier. In defense of his title, he finished a respectable tie for 10th. Elder would win three more times on the PGA Tour and play in another five Masters, his best finish a tie for 17th four years later. On Tour, his best year came in 1978 when he defeated Lee Trevino in a playoff at Milwaukee and birdied the final hole at Hartford to win by one. In 1979, he became the first black golfer to play on the U.S. Ryder Cup team.

In the dozen years following the 1975 Masters, Calvin Peete and Jim Thorpe were the only other black players to earn invitations to the tournament. For many reasons, the number of black golfers on Tour didn't rise; it declined. On December 30, 1975—eight-and-a-half months following the tournament—a black father and Thai mother welcomed a new infant into the world 2,060 miles away. Nineteen years later, a Masters invitation would be addressed to him, the next player who would truly challenge Jack Nicklaus's marks in the record book: Eldrick "Tiger" Woods, 6704 Teakwood Street, Cypress, California 90630.

SOME YEARS LATER, Frank Chirkinian wanted to re-create Nicklaus's putt on the 16th. It had taken on its own life. "Everybody tried that putt every year," says Roger Maltbie, who happened to hole a similar putt in the third round in 1987—but not at that moment Nicklaus did. They cut the hole in the same location, put a mark where the ball was, and had Nicklaus hit the same putt. Again, Tom Weiskopf watched. "I don't know how long he stood there, an hour, and hour-plus," says Weiskopf. "He never came close to making it. That's how hard that putt was."

It was another cruel reminder of how fate and fortune play a role in one's life. Weiskopf said that night he wouldn't let the finish of the 1975 Masters bother him, but it did. "A long time," responds Weiskopf when asked how long it took to get over that Sunday. "I don't know if I could really define it. A long time. Years. Years. It just never leaves you."

"For Weiskopf to be so close and always second to Nicklaus no matter what, that had to be a cross to carry I'm sure," says Scully.

"He hurt and suffered by never winning," says Wright. "For years he would talk about it ('75 Masters), how it killed him, really killed him."

Victory in the 1975 Masters could have meant a more confident, results-oriented Weiskopf. "Had he won, it might have propelled him to a few greater things," says Ed Sneed. Jack Nicklaus feel likewise: "It would have made a tremendous difference because he struggled to win."

Others aren't so sure. "I don't know if it would've changed a lot," says Maltbie. "I think he would've been driven by the same demons." Kaye Kessler agrees, "I'm not sure it would've been different, because Tom is Tom."

Later that summer, Weiskopf enacted some revenge on Nicklaus in a playoff for the Canadian Open, a tournament Nicklaus would finish runner-up in six times—the only significant event of the period that he never won. On the first playoff hole, Weiskopf had two feet for birdie and victory. He smiled, prompting Nicklaus to needle him, "What are you laughing at, you've got a lot of golf to play." Weiskopf said, "There's no chance I'm going to miss this one." And he didn't. "You'd have thought he'd inherited a billion dollars," says Wright, who remembers being with him that day. "It meant so much to him to beat Nicklaus."

After 1975, Weiskopf added only four more victories in his PGA Tour career. He was in the final-day hunt at a couple of U.S. Opens but never contended in another Masters. He shot a 63 in the opening round of the 1980 U.S. Open in Baltusrol, only for Nicklaus of all people to shoot the same number later in the day. For more than two decades, the trio of Miller, Weiskopf, and Nicklaus would be the only players to shoot 63 in a U.S. Open.

In 1978, he relocated his family from Columbus to Scottsdale, Arizona, a move he wished he'd made years earlier. Weiskopf thought about retiring several times until deciding to end it at the 1984 Western Open, the tournament in which he made his professional debut twenty years earlier and at which he won his final Tour title in 1982 with a birdie on the final hole. While he would play occasionally, his career as a touring professional was over at age forty-one. "In a way it ('75 Masters) probably had a lot to do with me retiring," says Weiskopf. "I just had to move on in a different way."

Instead, he took up a vocation that suited his personality to a tee—golf course design.

"I loved it. You're holding the purse strings in a lot of ways," says Weiskopf, who started in partnership with Jay Morrish in 1983 and went out on his own in 1994. He may not have been emotionally involved in every tournament he played, but he was in every course he designed. "It's lonely, which is nice, you're by yourself out there," he says, no longer having to answer to a flock of press every day.

Now one of the game's most respected golf course architects, the nickname Rembrandt is now a compliment.

Weiskopf has created more than sixty courses around the world in ten different countries, with celebrated layouts such as Troon, TPC Scottsdale, and Loch Lomond in Scotland. His biggest claim to fame was bringing the drivable par four back in vogue. "You hope you're leaving something of enjoyment for people in the future," he says.

Once he turned fifty in 1992, Weiskopf played the Champions Tour only sparingly. He won four times, including finally nabbing that elusive USGA championship—the 1995 U.S. Senior Open over

Nicklaus, after finishing second to him two years earlier when he couldn't make a putt. The victory at Congressional Country Club, where Weiskopf made the decision to turn professional three decades earlier, was made more special by Nicklaus returning greenside to congratulate him. "It means so much to me," Weiskopf told Nicklaus of his gesture.

The most significant milestone in Tom Weiskopf's life, however, didn't occur until the new millennium.

"January 2, 2000, I woke up, and on that day I quit drinking and started skiing all in the same day. And have never had a sip since," he says, having done it cold turkey without the assistance of any programs or rehabilitation clinics. "I do have a good constitution," he adds. "When I make up my mind, I can do just about anything that I'm capable of doing, good or bad."

Weiskopf wishes he would've stopped sooner. It was a contributing factor in the demise of his first marriage in the late-1990s. Now, he is able to deal with people and situations much easier.

"In a lot of ways, he's not the person that everybody used to know," says Ed Sneed. Chris Roderick, a long-time friend and business partner concurs, "He's more at peace with himself."

"Why me?" is no longer asked as frequently. A mellower Weiskopf splits his time between Scottsdale and Bozeman, Montana—re-married in 2007 to his new wife Laurie, sober, and comfortable with his life and himself.

"Things don't bother me like they used to," he says. Not even his place in the game.

Critics panned him as the biggest waste of talent the game had ever seen. If you separate perception from the reality of his achievements, Tom Weiskopf's record is quite remarkable. At the end of 2013, just fifty players in the game's history had more PGA Tour wins than Weiskopf and his sixteen titles. He won a major championship—something only 210 different players had achieved in 154 years. In

1981, he became the fourth player to pass the $2 million career earnings mark; and when he decided to quit playing full-time in 1984, he stood seventh on the all-time career money winners list.

Sixty-eight top-three finishes in his career stack up to the tallies of others who came just after—all whom played longer and are in the World Golf Hall of Fame: Ben Crenshaw (60), Lanny Wadkins (57), Curtis Strange (50), Nick Price (50), Hubert Green (40), and Larry Nelson (30). Even Johnny Miller totaled just 51. Maybe some of those players got more out of their careers than Weiskopf, but if not for that putt by Nicklaus, is there any doubt that Tom Weiskopf would be in the Hall of Fame?

And really, should one putt, one major win that didn't happen, keep someone out when his record and contributions to the game say otherwise.

Weiskopf had a significant influence on the modern game. His swing was emulated by youngsters such as Vijay Singh and Ernie Els. His name is still brought up in any conversation that leads off, "the best I ever saw..." If the Hall of Fame is truly for people who've succeeded at the highest level and contributed to their sport, then Weiskopf's name should be called.

"It doesn't mean that much to me," he says of the recognition. "It would mean a lot more to some people I could think about who were instrumental in various ways. I would be honored, but I don't expect it."

Weiskopf had a career others would dream of. Was he really an underachiever? "I've read stuff that people have said," admits Weiskopf. "Do I know that I was an extremely talented guy? Yes. Was I an emotional guy? Of course I was. That was just me. That was my makeup. I can't change the past. The future's always a mystery. All that's important is right now."

Jack Nicklaus says Weiskopf was "probably as talented a golfer as I've ever seen. Maybe he wasn't in the right place, the right time, to really have the reward I thought his talent deserved."

"If only I could be recycled," Weiskopf says. "There's one problem with playing this game of golf: when you finally figure it out you're too old to play it."

For a long time, Weiskopf thought about the 1975 Masters constantly. Now, it's only when early April rolls around or when someone asks him about the subject. "Now you see, Gil, I hadn't thought about those last four holes at Augusta until you asked me those questions today," he says while overlooking the finishing hole at Silverleaf, one of his award-winning designs in Scottsdale.

Weiskopf remembers little of the great shots he struck during the week. Instead, only five holes on Sunday stick in his head: 11, 15, 16, 17, and 18.

Would winning that Masters have changed his life? "I'm sure," says Weiskopf before hedging his answer. "But maybe not. Maybe not."

Asked to describe his lasting memories from the 1975 Masters, Weiskopf ponders to find the words: "Haunted comes to me first. Flashback. For years, I would remember those holes. I will never forget that. But there's other memories, too, just as hurtful that might not be related to golf. But that's all part of the journey that we're on."

Each year, Weiskopf sits down and watches the tournament on television. From 1984 to 1996, Weiskopf moonlighted as a commentator for CBS at the Masters. He hasn't been back to Augusta National since the final one he worked.

In 1986, he uttered one of the most honest comments in golf television history. As Nicklaus went through his pre-shot routine on the 16th tee during his final-nine charge, a rookie announcer named Jim Nantz brought in Weiskopf to ask him what was going through Nicklaus's mind. Weiskopf replied, "If I knew the way he thought, I would have won this tournament."

JUST AS NICKLAUS did after his first Masters appearance, Curtis Strange followed up his with a win in the prestigious North & South Amateur in Pinehurst four weeks later by defeating George Burns in the 36-hole final, 2 up. Strange felt like he became a better player from his experience at Augusta and playing with Nicklaus, a memory as clear today as in 1975. He continued his stellar amateur play and returned to the Masters in 1976 to capture low amateur honors, finishing tied for 15th. Strange went on to become the leading American player in the 1980s. Frequently, his mind wanders back to the 1985 Masters, a tournament in which he had shot 80 in the first round but by the 10th tee on Sunday was seven under and holding a four-shot lead with nine to play. Strange then got ahead of himself and going too fast. He hit shots in the water on holes 13 and 15. "I felt so bad afterwards I knew I didn't want to ever do that again," says Strange. "That hurt for a long time." Always keeping that day in the back of his mind, Strange used that experience to his advantage, particularly at the 1988 and 1989 U.S. Open, when he fulfilled another of his father's dreams, winning the national championship on Father's Day weekend.

Gary Koch turned professional later that year and won six times in his career. Roger Maltbie learned from Johnny Miller that "you can't make too many birdies." The rookie won back-to-back starts in July and drove down Magnolia Lane for the first time in 1976. "It was everything I thought it might be and more," he says. "One of the great memories of my life." In the 1987 Masters, Maltbie led at the halfway point only to finish one shot out of a playoff.

Gary Player kept jetting around the world, returning to play at Augusta each year until 2009 for his record fifty-second Masters start. He added one final major championship at the 1978 Masters, birdying seven of the last ten holes when no one paid him any attention.

Three weeks after the 1975 Masters, Arnold Palmer won the Spanish Open—his last win on a regular tour anywhere. Palmer would never seriously contend in another major championship on the weekend. Four years later, he turned fifty and was the pied piper of the new Champions Tour. Year after year, he returned to Augusta

National, staying in the limelight for a record fifty consecutive Masters until 2004.

In New Orleans five weeks later, Billy Casper captured the last of his fifty-one career PGA Tour wins. He still goes back each April for the Masters Club dinner. "It hasn't changed in all those years," he says. "You still have the same feeling when you turn onto Magnolia Lane."

Of all the people to have heartbreak befall them at the Masters since Weiskopf, the cruelest may have happened to, of all people, Ed Sneed. With three holes to play in 1979, he led by three shots. Without hitting a single shot that he considered poor, Sneed bogeyed 16, 17, and 18. He lost in a playoff to Fuzzy Zoeller.

"We sort of commiserated on it," says Sneed of his bond with Weiskopf's Augusta misfortunes. He went through the same emotions, received the same types of letters from President Ford, Ben Hogan, and complete strangers. "It's a tough thing to go through," says Sneed. "You can be a little overly philosophical about it. It is not a life and death situation. It is not a tragedy. At the same time, you never forget those things. You always wish you could've won."

Friday, June 27, 1975, remains a date three headliners from the Masters two-and-a-half months earlier will never forget. It had been overcast during the second round of the Western Open at Butler National Golf Club just west of Chicago before a storm suddenly appeared. The grouping of Bob Dickson, Tony Jacklin, and Bobby Nichols was playing the 4th hole along Teal Lake. On the other side was the 13th hole where Mike Fetchick, Jerry Heard, and Lee Trevino were. Just after 4:00 p.m., a bolt of lightning struck around the water.

"It knocked me to the ground," says Nichols. Startled, he was able to run 100 yards to a tent along with the group's standard bearer, who had a heavy metal standard ripped from his hands. Officials asked him if he was okay, but his breath smelled like burnt wire. With a headache and burns on his head, he was taken to the hospital where the doctor on call kept him forty-eight hours for observation. Nichols felt no lasting physical effects, but that first-round lead at the Masters would be his last ever on the PGA Tour and the tie for 4th his last top-five finish. He never won again. Nichols stayed at Firestone until the company sold the club in 1980. In a decade-and-a-half on the Champions Tour, he won once and eventually settled at Fiddlesticks Country Club in Ft. Myers, Florida. As a former major champion, he still enjoys returning each year to the Masters as an honorary invitee.

Across the lake, Lee Trevino was sitting by the water under an umbrella, waiting for the storm to pass, when he was struck. Trevino was also admitted to the hospital and held overnight for observation, but soon after leaving, immense back pains began. He conferred with a specialist, who believed fluid around his discs had been burnt by the electrical shock, and had surgery in late 1976. That decision probably saved his career. He won another nine times after 1975, including one more major championship at the 1984 PGA. Once he turned fifty, he dominated the Champions Tour in the first half of the 1990s with twenty-nine victories. But he would never contend in another Masters, that tie for 10th in 1975 remaining his best finish. He never completed the career Grand Slam and is the only player in the modern era to win the U.S. Open, British Open, and PGA and not the Masters. Long after he retired, Trevino would wonder what his career would've been like if he had learned the game somewhere other than the public tracks in Texas and developed a swing like Nicklaus or Weiskopf or Miller—a swing in his mind that could have won that tournament in Augusta, Georgia.

Jerry Heard had been beside Trevino. When the bolt struck, it went up the umbrella he was leaning against, right into his groin where the tip had been resting. Of the three, Heard was the only one who wasn't held for observation at the hospital. When play resumed the next day, Heard actually completed his round with a 74 and went on to finish tied for 4th. Little did he realize the strike would affect him the most. Once one of the young guns, Heard's career was virtually over. "Until I got hit by lightning, I never had a problem with my golf game," says Heard, who suffered severe back pain from a ruptured disk. "When I got hit by lightning, that shut me down for a while. I couldn't swing." He could no longer stay behind the ball to fade it and managed only one more win by slapping a hook around and holing putts in Atlanta in 1978. Unlike Trevino, he put off surgery for five years. "That was the biggest mistake I made," he says. "Looking back I should've been cut on, gotten well, and continued on. I quit way too early." Off the Tour by 1983, Heard now owns Silverthorn Country Club in Brooksville, Florida, where his body still feels the aftereffects four decades later.

For Heard, one of the most frustrating effects of that strike has been the crazy, vivid dreams he experiences. Heard gives one example: "I'm on the last hole playing with Ray Floyd. It's uphill. The pin's back on the left. It's a perfect 9-iron shot, and I'm going to win the tournament. I look down, and there's a trailer hitch right over my ball. Where'd that come from? I can't hit this ball with a trailer hitch over it. That's the kind of dreams I have. No matter what happens, I never get to win in my dreams.

"In John's dreams, probably, he's holed it out."

YEARS LATER, John Miller finds reliving his 276th stroke too tough. "I can't watch almost," he says of that final birdie putt that still doesn't go in. Had it, the fate of Johnny Miller's golf career may have been reversed. Part of Johnny Miller feels if he had won, maybe he would have been spurred to work a little harder at golf, and maybe his passion and resolve would have been rekindled as both a U.S. Open and Masters champion.

Instead on that Sunday night, Johnny Miller's time as golf's best player came to an end. "I started to get a little burned out around the middle of '75, right after the Masters," says Miller. "Maybe that Masters took something out of me." It was the zenith of his career. Going forward, there was no more talk about being the game's best player. No more talk about being better than Jack Nicklaus. Miller's reign as golf's "it" player was nearing its end.

His next close call at a major came at the British Open in July. Standing on the 72nd tee at Carnoustie one shot back, Miller hit his drive at the edge of a right fairway bunker, thinking the wind would carry it back in the fairway. Only it didn't, instead landing right in that bunker. Still aggressive, Miller tried to hit a 6-iron out of the pot bunker, but it hit the top of the lip and fell back in. Miller tried the same shot, this time extracting it toward the left side of the green. He made bogey and finished tied for 3rd, one shot out of a playoff for the second time in three majors. Since then, the hazard has been known as "Johnny Miller's bunker." He won only one more tournament in 1975 successfully defending the Kaiser tournament on his home course at Silverado that fall.

A series of events had catapulted Miller to the top of the golfing world in 1973, and another series would precipitate his downfall. It began just after the Masters with a decision Miller calls, "the biggest mistake I ever made in golf." Nicklaus, Weiskopf, and Miller (and Watson, too) had been carrying the Kelly green bags of MacGregor in the 1975 Masters. "The Greatest Name in Golf" was the company's slogan. They were contracted to play MacGregor irons and the Tourney golf ball. Miller's agent Ed Barner sold him on the idea that although the three biggest names in golf were all with MacGregor, the manufacturer wasn't big enough to properly utilize all three players. So Barner pursued other club deals, and later in the year while Nicklaus and Weiskopf remained with MacGregor, Miller signed a lucrative endorsement with Wilson. "I dropped my magical Tommy Armour irons and Tommy Armour woods and went to these crappy Wilson clubs," says Miller, who had to play a Wilson Staff ball he didn't like either. "That adjustment was like a shock to the nervous system."

At the same time, Miller's putting stroke, which hadn't been totally smooth at the Masters, was getting increasingly yippy. He won the 1976 British Open at Royal Birkdale by painting his wife's red nail polish on top of his putter. That allowed him to concentrate on the red dot going back and through at the same speed. He managed a total of three wins in 1976, but the nail polish trick didn't last long. The stabbiness in his stroke and rebound of the putter resurfaced.

A millionaire by now, Miller longed to be home. In Napa, he had purchased a 100-acre ranch and put all his efforts into restoring the property. "I couldn't believe how much I loved it," says Miller of his work. "I guess the pioneer part of me came out." Even ranching had passed golf in importance, and it showed. Miller returned to the Tour much bulkier in 1977 and couldn't swing the club like he used to. For the first time ever, he was in a slump. After six consecutive years in the top-twenty on the money list, he finished 48th. And it got worse. In 1978, he fell to 112th and, in his words, was "hitting it like a popcorn machine."

His press became a little more unfavorable. One of the most scathing stories came in the November 7, 1978 issue of *Esquire*. There on the cover was the line "Golf Johnny Miller: The Selling of a Loser."

"It was almost a relief to go into that slump," says Miller, who lost his Wilson contract in 1979 because he didn't play enough events. With five children now at home (and a sixth to arrive in 1980) and some money saved up, Miller thought about retiring. Then, a realization struck him. "It's not so much what you accomplish in life that matters as it is what you overcome that proves who you are," says Miller, who had never had to overcome anything. "Now the first thing that goes wrong, I'm just going to give up."

So Miller decided to work a little harder and rededicate himself. Even Jack Nicklaus offered words of encouragement. In the fall of 1979, Miller shot a 63—his lowest round in three years—and lost in a playoff to Tom Watson in the Hall of Fame Classic at Pinehurst. After three winless seasons, he triumphed again in 1980—the first of five victories in the next four years. He had one more close call at the Masters, finishing second in 1981 which was the first year in which the greens were bentgrass. "If they would have been bentgrass (in 1970s), I would have had more chances to win no doubt about it," he says. At age forty-seven, Miller won as a grandfather at the Pebble Beach National Pro-Am in 1994. That came after he'd all but given up playing competitively in 1990 to serve as NBC Sports' golf analyst. As of 2014, it was a position that he'd held longer than his playing career, and one that earned him eight Emmy nominations and critical praise for his candor and insight.

Miller reached the World Golf Hall of Fame in 1998, the same year the boy who watched him at the 1973 British Open was inducted—Nick Faldo. Soon after the 1975 Masters, Faldo turned professional. He earned his first Masters invitation in 1979 and went on to win three green jackets in 1989, 1990, and 1996.

Miller remains good friends with Nicklaus. "Even to this day we're like younger brother, older brother," says Miller. Maybe Nicklaus is looking for the younger brother he never had; maybe Miller is longing for the older brother he lost. "He needles me," Miller continues. "There's something about the two of us. If I lived near him, we'd probably be best friends, fishing and hunting and messing around together. There's something there. I haven't figured it out. Sort of like Forrest Gump, peas and carrots."

When Miller runs into Weiskopf on occasion, a mutual respect surfaces. They were two players who in retrospect were more similar to each other than to Nicklaus. They were seekers, players whose flames burned too bright to last long, but whose brightness still cast a shadow over the game today.

"I don't think the Masters has ever had three guys at the very top of their game go down the wire like that," says Miller. "That's why that tournament is so revered. It doesn't get a lot better than that. To be included, I get a thrill that people still talk about that Masters."

"YOU CAN NOW, if you will, go to the blackboard and write 100 times, 'Jack Nicklaus is the greatest golfer in the world'," wrote Jim Murray in Monday's *Los Angeles Times*.

Nicklaus, however, had little time to read or celebrate. In victory or defeat, the schedule had been set. Monday morning, he was off to Columbus for a little work on Muirfield Village. From there, he was flying to Birmingham, Alabama, for another site visit. He was designing a new private course there for a man named Hall Thompson. It would be called Shoal Creek. Then, he would be home for the weekend in Florida before his next competitive stop at the Tournament of Champions in California. After that, some fishing in Mexico was on the calendar before going back to Columbus again.

Once again, he stood as the undisputed king of golf. His confidence was bolstered; the psyches of his rivals were dented—some beyond repair. It was the first time in his career that he won three consecutive starts. This was the best golf of his life, and preparations began immediately for the next major in ten weeks—the U.S. Open at Medinah Country Club outside Chicago.

"It's a possibility, not a probability," said Nicklaus of the Grand Slam. "One thing, there were seventy-six who could do it at the start of the week and now there's one." He had said he wanted to get some of that '72 talk going again, and for the next two months he got his wish. Nicklaus went to the Open feeling confident, but once there he didn't play particularly well. Going into the final round, he was seven shots behind. On the final day, he teed off two hours in front of the final group with, of all people, Arnold Palmer, the last man to come from that far behind and win. Nicklaus turned it around. By the time he walked on the 16th tee, he was two under for the round and just a shot out of the lead. Then, similar to four years earlier at the British Open, his Grand Slam aspirations dissipated on the final three holes. Unable to consistently fade the ball all week, Nicklaus tried to force a cut on a dogleg-left par four, but he pull-hooked it left into the woods. He bogeyed the final three holes to finish tied for 7th, two shots out of the Lou Graham/John Mahaffey playoff. Three pars would have given him the outright victory. "That absolutely killed me," he says.

At the British Open in July, he began the final round four shots out of the lead. As the field fought blustery conditions, he soon climbed up the leaderboard. Unlike at the Masters, the par-three 16th hole at Carnoustie was unkind, making bogey. Standing on the 17th tee, he thought to himself a birdie on one of the final two holes could be good enough to win. He nearly holed a chip shot on the 17th and couldn't get close enough for a good birdie look on the 18th. He was right. His tie for 3rd was just one shot out of another playoff. "I didn't finish it properly," he says.

In August, he won the PGA Championship at Firestone by two shots over Bruce Crampton and three over Weiskopf. Roger Maltbie, starting in his very first major championship, was grouped with Nicklaus in the first two rounds. Firestone was the hardest course he'd ever seen, so when he saw a scoreboard posting Ed Dougherty at six under, Maltbie was flabbergasted. Nicklaus looked at him and said, "It doesn't matter. Four under par will win." And that's what Nicklaus finished on.

Nicklaus was only three shots from a possible Grand Slam in 1975—stroke-wise, no one has come closer since then. The Player of the Year with five victories, he would never again come close to winning all four majors in a year. He would never win three tournaments in a row again. And he would never play golf as well as he did in April 1975.

The following year, the superstitious Nicklaus wore the same Sunday outfit in the Masters in a bid to win back-to-back titles. He shot a pair of 73s on the weekend and was unable to keep up with Raymond Floyd's blistering 271 total that tied Nicklaus's tournament record set in 1965. The tie for 3rd marked Nicklaus's thirteenth consecutive top-ten finish in a major championship—still the all-time record.

The man who wound up challenging Nicklaus in the later part of his career wouldn't be Miller or Weiskopf, but the person who played with Nicklaus that final day in 1975. Tom Watson may have been the forgotten figure among the final four at the Masters, but a victory three months later in the British Open at Carnoustie boosted his confidence even more and propelled him on a remarkable run over the next decade. "I think Watson was a young guy who came along with blinders who just wanted to beat everybody and didn't care who was on the sideline," says Nicklaus. Watson combined his high-ball flight with a short game that was one of the best in golf. Nearly ten years younger than Nicklaus, their tussles resembled Nicklaus's rivalry with Palmer, only with the roles reversed. Watson would get the better of Nicklaus at the 1977 Masters, 1977 British Open, 1981 Masters, and 1982 U.S. Open with an incredible chip-in on the 71st hole at Pebble Beach.

When some Augusta National caddies didn't show up for a rain-delay restart in 1982, Masters participants had their opening to bring their own caddies the next year. So Nicklaus let Jack Nicklaus II start carrying his bag. Eleven years after walking all 18 holes on Sunday as a thirteen-year-old to see his dad win Masters number five, he was inside the ropes to witness number six. At age forty-six, Nicklaus produced a spine-tingling back-nine 30 to come from behind and capture his eighteenth, and final, professional major at the 1986 Masters. It was unlike in 1975 or any other win. Instead of controlling his emotions, he rode the high of the moment throughout the second nine. No longer in his prime, he had to recall the player he had been in 1975. This time, all the competitors around him melted under the pressure of playing for a Masters title with the Nicklaus name on the leaderboard. It was also the only Masters other than his first in 1959 that his mother and sister attended.

In 2001, Nicklaus became only the second Masters champion to become a member of the Augusta National Golf Club, joining Arnold Palmer. Nicklaus played in his last Masters in 2005 with little pomp and circumstance, his final hole actually being the 9th hole on a Saturday morning because of weather delays. In 2010, he joined Palmer as an honorary starter. Gary Player made it a threesome in 2012.

"I go back and look at the record and say, 'That wasn't too bad'," said Nicklaus. "And I don't mean that in a braggy sort of way. But I was very proud of that. But it was fun. I enjoyed it. I enjoyed playing the game for the game. And I enjoyed getting better to get better. I enjoyed the work that I put into it to get something out of it. And I think that anybody who's good at something enjoys that. He better enjoy it, if you don't you're not going to be around long."

Sitting in his office thirty-six years later, Nicklaus enjoys reminiscing. "1975 was fun because I was under control of my golf game," he says. "Weiskopf was in control of his game, and Miller was in control of his game. It was not an event where we were giving stuff away. It was each of us taking the challenge of the next guy, and that was fun being on both the receiving end and giving end. Of course, obviously, I ended up giving more to them at the end than receiving."

A bit of frustration seeps into the air. Nicklaus competed in forty-five Masters, played 163 competitive rounds, and hit 11,733 shots. He can't remember them all, and even some important ones slip from his mind occasionally as a septuagenarian. The feeling of that final day of the 1975 Masters is still present. "It was probably the most exciting and best tournament and most fun I had finishing a golf tournament," he says.

Nobody seeks to emulate Bobby Jones today. It's Jack Nicklaus who's the all-around benchmark. Emulating his respect for his game, his sportsmanship, and his record are the goals of aspiring golfers. He took the best shots from golf's golden generation—Palmer, Casper, Trevino, Watson, Miller, Weiskopf, and others—but no one could dislodge him from the throne.

Nicklaus's affair with Jones, the Masters, and golf began with that simple invitation mailed to his parents' house in 1959. It's not forgotten. Today it resides in the Jack Nicklaus Museum on the campus of Ohio State University in Columbus, along with the clubs, trophies, medal, and green shirt from the 1975 Masters.

1975 MASTERS TOURNAMENT

	RD 1	RD 2	RD 3	RD 4	TOTAL	TO PAR
1. Jack Nicklaus	68	67	73	68	276	−12
2. Johnny Miller	75	71	65	66	277	−11
Tom Weiskopf	69	72	66	70	277	−11
4. Hale Irwin	73	74	71	64	282	−6
Bobby Nichols	67	74	72	69	282	−6
6. Billy Casper	70	70	73	70	283	−5
7. Dave Hill	75	71	70	68	284	−4
8. Hubert Green	74	71	70	70	285	−3
Tom Watson	70	70	72	73	285	−3
10. Tom Kite	72	74	71	69	286	−2
J.C. Snead	69	72	75	70	286	−2
Lee Trevino	71	70	74	71	286	−2
13. Larry Ziegler	71	73	74	69	287	−1
Arnold Palmer	69	71	75	72	287	−1
15. Bobby Cole	73	71	73	71	288	E
Rod Curl	72	70	76	70	288	E
Bruce Devlin	72	70	76	70	288	E
Allen Miller	68	75	72	73	288	E
Art Wall	72	74	72	70	288	E
20. Bud Allen	73	69	73	74	289	+1
Ralph Johnston	74	73	69	73	289	+1
22. Hugh Baiocchi	76	72	72	70	290	+2
Pat Fitzsimons	73	68	79	70	290	+2
Gene Littler	72	72	72	74	290	+2

Graham Marsh	75	70	74	71	290	+2
26. Miller Barber	74	72	72	73	291	+3
Maurice Bembridge	75	72	75	69	291	+3
Jerry Heard	71	75	72	73	291	+3
Dave Stockton	72	72	73	74	291	+3
30. George Burns (a)	72	72	76	72	292	+4
Ben Crenshaw	72	71	75	74	292	+4
Forrest Fezler	76	71	71	74	292	+4
Raymond Floyd	72	73	79	68	292	+4
Gary Player	72	74	73	73	292	+4
Victor Regalado	76	72	72	72	292	+4
Bert Yancey	74	71	74	73	292	+4
37. Jerry Pate (a)	71	75	78	69	293	+5
38. Tommy Aaron	71	75	76	72	294	+6
Gary Groh	72	76	71	75	294	+6
40. Charles Coody	72	75	75	73	295	+7
Lou Graham	72	72	77	74	295	+7
42. Bob Murphy	70	72	80	74	296	+8
43. Homero Blancas	72	69	79	77	297	+9
Lu Liang-Huan	73	74	78	72	297	+9
Masashi Ozaki	73	73	83	68	297	+9
46. Richie Karl	72	75	79	76	302	+14
mc Gay Brewer	77	72			149	
Roberto De Vicenzo	74	75			149	
Mac McLendon	71	78			149	
Mike Reasor	74	75			149	
Phil Rodgers	77	72			149	
Chi Chi Rodriguez	74	75			149	
Frank Beard	76	74			150	
Bob Charles	76	74			150	
Jim Colbert	75	75			150	
Terry Diehl	72	78			150	
Al Geiberger	79	71			150	
Ed Sneed	74	76			150	
Isao Aoki	75	76			151	

Dale Hayes	77	74	151
Tony Jacklin	77	74	151
Gary Koch (a)	77	74	151
Peter Oosterhuis	79	72	151
George Archer	80	72	152
Lee Elder	74	78	152
Doug Ford	78	74	152
John Mahaffey	77	75	152
Curtis Strange (a)	75	77	152
Bob Goalby	81	72	153
Dick Siderowf (a)	75	78	153
John Grace (a)	79	75	154
Bruce Crampton	76	79	155
Craig Stadler (a)	80	76	156
Bob Menne	76	82	158
Dan Sikes	76	82	158
Sam Snead	71	w/d	

HOLE-BY-HOLE SCORES OF TOP-THREE PLAYERS

Jack Nicklaus

HOLE	1	2	3	4	5	6	7	8	9	OUT	10	11	12	13	14	15	16	17	18	IN	TOTAL
PAR	4	5	4	3	4	3	4	5	4	36	4	4	3	5	4	5	3	4	4	36	72
ROUND 1	4	4	3	3	4	3	4	5	4	34	4	4	3	4	4	4	3	4	4	34	68
ROUND 2	4	5	4	3	4	2	3	5	4	34	4	3	2	4	4	4	3	4	5	33	67
ROUND 3	5	4	4	3	4	3	4	5	5	37	4	5	2	5	4	5	3	4	4	36	73
ROUND 4	5	4	3	3	3	3	4	5	3	33	4	4	3	5	5	4	2	4	4	35	68

Johnny Miller

HOLE	1	2	3	4	5	6	7	8	9	OUT	10	11	12	13	14	15	16	17	18	IN	TOTAL
PAR	4	5	4	3	4	3	4	5	4	36	4	4	3	5	4	5	3	4	4	36	72
ROUND 1	5	5	5	4	4	2	5	4	4	38	4	4	3	5	4	5	3	5	4	37	75
ROUND 2	4	4	4	3	4	4	4	4	4	35	4	4	4	4	4	4	3	4	5	36	71
ROUND 3	4	4	3	2	3	2	3	5	4	30	4	4	3	4	4	5	3	4	4	35	65
ROUND 4	4	4	5	2	4	2	4	4	3	32	4	5	3	4	4	4	3	3	4	34	66

Tom Weiskopf

HOLE	1	2	3	4	5	6	7	8	9	OUT	10	11	12	13	14	15	16	17	18	IN	TOTAL
PAR	4	5	4	3	4	3	4	5	4	36	4	4	3	5	4	5	3	4	4	36	72
ROUND 1	4	4	4	3	4	3	4	4	4	34	4	4	3	4	4	4	3	4	5	35	69
ROUND 2	5	4	4	3	4	2	3	5	4	34	4	4	3	6	4	6	3	4	4	38	72
ROUND 3	4	4	5	3	4	2	4	4	4	34	3	4	3	4	4	5	2	4	3	32	66
ROUND 4	4	5	3	3	4	2	4	5	4	34	4	5	3	5	3	4	4	4	4	36	70

A NOTE ON SOURCES
AND BIBLIOGRAPHY

In writing this book, I was fortunate to have such a wide variety of sources to use. I was able to watch the live broadcast of the final two rounds. I was able to speak with the actual participants. I was able to delve into endless newspaper clipping and magazine articles.

At times, I nearly had the feeling that there was too much material because the more you research, the more things you discover that don't match. In any instances that memories and/or reports varied, I carefully weighed the research and evidence before coming to any conclusions, if I came to one at all.

Being able to talk with so many people involved with the game at that time presented another problem: how to distinguish between present-day quotes and those of almost four decades ago. To delineate between them, I have written quotes in two different tenses. Any quotation that is preceded or followed by a verb in the present tense is from a personal interview I conducted. Those associated with a verb in the past tense come from sources during that period of time.

BOOKS

Augusta National Golf Club. *Masters: The First Forty One Years*. Augusta, Ga.: Augusta National Golf Club, 1978.

Barkow, Al. *Golf's Golden Grind: The History of the Tour*. New York: Harcourt Brace Jovanovich, 1974.

————. *The Golden Era of Golf: How America Rose To Dominate The Old Scots Game*. New York: Thomas Dunne Books, 2000.

Bisher, Furman. *The Masters & Augusta Revisted: An Intimate View*. Birmingham, Ala.: Oxmoor House, 1976.

Byrdy, Stan. *The Augusta National Golf Club: Alister MacKenzie's Masterpiece*. Ann Arbor, Mich.: Sports Media Group, 2005.

Clayton, Ward. *Men on the Bag: The Caddies of Augusta National*. Ann Arbor, Mich.: Sports Media Group, 2004.

D'Antonio, Michael. *Tour '72: Nicklaus, Palmer, Player, Trevino. The Story of One Great Season*. New York: Hyperion, 2002.

Delaney, Tim and Tim Madigan. *The Sociology of Sports: An Introduction*. Jefferson, N.C.: McFarland, 2009.

Editors of *Golf Magazine. Golf Magazine's Encyclopedia of Golf: The Complete Reference*. 2nd ed. New York: Harper Collins Publishers, 1993.

Flaherty, Tom. *The Masters: The Story of Golf's Greatest Tournament*. New York: Holt, Rinehart and Winston, 1961.

Hobbs, Michael with Peter Alliss. *Golf To Remember*. Garden City, N.Y.: Doubleday & Company, 1978.

Jones Jr., Robert T. *Golf Is My Game*. New York: Doubleday, 1960.

Jones Jr., Robert T. *Spectator Suggestions for the Masters Tournament*. 1975 ed. Augusta, Ga.: Augusta National Golf Club, 1975.

Kirsch, George B. *Golf In America*. Champaign, Ill.: University of Illinois, 2009.

Lazarus, Adam and Steve Schlossman. *Chasing Greatness: Johnny Miller, Arnold Palmer, and the Miracle at Oakmont*. New York: New American Library, 2010.

MacKenzie, Alister. *The Spirit of St. Andrews*. Chelsea, Mich.: Sleeping Bear Press, 1995.

McCormack, Mark. *The World of Professional Golf, Mark H. McCormack's Golf Annual 1976*. New York: Antheneum, 1976.

McDaniel, Pete. *Uneven Lies: The Heroic Story of African-Americans in Golf*. Greenwich, Conn.: The American Golfer, 2000.

Nicklaus, Jack with Ken Bowden. *Golf My Way*. New York: Simon and Schuster Paperbacks, 2005.

———. *My Most Memorable Shots in the Majors*. Trumbull, Conn.: Golf Digest, 1988.

———. *My Golden Lessons*. New York: Simon and Schuster, 2002.

———. *My Story*. New York: Simon and Schuster Paperbacks, 2007

Nicklaus, Jack with Herbert Warren Wind. *The Greatest Game of All: My Life in Golf*. New York: Simon and Schuster, 1969.

O'Connor, Ian. *Arnie & Jack: Palmer, Nicklaus, and Golf's Greatest Rivalry*. Boston: Houghton Mifflin Co, 2008.

Owen, David. *The Making of The Masters*. New York: Simon & Schuster Paperbacks, 2003.

Peper, George, ed. *Golf In America: The First One Hundred Years*. New York: Abradale Press, 1994.

Post, Peggy, et. al. *Emily Post's Etiquette*. 16th ed. New York: William Morrow, 1997.

————. *Emily Post's Etiquette: Manners For A New World*. 18th ed. New York: William Morrow, 2011.

Price, Charles. *A Golf Story: Bobby Jones, Augusta National, and the Masters Tournament*. New York: Antheneum, 1986.

Roberts, Clifford. *The Story of Augusta National Golf Club*. Garden City, N.Y.: Doubleday, 1976.

Roberts, Jimmy. *Breaking The Slump*. New York: Harper Collins, 2009.

Sampson, Curt. *The Masters: Golf, Money, and Power in Augusta, Georgia*. New York: Villard, 1999.

Shipnuck, Alan. *The Battle for Augusta National: Hootie, Martha, and the Masters of the Universe*. New York: Simon & Schuster, 2004

Sifford, Charlie, and James Gullo. *Just Let Me Play*. New York: British American, 1992.

Sinnette, Calvin H. *Forbidden Fairways: African Americans and the Game of Golf*. Chelsea, Mich.: Sleeping Bear Press, 1998.

Sounes, Howard. *The Wicked Game: Arnold Palmer, Jack Nicklaus, Tiger Woods, and the Story of Modern Golf*. New York: William Morrow, 2004.

Taylor, Dawson. *The Masters: An Illustrated History*. 3rd ed. New York: A.S. Barnes & Co., 1981.

Trevino, Lee and Sam Blair. *They Call Me Super Mex*. New York: Random House, 1982.

Wexler, Daniel. *The Book of Golfers: A Biographical History of the Royal & Ancient Game*. Ann Arbor, Mich.: Sports Media Group, 2005.

Wright, Ben with Michael Patrick Shields. *Good Bounces & Bad Lies*. Chelsea, Mich.: Sleeping Bear Press, 1999.

PRESS GUIDES

European Tour Media Guide
Masters Media Guide
(British) Open Championship Media Guide
PGA of America Media Guide
PGA Tour Media Guide
USGA Media Guide
U.S. Open Almanac
USGA Record Book, 1895–1959, 1960–1980, 1981–1990, 1991–1995, 1996–2000, 2001–2005

PERSONAL INTERVIEWS

James Black, Billy Casper, Brandel Chamblee, Earnie Ellison, Nick Faldo, Jerry Heard, Kaye Kessler, Bob Kletcke, Gary Koch, John Mahaffey, Roger Maltbie,

Johnny Miller, Bob Murphy, Bobby Nichols, Barbara Nicklaus, Jack Nicklaus, Peter Oosterhuis, Chris Roderick, Vin Scully, Ed Sneed, Curtis Strange, Tom Weiskopf, Chuck Will, Ben Wright.

TELEVISION/FILM

ABC World News

CBS Evening News

"Feherty." With David Feherty, Jack Nicklaus. Golf Channel. 26 Feb. 2013.

"Jim Nantz Remembers Augusta: The 1975 Masters." Prod. and dir. Chris Svendsen. CBS. 10 April 2011.

Masters films. 1960, 1961, 1962, 1963, 1964, 1965, 1966, 1967, 1968, 1969, 1970, 1971, 1972, 1973, 1974, 1975, 1976.

NBC Nightly News

Tournament Broadcast, 1975 Masters, CBS. 12–13 April 1975.

NEWSPAPERS

Atlanta Constitution

Atlanta Journal Constitution

Augusta Chronicle

Boston Globe

Charleston (S.C.) News and Courier

Charlotte Observer

Charlotte News

Chicago Tribune

Christian Science Monitor

Columbus (Ohio) Citizen-Journal

Columbus (Ohio) Dispatch

Dallas Morning News

Daytona Beach Morning Journal

Florence (Ala.) Times-Daily

Fort Lauderdale Sun-Sentinel

Fort Myers News-Press

Greenville (S.C.) News

Hartford Courant

Irish Independent

Lakeland (Fla.) Ledger

Lexington (N.C.) Dispatch

Los Angeles Times

Miami Herald

Montreal Gazette

Nashville Tennessean
New York Times
New York Post
North County (Calif.) Times
Palm Beach Post
Paterson (N.J.) News
Pittsburgh Post-Gazette
Raleigh News and Observer
Reading (Penn.) Eagle
Rome (Ga.) News-Tribune
Sacramento Bee
Salt Lake Tribune
San Francisco Chronicle
Sarasota (Fla.) Herald Tribune
The Scotsman
St. Petersburg Times
The Times of London
USA Today
Wall Street Journal
Washington City Paper
Washington Post

MAGAZINES

The American Golfer
Colorado Avid Golfer
Ebony
The Economist
Esquire
Golf Digest
Golf Illustrated
Golf Journal
Golf Magazine
Golf World
Golfweek
Jet
Life
Newsweek
New Yorker
People
Saturday Evening Post
Sport

Sporting News
Sports Illustrated
Time

WEBSITES

asap.com
augusta.com
bbc.co.uk
espn.com
fordlibrarymuseum.gov
golf.com
golfchannel.com
golfdigest.com
masters.com
nicklaus.com
pgatour.com
va.gov

ACKNOWLEDGMENTS

The idea for this project sprouted from a dinner in 2009 with Jimmy Roberts. The multiple Emmy award-winning announcer for NBC Sports had just released his hugely successful book *Breaking the Slump*. We were discussing the most compelling subjects in golf that hadn't been tackled in book form when I raised the 1975 Masters. Jimmy leaned forward and expressed unbridled enthusiasm for the topic. But he said pointedly to me, "You *really* should write one." Thanks Jimmy.

From there, Farley Chase—formerly of Waxman Literary Agency, now of Chase Literary Agency (yea Farley!)—guided this novice through the complex world of book publishing with nary a stumble. At Da Capo Press, Jonathan Crowe purchased the idea with more excitement than I could have wished. Bob Pigeon shepherded the project into its final form with assistance from Marco Pavia and others.

Writing this story properly would not have been possible without the full cooperation of the three protagonists: Jack Nicklaus, Johnny Miller, and Tom Weiskopf. I am grateful to each for being exceedingly generous with his time and forthright in answering every question. Their exclusive insights into that Masters, golf at the time, and themselves made the book. I can say honestly that I really wish all three could have won!

In regard to Nicklaus and Weiskopf, I am indebted to the assistance of Scott Tolley and Chris Roderick, respectively, in procuring my time with those men and in answering countless questions themselves. Thank you both.

In addition to the three headliners, I greatly appreciate the other people who took an hour or two (or three) out of their busy schedules to help me paint the full landscape of that week. Alphabetically, they were James Black, Billy Casper, Brandel Chamblee, Earnie Ellison, Nick Faldo, Jerry Heard, Kaye Kessler, Bob Kletcke, Gary Koch, John Mahaffey, Roger Maltbie, Bob Murphy, Bobby Nichols, Barbara Nicklaus, Peter Oosterhuis, Vin Scully, Ed Sneed, Curtis Strange, Chuck Will, and Ben Wright.

Thank you to the assistance provided by the Masters Tournament and the Augusta National Golf Club, starting with (now-retired) executive director Jim Armstrong and the trio of Steve Ethun, Melissa Lyles, and Lee Bennett.

ACKNOWLEDGMENTS

Steve Auch proved to be a great resource at the Jack Nicklaus Museum, allowing me to roam the premises and even peruse some of Nicklaus's personal scrapbooks. When in the Columbus area, the museum is a must visit.

My primary work home for nearly two decades has been on the road with the NBC Sports golf crew—the best team in sports television I say with a slight bias. There are too many friends and colleagues to list, but one would start with Tom Roy, our producer and esteemed leader; former spotting coordinator Lou Serafin, who first hired me all those years ago; and John Goldstein, who showed me the ropes. In particular, I owe a debt of gratitude to the play-by-play hosts I've been privileged to sit alongside, beginning briefly with Jim Lampley and continuing with master storytellers and scene setters Dick Enberg and Dan Hicks. A second thank you is still not enough for Johnny Miller. So much of my knowledge in golf and in telling its story comes from the thousands of hours I've joyfully spent with him in the NBC booth.

Now, I have a second work family with Golf Channel led by President Mike McCarley. My boss Geoff Russell was instrumental with his support of my completing this project after our lives were uprooted and hastily transplanted to the Sunshine State. The ability to lean on his expertise from his previous world of print media was a true asset as well.

For a decade, Bill Macatee allowed me to work beside him atop the 14th tower for the CBS broadcasts of the Masters. Thanks Bill for taking me along for the ride.

Also on the television front, I'm grateful for the assistance provided by Robin Brendle at CBS and Chris McClosky at NBC in fielding my requests so efficiently.

Many contributed along this book's journey in ways big and small, and I appreciate the help of all: Tom Alter, Ron Borolla, Bobby Bowers, Mark Carlson, Kelly Elbin, David Fay, Bill Hensley, Joe Jareck, Rand Jerris, Kathy Jordan, Pete Kowalski, David Marr, Frank Nobilo, Harris Prevost, Del Ratcliffe, Simon Roper, Tim Rosaforte, Ron Thow, Ben Vernon, and Henry Ward.

Even in the digital age, book research cannot be accomplished solely online, and the access afforded me at the following institutions was invaluable: Probst Library at the PGA Museum, Vanderbilt Television News Archives, Davidson College Library, Charlotte-Mecklenburg Public Library, Mooresville Public Library, Winter Park Public Library, and the Orange County Public Library. Long live bricks and mortar.

And of course, none of these thank yous would be possible without the love and support of my family, beginning with my father, mother, and sister Addria. Both my parents encouraged me to follow my dreams and have always been supportive of whatever turns I chose to make in life. I try my best to reciprocate that gift to my two daughters, Katie and Ellie, who make time go by way too quickly. And finally, thank you to my wife Julie, who put up with the early mornings, late nights, stressful moments, and constant requests for solitude. I couldn't have done it without you. I love you all!

INDEX

Aaron, Hank, 32, 42
Aaron, Tommy, 40, 46
alcohol use, by Weiskopf, T., 223–225, 273
Allin, Bud, 205
amateurs
    dinner for, 104
    Jones, B., as, 19
    at Masters Tournament, 5, 49–50, 104
    in Pro-Am, 54–55
Amen Corner
    Miller, J., at, 157–158
    Nicklaus, J., at, 149–150
    Palmer at, 135
    Watson at, 197
American Golf Classic, 34, 172, 227
Andrews, Gene, 183
Andy Williams San Diego Open, 27
Aoki, Isao, 75–76
approach shots, 53
    by Miller, J., 63
Archer, George, 46, 168, 207–208
Argea, Angelo, 181
Arnie's Army, 133, 136, 185
Ashe, Arthur, 42
Aspley Guise & Woburn Sands Golf Club, 266
Atlanta Athletic Club, 269
The Atlanta Constitution, 173
Augusta, Georgia, 17–18
Augusta Chronicle, 11, 16, 61, 141, 266

Augusta Chronicle-Herald, 4
Augusta Gazette, 16
Augusta Herald, 16
Augusta National Golf Club
    caddies at, 181–183
    draws on, 51–52
    Jones, B., and, 20–21
    layout of, 23
    length of, 50
    links-style golf course and, 23, 51, 53
    Nicklaus, J., and, 116–117, 285
    Palmer and, 134
    par for, 50
    putting at, 153
    Senior PGA Championships at, 77
    Trevino and, 89–91
    U.S. Open and, 20–21
    water hazards on, 191
    yardage book for, 182–183
    See also specific holes and features
Augusta National Invitation Tournament, 22
Austin, J. Paul, 39
Azalea Open, 4, 70

Ball, Clarence, 47
Baltusrol, 11, 271
Barbarossa, Bob, 170
Barber, Miller, 124, 140
Barner, Ed, 280
Barnes, Brian, 72

Barton, Bob, 116
Barton, Linda, 116
Beman, Deane, 28–29, 39, 183, 221
Beman, Elder, L., and, 39
Bembridge, Maurice, 74, 241
bentgrass, 171, 281–282
Berg, Patty, 210
Bermuda grass, 10, 36, 52–54, 99, 171,
    172–173
Big Three, 44
    See also Nicklaus, Jack; Palmer, Arnold;
    Player, Gary
Bing Crosby Pro-Am, 27, 28
    Littler at, 81
    Miller, J., at, 65–66, 176
    Nicklaus, J., at, 65–66
    Weiskopf, T., at, 225–226
Black, Joe, 4
black caddies, 181–183
black golfers, 30, 32, 33, 270
    See also Elder, Lee
Blancas, Homero, 143
Bob Hope Desert Classic, 27, 63, 68, 88,
    134
Bolt, Tommy, 218–219, 222, 236
Boros, Julius, 196
Brewer, Gay, 46, 86, 116
Las Brisas, 175–176
British Amateur Championship, 3, 19
British Open, 232
    Jones, B., at, 19
    Nicklaus, J., at, 283–284
British Open (1926), 102–103
British Open (1964), 169
British Open (1970), 117
British Open (1972), 89, 125
British Open (1973), 15, 203, 227
British Open (1975), 280, 284
British Open (1976), 280–281
Brown, Henry, 40, 140
Brown, Jim, 42
Brown, Pete, 30
Bryant, Bear, 85
Buick Open, 34, 206
bunkers, 50, 117
    on 2nd hole, 239
    on 13th hole, 245
    on 14th hole, 246

on 16th hole, 202
on 18th hole, 94
sand in, 79–80
Burke, Jackie, 7
Burning Tree Country Club, 263
Burns, George, 58, 142, 275
Butler, Peter, 72
Butler Cabin, 131, 258–259
Byron Nelson Classic, 226

caddies, 285
    Peterson, 60, 181–183, 252
    Schultz, 200–201, 253
Calcutta (party), 132
Canadian Open, 227, 271
career Grand Slam, 91
    Trevino and, 278
Carling World Open, 85
Carnoustie, 284
Carolan, Ernest "Creamy," 186
Carter, Ed, 4
Casper, B., putting by, 138
Casper, Billy, 26, 29, 276–277
    Hogan and, 138
    in Masters Parade, 5
    at Masters Tournament (1975),
        136–140, 197, 241
    Miller, J., and, 9, 97, 139–140, 156,
        172, 187
    putting by, 138
    at U.S. Open (1966), 137
Casper, Shirley, 139, 187
Cerrudo, Ron, 169
Champions Tour, 272–273, 276, 278
Charlotte News, 266
Chirkinian, Frank, 128–131, 241–242,
    266, 268
Citizen-Journal, of Columbus, Ohio, 71
Citrus Open, 12, 88, 91
Civil Rights Bill, 30
Clark, Clive, 72
Cobb, George, 75
Colbert, Jim, 69
Cole, Bobby, 75
Columbia Country Club, 78
Columbus, Ohio
    Citizen-Journal of, 71
    Evening Dispatch of, 71

Muirfield Village in, 123, 283
Nicklaus, J., in, 106
Columbus Country Club, 83, 85, 122
Congressional Country Club, 272–273
Coody, Charles, 46, 153, 158, 159
Corcoran, Fred, 37
corporate sponsorships, 27–28
    at Masters Tournament (1975), 132
    Miller, J., and, 153, 173, 237, 280
    Nicklaus, J., and, 237
Courville, Jerry, 48
Crampton, Bruce, 97
Crooks, Stanley, 103
Crow's Nest, 9, 49
cut
    at Masters Tournament, 23
    at Masters Tournament (1975), 141–142
    Nicklaus, J., and, 44, 117

Danny Thomas Memphis Classic, 27
De Vicenzo, Robert, 40
Dean Martin Tucson Open, 27
DeLeone, Jim, 216
Demaret, Jimmy, 5–6, 9–10, 24, 52
Denlinger, Kenneth, 155
"Desert Fox," Miller, J., as, 63
Devlin, Bruce, 183
Dickinson, Gardner, 12, 57
Dill, Terry, 216
Doral Open, 12, 59, 190, 207
Dougherty, Ed, 284
Drago, George, 243
draws, on Augusta National Golf Course,
    51–52
driver
    Miller, J., and, 189
    Nicklaus, J., and, 59–60, 99–100
    Weiskopf, T., and, 200
driving contest, at Masters Tournament
    (1934), 75

East Lake Country Club, 19
Ebony (magazine), 37
The Economist (magazine), 266
18th hole, 94
    Casper, B., and, 140
    Miller, J., at, 256–258
    Nicklaus, J., at, 150–151, 254–256

Scully at, 131
on television, 9, 131
Watson at, 197, 255
Weiskopf, T., at, 202–203, 209,
    256–258
Eisenhower, Dwight D., 24
Elder, Lee, 32–43
    at American Golf Classic, 34
    Beman and, 39
    Bermuda grass and, 36
    at Buick Open, 34
    early life of, 33
    Ford and, 38
    Green, H., and, 36
    invitation to, 30, 37
    Littler and, 81–82
    at Masters Tournament (1972), 37
    at Masters Tournament (1975), 39–43,
        81–83, 140–141
    Monsanto Open and, 32, 37–38
    Nicklaus, J., and, 34
    Oosterhuis and, 34–36
    Order of Merit and, 34
    in Par Three Contest, 75
    Player and, 32
    Qualifying Tournament and, 33
    Ryder Cup and, 34, 270
Elder, Rose, 32, 36, 39, 42, 141
11th hole
    contour of green on, 54
    Miller, J., at, 245
    Nicklaus, J., at, 149, 194, 245
    Rae's Creek and, 50
    Weiskopf, T., at, 244–245
Els, Ernie, 274
Esquire (magazine), 281
Eubanks, Mark, 191
Eubanks, Robert, 11, 141, 266
Evans, Chick, 7
Evening Dispatch, of Columbus, Ohio, 71

fade, 51, 52
    of Murphy, 89
    of Nicklaus, J., 114
fairways
    fescue grass on, 53
    grass length on, 50
    overseeding on, 53

Faldo, George, 233
Faldo, Joyce, 231
Faldo, Nick, 231–233, 282
fescue grass, 53
15th hole
 Miller, J., at, 158
 Nicklaus, J., at, 144, 195, 247–248
 Sarazen at, 22
 on television, 9, 131
 Watson at, 197
 Weiskopf, T., at, 144, 201, 208, 209,
  249–250
 Wright at, 266
5th hole, Nicklaus, J., at, 239
Financial Times, 18
Finsterwald, Dow, 184
Firestone Country Club, 86, 284
1st hole
 Miller, J., at, 97
 Nicklaus, J., at, 147, 238
 Palmer at, 193
 Trevino at, 91
 Weiskopf, T., at, 78
first-round leaders, 94–95
Fitzsimons, Pat, 143
Five Young Thunderbirds, 173, 175
Fleck, Jack, 119
The Flip Wilson Show (TV program),
 37
Floyd, Raymond, 29, 279, 284
Ford, Gerald, 27, 38, 263–264
forecaddies, 182
foreign players, at Masters Tournament
 (1975), 43
Foster, Dan, 196
14th hole
 Miller, J., at, 158, 246–247
 Nichols at, 198
 Nicklaus, J., at, 195, 246
 television at, 131
 Weiskopf, T., at, 247
Fruitlands Nurseries, 20

Gabrielsen, Jim, 39
Gardner, Bob, 104
Garrett, Dick, 108
Geertsen, John, 164–165
Georgia Highway 28, 18

Gillette Cavalcade of Champions 1974,
 68
Glen Campbell Los Angeles Open, 27
Glen Garden Golf and Country Club, 107
Glieber, Frank, 131
Glosser, Larry, 108
Go For The Flag (Miller), 71
Goalby, Bob, 40, 143
Golden Bear, Nicklaus, J., as, 14
golf clubs
 of Miller, J., 188–189, 280
 of Nichols, 87
 of Nicklaus, J., 58–60, 107
 steel-shafted, 51
 of Weiskopf, T., 199–200
 See also driver; hickory-shafted clubs;
  putting; sand wedge
Golf Digest, 37, 64, 71
Golf Is My Game (Jones, B.), 20
Golf Magazine, 37, 153, 227
Golf My Way (Nicklaus, J.), 123
Golf World, 64, 79
Graham, Lou, 174
grain, of greens, 53–54
Grand Slam
 of Jones, B., 103, 125
 Nicklaus, J., and, 126, 283
 See also career Grand Slam
Grandfather Golf & Country Club, 80
grass
 bentgrass, 171, 281–282
 Bermuda, 10, 36, 52–54, 99, 171,
  172–173
 fescue, 53
 ryegrass, 52–53, 99
Great Depression, 20
Greater Greensboro Open, 48, 56,
 69–70, 88, 139, 207, 226
Greater Jacksonville Open, 156
The Greatest Game of All: My Life in Golf
 (Jones, B.), 105
Green, Hubert, 29, 36
Green, Ron, 266
Green Island Country Club, 172
green jackets, 24, 259
greens
 Bermuda grass on, 10, 52–54, 99, 171,
  172–173

contour of, 53–54
grain of, 53–54
grass length on, 50
at Greater Greensboro Open, 69–70
overseeding on, 52–53
ryegrass on, 52–53, 99
Tifton 328 hybrid Bermuda grass on, 52–53
Greenville News, 196
Greenwald, Phil, 60
Gregoire, Leon, 167
Gregoire, Steve, 7, 167
Grout, Jack, 107–110, 151

Hall of Fame Classic, 281
Harbour Town Golf Links, 60
Harding Park, 166–167
Harmon, Claude, 158
Harris, Labron, Jr., 216
Harvey, Neal, 90
Hawaiian Open, 173–175
Hayes, Woody, 110
Heard, Jerry, 278–279
at American Golf Classic, 172
fade of, 52
in Five Young Thunderbirds, 173, 175
lightning strike to, 278–279
Miller, J., and, 152, 172
Nicklaus, J., and, 146, 151
Palmer and, 134
Trevino and, 91
on Weiskopf, T., 209
Hearst, Patricia, 27
Hendrix, Johnny, 4
Heritage Classic, 60, 199
Hershey Country Club, 107
hickory-shafted clubs
Jones, B., and, 51
Nicklaus, J., and, 147
Hill, Dave, 34
Hit 'em a Mile (Thompson), 162
Hoag, Bob, 122
Hogan, Ben, 44, 60–61, 87, 112, 116
Casper, B., and, 138
at Glen Garden Golf and Country Club, 107
Masters Tournament wins by, 24
Miller, J., and, 162

Nichols and, 84–85
Nicklaus, J., and, 91, 111
at U.S. Open (1955), 119
Hogan Bridge, 150
Hornung, Paul, 71
Hound Ears Club, 229
How to Play Golf (Snead, S.), 162
Hutchison, Jock, 77–78

Inverness Club, 211
Inverrary Golf & Country Club, 185–186
See also Jackie Gleason Inverrary Classic
invitations
to Elder, L., 30
to Masters Tournament, 26, 30, 37
to Masters Tournament (1959), 1–3
to Masters Tournament (1975), 31, 48
to Nicklaus, J., 1–3
to Palmer, 133
to Strange, C., 48
iron contest, in Masters Tournament (1934), 75
Irwin, Hale, 29, 190, 240

Jackie Gleason Inverrary Classic, 27, 59, 72, 88, 264
Jacklin, Tony, 74
Jack's Pack, 184
Jacobs, John, 205
Jacobs, Tommy, 116
Jaycee Tournament, 104
Jenkins, Dan, 157
Jet (magazine), 37
Jones, Bobby
as amateur, 19
Augusta National Golf Club and, 20–21
at British Amateur Championship, 19
at British Open, 19, 102–103
fame of, 18–19
Grand Slam of, 103, 125
hickory-shafted clubs and, 51
on invitation to Masters Tournament, 2
as long hitter, 52
Maiden and, 109

Jones, Bobby (*continued*)
  in Masters Parade, 5
  in Masters Tournament (1934),
    21–22
  Memorial Tournament and, 123
  Nicklaus, C., and, 102–103
  Nicklaus, J., and, 103–106, 111
  retirement of, 121
  rough and, 52
  *Spectator Suggestions for the Masters
    Tournament* by, 235
  at U.S. Open (1923), 19
  at U.S. Open (1926), 102–103
  Weiskopf, T., and, 12
Jones, Grier, 173, 175
Jones, Robert Trent, 202
Jupiter Hills Club, 59–60

Keeler, O.B., 21
Keiser, Herman, 151
Kellerman, Ernie, 211, 213
Kemper Insurance, 27
Kepler, Bob, 3, 214–216, 229
Kerr, Bill, 131–132
Kessler, Kaye, 71, 74, 106
  on Nicklaus, J., 107–109, 220
  on Palmer, 185
  on Weiskopf, T., 220, 221
Kite, Tom, 29
Kletcke, Bob, 25, 26, 268–269
  on caddies, 182
  Nicklaus, J., and, 57
  on ryegrass, 99
  sand and, 80
  Scioto at, 110
Knudson, George, 12, 95, 97
Koch, Gary, 42–43, 49, 53, 128, 133,
    276
  at Masters Tournament (1975), 142
  Strange, C., and, 48
  Weiskopf, T., and, 217

lawn chairs, for spectators, 235
Lee Elder Scholarship Fund, 42
Lema, Tony, 164, 169
Leonard, Stan, 6
lightning strike, 277–279
links-style golf course

Augusta National Golf Club and, 23,
    51, 53
  at Muirfield, 125
Littler, Gene, 81–82, 139, 156, 207
Loch Lomond, 272
Long, Jeretta, 116
Long, Jim, 116
long hitters, 52
  Miller, J., as, 189
  Nicklaus, J., as, 113
Longhurst, Henry, 131–132, 243,
    266–267
Los Angeles Times, 282
Lotz, Dick, 169
Lotz, John, 169
Low, George, 147
Lu Liang-Huan, 40
Lunn, Bob, 169

MacKenzie, Alister, 12, 20, 51
Magnolia Lane, 18, 26, 276
Mahaffey, John, 40, 53, 120, 142
  on alcohol use, 223
  on Hogan, 112
Maiden, Stewart, 109
major championships
  Miller, J., and, 179
  Nicklaus, J., and, 112–118, 123
  See also Grand Slam; *specific
    tournaments*
Malatin, Marty, 211, 213
Maltbie, Miller, J., and, 62
Maltbie, Roger, 62, 276
  on Nicklaus, J., 101, 119–120, 151
  on Palmer, 133
  on Trevino, 90–91
  on Weiskopf, T., 217–218, 219, 220,
    222
Mangrum, Lloyd, 240
Mangrum, Ray, 33
Marr, Dave, 26
Martinez, Andy, 172, 181
Masters Club Dinner, 60–61
Masters Edition supplement, in *Sunday
    Chronicle-Herald*, 16–17
Masters Parade, 5, 17
Masters Tournament
  amateurs at, 5, 49–50, 104

calendar position of, 25
cut at, 23
green jackets at, 24, 259
invitations to, 26, 37
pairings at, 77
playoff for, 265
prize money at, 23
prominence of, 29
scoreboards at, 23
spectators at, 24
Masters Tournament (1934), 21–22, 75
Masters Tournament (1935), 22
Masters Tournament (1938), 107
Masters Tournament (1956), 7
Masters Tournament (1959), 1–6
   Nicklaus, J., at, 1–3, 104
Masters Tournament (1961), 45
Masters Tournament (1963), 56
Masters Tournament (1964), 115
Masters Tournament (1967), 86
Masters Tournament (1968), 11–15
Masters Tournament (1969), 207–208
Masters Tournament (1970), 136–137
Masters Tournament (1971), 156–159
Masters Tournament (1972), 37, 125,
   209
Masters Tournament (1974), 209
Masters Tournament (1975)
   caddies at, 181–183
   Casper, B., at, 136–140, 197, 241
   corporate sponsorships at, 132
   cut at, 141–142
   Elder, L., at, 39–43, 81–83, 140–141
   foreign players at, 43
   importance of, 269
   invitations to, 31, 48
   Koch at, 142
   Miller, J., at, 62–69, 95–98, 152–154,
      187–192, 231–264
   Murphy at, 87–92, 197
   Nichols at, 83–87, 142–143, 198–199,
      241
   Nicklaus, J., at, 46, 55–61, 102–126,
      145–152, 181–187, 231–264
   pairings at, 78, 235–236
   Palmer at, 44–45, 132–136, 183–187,
      192–197, 241
   Player at, 45–46

   prize money for, 259
   qualifications for invitation to, 31
   Snead, J.C., at, 93, 196–197
   Snead, S., at, 92–93
   Strange, C., at, 47–50, 98–101
   television at, 127–132, 241–242,
      266–268
   tickets for, 55, 234–235
   Trevino at, 44, 87–92, 142, 197–198,
      241
   Watson at, 197
   Weiskopf, T., at, 69–75, 93–94,
      143–145, 199–204, 231–264
Masters Tournament (1975), days of
   Monday, April 7th, 32–46
   Tuesday, April 8th, 47–61
   Wednesday, April 9th, 62–76
   Thursday, April 10th, 77–101
   Friday, April 11th, 127–154
   Saturday, April 12th, 181–204
   Sunday, April 13th, 231–264
Masters Tournament (1976), 284–285
Masters Tournament (1981), 281–282
Masters Tournament (2005), 285
McLeod, Fred, 77–78
McManus, Roger, 6
McPhail, Bill, 131
Medinah Country Club, 283
Meihaus, Johnny, 85
Memorial Tournament, 123
Mezzrow, Milton "Mezz," 149
Middlecoff, Cary, 24, 198, 213
military draft
   Nicklaus, J., and, 13
   Weiskopf, T., and, 13–14, 205–207
Miller, Allen, 79, 142
Miller, Ida Meldrum, 160–161
Miller, Johnny, 6–10, 26, 155–180,
   279–282
   at Amen Corner, 157–158
   Bermuda grass and, 171, 172–173
   at Bing Crosby Pro-Am, 65–66, 176
   at Bob Hope Desert Classic, 63, 68
   at British Open, 280–281
   Casper, B., and, 9, 97, 139–140, 156,
      172, 187
   childhood of, 160–166
   corporate sponsorships and, 237

Miller, Johnny (*continued*)
Demaret and, 9–10
as "Desert Fox," 63
driver and, 189
Faldo, N., and, 232–233
in Five Young Thunderbirds, 173, 175
golf clubs of, 188–189
Heard and, 152, 172
Hogan and, 162
Knudson and, 95, 97
major championships and, 179
Maltbie and, 62
at Masters Tournament (1971),
156–159
at Masters Tournament (1975),
62–69, 95–98, 152–154, 187–192,
231–264
as Mormon, 8, 10, 163, 166
Murphy and, 63, 152
Nelson, B., and, 162
Nicklaus, J., and, 64–67, 112,
124–126
on Palmer, 133
par fives and, 249–250
at Par Three Contest, 9
Player and, 45
as Player of the Year, 177, 179
practice rounds of, 68, 95, 172
putting by, 96, 153, 189, 191, 226,
243–244, 280–281
at Qualifying Tournament for PGA
Tour, 170
Rosburg and, 168
Snead, S., and, 9, 162, 172
on Sunday of Masters Tournament
(1975), 231–264
at Tournament of Champions, 79
at U.S. Open, 95, 174–175, 240
Venturi and, 168, 169
Watson and, 281
Weiskopf, T., and, 70–75, 152
wins by, 14–15
World Cup of Golf and, 175–176
Yancey and, 175
Miller, Larry, 160–166, 178
Miller, Linda, 173, 174, 175, 187
Miller, Ronnie, 165–166
Miss Golf Pageant, 5, 17

Mizell, Hubert, 266
Monsanto Open, 32, 37–38
Montgomery, John, 145, 172
Montgomery, Nancy, 145
MONY, 27
Morgan, Walter, 205
Mormons, 8, 10, 163, 166
Morris, William S., Jr., 16
Morrish, Jay, 272
moving day, 187
Muirfield, 73, 89, 125
Muirfield Village, 123, 283
Murphy, Bob, 33, 38, 51, 114, 224
at Masters Tournament (1975), 87–92,
197
Miller, J., and, 63, 152
on Palmer, 186
on Weiskopf, T., 218
Murray, Jim, 87, 282
Musburger, Brent, 242

Nelson, Byron, 5, 44, 107, 151
at Masters Tournament (1975),
235–236
Miller, J., and, 162
Nelson, Larry, 205
New York Times, Elder, L., in, 37
Newsweek, 64
Nichols, Bobby, 52, 122, 277–278
Hogan and, 84–85
lightning strike to, 277
at Masters Tournament (1975), 83–87,
142–143, 198–199, 241
Middlecoff and, 198
Nicklaus, J., and, 83
Weiskopf, T., and, 200, 209–210
Nicklaus, Barbara, 5, 115, 145–146, 185
Nicklaus, Charlie, 2–3, 102–103,
106–107, 117
Nicklaus, Helen Schoener, 106
Nicklaus, Jack, 102–126, 282–286
at Amen Corner, 149–150
at American Golf Classic, 34
approach shots by, 53
Augusta National Golf Club and,
116–117, 285
in Big Three, 44
at Bing Crosby Pro-Am, 65–66

at British Open, 283–284
caddie of, 60, 181–183, 252
childhood of, 105–107
clothing of, 237–238
in clubhouse, 49
competitiveness of, 119–121
corporate sponsorships and, 237
cut and, 44
driver and, 59–60, 99–100
Elder, L., and, 34
fairway shots by, 53
as Golden Bear, 14
golf clubs and, 58–60
Grand Slam and, 126
at Greater Jacksonville Open, 156
green jackets to, 259
Heard and, 146, 151
hickory-shafted clubs and, 147
Hogan and, 91, 111
invitations to, 1–3
at Jackie Gleason Inverrary Classic, 59, 72, 264
Jones, B., and, 103–106, 111
Kessler on, 107–109, 220
Kletcke and, 57
major championships and, 112–118, 123
Maltbie on, 101, 119–120, 151
at Masters Tournament (1959), 1–3, 104
at Masters Tournament (1971), 159
at Masters Tournament (1975), 46, 55–61, 145–152, 181–187, 231–264
military draft and, 13
Miller, J., and, 64–67, 112, 124–126
Nichols and, 83
at North & South Amateur, 111
1-iron and, 248–249
Palmer and, 183–187, 192–197
par fives and, 6, 194–195
Peterson and, 60, 181–183, 252
as Player of the Year, 284
playing schedule of, 55–56
practice rounds of, 56–58, 104
putting by, 100, 113, 147–149, 251–252, 255–256
Ryder Cup and, 73

Spencer and, 57
Strange, C., and, 55, 98–101
at U.S. Open (1962), 184
Watson and, 238, 284–285
Weiskopf, T., and, 12, 60, 70–75, 120, 209, 218, 227, 252, 271
wink of, 118
wins by, 14
Nicklaus, Marilyn, 106
9th hole, Nicklaus, J., at, 239, 242
Nixon, Richard, 38, 263
North & South Amateur, 6, 77, 111, 275

Oakland Hills, 85
Oakmont, 174–175, 192, 227, 240
Obetz, Robin "Bob," 3–4
Ohio State University, 3, 12, 70–71, 214–216
Old Course, in St. Andrews, Scotland, 23
Olympic Club, 7, 64, 119, 137, 167–168
1-iron, 248–250
Oosterhuis, Peter, 34–36, 75
at Masters Tournament (1975), 142
Snead, S., and, 93
Weiskopf, T., and, 233
Order of Merit, Elder, L., and, 34
Osborne, Alec, 3–4
overseeding, 52–53

pairings
at Masters Tournament, 77
at Masters Tournament (1975), 78, 235–236
Palmer, Arnold, 29, 115
at Amen Corner, 135
Augusta National Golf Club and, 134
in Big Three, 44
at Bob Hope Desert Classic, 134
Champions Tour and, 276
at Greater Jacksonville Open, 156
Heard and, 134
Kessler on, 185
Koch and, 133
major championships and, 123
Maltbie on, 133
Master Tournament wins by, 7
in Masters Parade, 5
at Masters Tournament (1959), 6

Palmer, Arnold (*continued*)
  at Masters Tournament (1975), 44–45,
    132–136, 183–187, 192–197, 241
  Miller, J., and, 174
  Nicklaus, J., and, 183–187, 192–197
  putting by, 134
  Sneed and, 133
  Stadler and, 136
  Strange, C., and, 133
  at U.S. Open (1962), 184
  at U.S. Open (1966), 137
  Watson and, 136–137
  Weiskopf, T., and, 74
par fives
  Miller, J., and, 249–250
  Nicklaus, J., and, 6, 194–195
Par Three Contest, 9, 61, 75–76
Pate, Jerry, 49, 52, 101
Pebble Beach, 63, 118, 125, 176,
  225–226
Pebble Beach National Pro-Am, 282
Peete, Calvin, 270
People (magazine), 37, 96, 177
Perry, Gaylord, 42
Peterson, Nicklaus, J., and, 60, 181–183,
  252
Peterson, Willie, 60, 181–183, 252
PGA Championship (1964), 83, 85, 122
PGA Championship (1968), 196
PGA Championship (1973), 91, 122,
  227
PGA Championship (1974), 88, 93, 221
PGA Championship (1975), 284
PGA Championship (1984), 278
PGA of America, 28
PGA Tour, 28
  Masters Tournament invitations and,
    37
  See also specific tournaments and players
PGA Tour Qualifying Tournament
  Elder, L., at, 33
  Miller, J., at, 169–170
Phoenix Open, 171–172
Picard, Henry, 107, 151
Pierman, Putnam, 123
Pinehurst, 6, 111, 177, 275
Player, Gary, 29, 115, 276
  in Big Three, 44

Elder, L., and, 32
  at Greater Jacksonville Open, 156
  at Masters Tournament (1961), 45
  at Masters Tournament (1975),
    45–46
  Miller, J., and, 45, 189–192
  Nicklaus, J., on, 67
  as short hitter, 67
  Weiskopf, T., and, 209
Player of the Year
  Miller, J., as, 177, 179
  Nicklaus, J., as, 284
  Weiskopf, T., as, 227
Poe, Henry, 29
Polland, Eddie, 72
popularity of golf, 27
Posey, Dudley, 187
Posey, Marie, 187
Post, Emily, 26
Power Golf (Hogan), 162
Powers, Bill, 169
practice rounds
  of Miller, A., 79
  of Miller, J., 68, 95, 172
  of Nicklaus, J., 56–58, 104
  of Weiskopf, T., 74
prize money
  increases in, 28
  at Masters Tournament, 23
  at Masters Tournament (1975), 259
  television and, 131
Pro-Am, amateurs in, 54–55
putting
  at Augusta National Golf Course, 153
  by Casper, B., 138
  importance of, 6
  by Miller, J., 96, 153, 189, 191, 226,
    243–244, 280–281
  by Nicklaus, J., 100, 113, 147–149,
    251–252, 255–256
  by Palmer, 134
  speed, 54
  by Weiskopf, T., 209, 221, 226–227,
    251–252, 255

Qualifying Tournament, for PGA Tour
  Elder, L., at, 33
  Miller, J., at, 169–170

Rae's Creek, 50, 149, 150
Reese, Pee Wee, 84
Regalado, Victor, 120
Reuter, John, 189
Rhodes, Ted, 33
Rice, Grantland, 21
Ridgewood Country Club (N.J.), 48
Roberts, Charlie, 173
Roberts, Clifford, 19, 21, 25–26, 37, 39,
    55, 259, 265, 268
  Casper, B., and, 139
  death of, 269
  on Nicklaus, J., 115
  Par Three Contest and, 75
  sand and, 80
  Scully and, 128
Robinson, Frank, 41–42
Robinson, Jackie, 42
Roderick, Chris, 273
Rodgers, Phil, 49
Rodriguez, Chi Chi, 146
Rosburg, Bob, 168, 216
Ross, Donald, 110
rough, 23, 50, 52, 125
Royal Birkdale, 280–281
Runyan, Paul, 137
Ryder Cup, 34, 73, 102, 270
ryegrass, 52–53, 99

Salt Lake Country Club, 7
Sammy Davis Jr. Greater Hartford Open,
  27
San Diego Open, 12
San Francisco Chronicle, 6–7
San Francisco Examiner, 6–7
San Francisco Golf Club, 7, 64–65,
  164–165, 167, 169
sand, in bunkers, 79–80
sand wedge, 60
Sarazen, Gene, 12, 22, 60, 132
Savic, Janice, 145
Savic, Pandel, 122, 145
Sayers, Ben, 147
scalpers, 234–235
Scarlet Course, 12
Schultz, LeRoy, 200–201, 253
Scioto Country Club, 103, 105, 107, 110
Scully, Vin, 127–132, 241–242, 267–268

2nd hole, Nicklaus, J., at, 238–239
Sedgefield Country Club, 69
segregation, in Augusta, Georgia,
  17–18
Senior PGA Championships, 77
series badges, 55
17th hole
  Casper, B., and, 140
  Coody at, 159
  Miller, J., at, 192
  Nicklaus, J., at, 254
  on television, 9, 131
  Weiskopf, T., at, 202, 255
Shell's Wonderful World of Golf (TV show),
  206
Shepard, Alan, 27
Sherman, William, 19
Shoal Creek, 283
short hitters, 52
  Player and Trevino as, 67
Sifford, Charlie, 30, 38
Sikes, Dan, 12, 216
Simons, Jim, 173, 175
Simpson, O.J., 165
Singh, Vijay, 274
16th hole
  Longhurst at, 243, 266
  Miller, J., at, 158–159, 255
  Nicklaus, J., at, 249, 250, 251–252
  on television, 9, 131
  Watson at, 250
  Weiskopf, T., at, 202, 209, 250–251,
    253–254
6th hole, Weiskopf, T., at, 200, 239
Slingers, 41
Smith, Horton, 22
Smith, Philip, 39
Snead, J.C., 86, 93, 142, 196–197
Snead, Sam, 44, 87
  at Masters Tournament (1975), 92–93,
    142
  Masters Tournament wins by, 24
  Miller, J., and, 9, 162, 172
  in Par Three Contest, 75
  Weiskopf, T., and, 218
Sneed, Ed, 74, 114, 120, 277
  at Masters Tournament (1975), 142
  on Miller, J., 152

Sneed, Ed (*continued*)
  Palmer and, 133
  Weiskopf, T., and, 218, 222, 271, 273
Snyder, Jimmy "the Greek," 75
Spanish Open, 276
*Spectator Suggestions for the Masters
  Tournament* (Jones, B.), 235
spectators
  increasing numbers of, 27
  lawn chairs for, 235
  at Masters Tournament, 24
Spencer, Dave, 57
Sport (magazine), 177
The Sporting News, 64, 177
Sports Illustrated, 37, 149, 157, 170, 177
St. Andrews, 23
St. Petersburg Times, 266
Stadler, Craig, 49, 136
Stanford, Maxell, 34
steel-shafted clubs, 51
Sterling, Enrique, 170
Stockton, Dave, 45, 209
Stokes, Pappy, 182
Stonehouse, R.S., 22
The Story of Augusta National Golf Club
  (Roberts), 25
Strange, C., U.S. Amateur and, 48
Strange, Curtis, 275–276
  on greens, 54
  Koch and, 48
  at Masters Tournament (1975), 47–50,
    98–101
  Nicklaus, J., and, 55, 98–101
  Palmer and, 133
Strange, Tom, 47–48
Summerall, Pat, 131, 259
Sunday Chronicle-Herald, Masters Edition
  supplement in, 16–17
Swaelens, Donald, 43
Swanson, Johnny, 64

Tanglewood Park, 88
Taylor, Converse Chuck, 181–182
tees
  grass length on, 50
  See also specific holes
television, 28
  at Masters Tournament (1956), 7

  at Masters Tournament (1975),
    127–132, 241–242, 266–268
  prize money and, 131
10th hole
  Miller, J., at, 244
  Weiskopf, T., and, 200, 244
Texas Open, 171
Thacker, Jim, 131
13th hole
  Miller, J., at, 245
  Nichols at, 198
  Nicklaus, J., at, 150, 245
  television and, 131
  Weiskopf, T., at, 144, 200
Thompson, Hall, 283
Thompson, Jimmy, 162
Thompson, Titanic, 33
Thorpe, Jim, 270
tickets, 5, 55, 234–235
Tifton 328 hybrid Bermuda grass,
    52–53
Tillinghast, A.W., 164
Time (magazine), 177
Toscano, Harry, 7
Toski, Bob, 79
Tournament Improvements Committee,
    26
Tournament of Champions, 79, 176
Tournament Players Championship
    (TPC), 28–29
Tournament Players Division (TPD), 28
TPC. *See* Tournament Players
    Championship
TPC Scottsdale, 272
TPD. *See* Tournament Players Division
Trevino, Lee, 7, 29
  Augusta National Golf Club and,
    89–91
  at British Open (1972), 89, 125
  career Grand Slam and, 278
  Elder, L., and, 270
  Heard and, 91
  lightning strike to, 278
  Maltbie on, 90–91
  at Masters Tournament (1975), 44,
    87–92, 142, 197–198, 241
  Miller, J., and, 172
  Nicklaus, J., and, 67, 91, 124

1-iron and, 248
  as short hitter, 67
Troon, 232, 272
Tucker, Carl, 8
Tucson National, Miller, J., at, 63, 192
Tucson Open, Weiskopf, T., at, 221
Turnesa, Joe, 103
12th hole
  Miller, J., at, 157–158, 192
  Nichols at, 198
  Nicklaus, J., at, 149, 194
  Palmer at, 241
  Rae's Creek and, 149
  Weiskopf, T., at, 200, 245

UGA. *See* United Golfers Association
United Golfers Association (UGA), 33
U.S. Amateur, 8, 49, 88
  Nicklaus, J., at, 104, 112
  Strange, C., and, 48
U.S. Junior Amateur, 8, 169–170
U.S. Open, 9
  Augusta National Golf Club and,
    20–21
  at Baltusrol, 11, 271
  Jones, B., at, 19
  at Medinah Country Club, 283
  Miller, J., and, 95
  Nicklaus, J., at, 83, 113
  Weiskopf, T., at, 11, 213
U.S. Open (1908), 77
U.S. Open (1923), 19
U.S. Open (1926), 102–103
U.S. Open (1955), 119
U.S. Open (1959), 138
U.S. Open (1960), 111
U.S. Open (1962), 184
U.S. Open (1964), 216
U.S. Open (1966), 7–8, 89, 137
U.S. Open (1972), 118, 125
U.S. Open (1973), 174–175, 227, 240
U.S. Open (1974), 137
U.S. Open (1975), 65
U.S. Open (1976), 269
U.S. Senior Open, 272–273

Venturi, Ken, 7, 168, 169
Vietnam, 13–14, 26–27

Wadkins, Lanny, 29, 173, 175
Wahl, Phil, 24
Walker Cup, 3
Wall, Art, 4, 6, 70, 240
Wallace, Fielding, 21
Ward, Harvie, 169
Ward-Thomas, Pat, 118
Washington Post, 155
Washington Road, 18
water hazards, 191
Watson, Tom, 29
  at Amen Corner, 197
  at British Open (1975), 284
  at Masters Tournament (1970),
    136–137
  at Masters Tournament (1975), 197
  Miller, J., and, 281
  Nicklaus, J., and, 238, 284–285
  Palmer and, 136–137
  at U.S. Open (1974), 137
  at Western Open (1974), 137
Weiskopf, Eva, 210
Weiskopf, Jeanne Ruth, 221
Weiskopf, Tom, 205–230, 270–275
  alcohol use by, 223–225, 273
  at American Golf Classic, 227
  approach shots by, 53
  at Bing Crosby Pro-Am, 225–226
  at British Open (1973), 15, 203, 227
  at Buick Open, 206
  caddie of, 200–201, 253
  on Champions Tour, 272–273
  childhood of, 210–214
  at Citrus Open, 12
  clothing of, 236–237, 259
  at Doral Open, 12
  driver and, 200
  Faldo, N., and, 232–233
  at Greater Greensboro Open, 226
  at Jackie Gleason Inverrary Classic,
    72
  Jones, B., and, 12
  Kepler and, 229
  Kessler on, 220, 221
  Koch and, 217
  Littler and, 207
  Maltbie on, 217–218, 219, 220, 222
  at Masters Tournament (1968), 11–15

Weiskopf, Tom (*continued*)
  at Masters Tournament (1975),
    69–75, 93–94, 143–145, 199–204,
    231–264
  Middlecoff and, 213
  military draft and, 13–14, 205–207
  Miller, J., and, 70–75, 152
  at Muirfield Village, 123
  Nichols and, 200, 209–210
  Nicklaus, J., and, 12, 60, 70–75, 120,
    209, 218, 227, 252, 271
  1-iron and, 249–250
  as Player of the Year, 227
  practice rounds of, 74
  putting by, 209, 221, 226–227,
    251–252, 255
  retirement of, 271
  Ryder Cup and, 73
  at San Diego Open, 12
  Schultz and, 200–201, 253
  Sikes and, 216
  Snead, S., and, 218
  Sneed and, 218, 222
  Stockton and, 209
  on Sunday of Masters Tournament
    (1975), 231–264
  at U.S. Open, 11, 213
  Yancey and, 226
Weiskopf, Tom (father), 210, 211–213,
    223, 225
Westchester, 176–177
Western Amateur, 216

Western Open (1964), 218
Western Open (1974), 137
Whitaker, Jack, 128
Wiechers, Jim, 169
Will, Chuck, 268
Wind, Warren, 149, 266
Winged Foot, 138
Winning Golf (Nelson), 162
Woods, Tiger, 270
World Cup of Golf, 175–176
World Golf Hall of Fame, 27
  Faldo, N., in, 282
  Miller, J., in, 282
  Nicklaus, J., in, 123
  Weiskopf, T., and, 274
World Open (1974), 221
World Series of Golf, 28–29, 227
World War II, 22–23
Wright, Ben, 18, 50, 72, 118, 128, 243,
    266–267
  Calcutta and, 132
  on Chirkinian, 130
  on Nicklaus, B., 146
  on Nicklaus, J., 74
  on Weiskopf, T., 224

Yancey, Bert, 45, 175, 226
yardage book, for Augusta National Golf
    Club, 182–183
Young, Ivor, 122

Zoeller, Fuzzy, 132, 277